ALL ABOUT PUBLIC RELATIONS
SECOND EDITION

D0557652

ALL ABOUT PUBLIC RELATIONS
SECOND EDITION

How To Build Business Success on Good Communications

ROGER HAYWOOD

The McGraw-Hill Companies

London · New York · St Louis · San Francisco · Auckland
Bogotá · Caracas · Lisbon · Madrid · Mexico · Milan
Montreal · New Delhi · Panama · Paris · San Juan
São Paulo · Singapore · Sydney · Tokyo · Toronto

Published by
McGRAW-HILL Publishing Company
Shoppenhangers Road, Maidenhead, Berkshire, SL6 2QL, England
Telephone 01628 23432
Fax 01628 770224

British Library Cataloguing in Publication Data
Haywood, Roger
   All about public relations. – 2nd ed.
   1. Public relations. Business firms
   I. Title
   659.2

   ISBN 0–07–707230–8

Library of Congress Cataloging-in-Publication Data
Haywood, Roger
   All about public relations: how to build business success on good
communications / Roger Haywood, – 2nd ed.
      p. cm.
   Rev. ed. of All about PR. 1st ed. c1984.
   Includes index.
   ISBN 0–07–707230–8
   1. Public relations. I. Haywood, Roger. All about PR.
II. Title.
HM263.H425   1990
659.2 – dc20   90–39247
                                                    CIP

McGraw-Hill

A Division of The McGraw·Hill Companies

First edition © 1984 McGraw-Hill Book Company (UK) Limited

Printed and bound in Great Britain at the University Press, Cambridge.

CONTENTS

ACKNOWLEDGEMENTS

I must express my appreciation to the many colleagues who helped me with their professional observations on the contents of this book including David Bernstein, Martyn Bond, Harold Burson, Roddie Dewe, John Drew, Julie Ganner, Peter Gummer, Roger Hayes, Harry Hemens, Marianne Neville-Rolfe, Douglas Smith, Ilsa Vermuch, Reginal Watts and Bob Worcester. My thanks also go to John Lavelle of the IPR and Colin Thompson of the PRCA for constant assistance and to those who compiled the contents, particularly Sue Furness, Emma Angus and Katie Montague-Johnstone.

Above all, my thanks go to the demanding and critical clients with whom I have had the challenge of working over the years and without whom, certainly, none of this would have been possible—and to the demanding and critical colleagues who have had the 'challenge' of working with me over the years and without whom, maybe, none of this would have been necessary.

Cartoons by Tom Bailey

SECTION
ONE

Figure 1.1 Members of The All-Party Parliamentary Construction Group regularly visit UK sites. This organization was set up by Douglas Smith of Political Communications on behalf of the Builder Group to act as a link between parliament and the construction industry.

PUBLIC RELATIONS, A BUSINESS WAY OF LIFE

ORGANIZATIONS NEED PERSONALITY, TOO

An organization that succeeds without public relations is as likely as, say, a salesman, a politician, a lawyer (or any other professional persuader) succeeding without a personality. There are very few whose brilliance can overcome the need for an effective, appealing personality. Equally, there are few organizations that have such a revolutionary product or unassailable monopoly or privileged role in society that they can afford not to bother about making friends and influencing people.

A few fortunate people have such a natural, positive personality that they never need to think about their attitudes, approach or behaviour. Perhaps an occasional company falls into this category.

But most of us like to be understood, like to be well-regarded, like to be influential. Our success is dependent upon the understanding and support we are able to create; it is as true in the circles of the lathe-operator as the corridors of the cabinet minister.

And it is exactly the same for our company, our local council, our church, our favourite charity and any other organized body. The personality of an organization, demonstrated through the attitudes it adopts, is a critical factor in its success—or failure. It *can* be more important than, for example, the price of the products it offers or, in the case of a charity, the worthiness of its cause.

PUBLIC RELATIONS STARTS BEFORE THE ACTION

One view of public relations describes the craft as the projection of the personality of the organization. As it is doubtful that any person could build a reputation without a personality, so it is with organizations. The corporate personality is what the organization *is*, reflects what it believes in, determines where it is heading. But above all the personality, agreed by the management, is the central factor in the building of the corporate reputation ... and, perhaps, the most satisfactory practical definition of public relations is that it is *the management of corporate reputation.*

Another definition of public relations describes it as the organized two-way communications between the organization and the audiences critical to its success. Such organizational communications are designed to create understanding for the organization's aims, policies and actions, though public relations is *not* the universal problem-solver. Those definitions of public relations that only cover 'mutual understanding' are talking about *information* activities and not public relations. Information can change knowledge but not necessarily opinions and attitudes. Information is only part of communications and communications is only part of public relations. What the company does is as important as what it says.

Effective public relations is much more than communications: it should be more fundamental to the organization. Public relations should begin before the decision-making stage—when attitudes towards the issues are being developed by management and policies are being formulated.

For this reason, public relations is an essential top-management responsibility—not an optional extra or a bolt-on publicity goody. Nor should public relations policies be developed by instinct; there is no room for optimism in the sensitive and critical areas of human relations. No organization should rely on luck for success.

Good public relations needs thought, planning and organization. No manager should expect to have a 'natural' public relations talent. Those that claim it, rarely have it. (What manager might expect to be a 'natural' financial, production or personnel expert?) The development of a worthwhile public relations policy needs as much thought, attention and professional skill as does the financial or personnel policy.

Of course, there are many other factors that are essential to success. If we consider a trading company, it must have the right products or services at the right price, with the right service and back-up. It must be able to produce these efficiently, reliably, safely. The company must be able to attract the right personnel, train, develop and motivate them. The best public relations will not compensate for weakness in these and many other important business areas. Indeed it is likely that an active public relations policy will expose rather than hide such weaknesses.

Public relations must be a two-way activity and is all about creating both goodwill and understanding. Hitler *understood* Churchill and vice versa ... but that does not mean there was much goodwill between them! And so it can be with some organizations and the public upon which they depend for success. If public relations is all about generating goodwill, then it follows that public relations efforts can only be effective where the aims of the organization are compatible with the aims of the public. The concept of the hidden persuader in public relations is nonsense.

It is the responsibility of the public relations professional to ensure that the company behaves properly. In a commercial democracy, an organization perhaps can deceive some of the public all of the time and all of the public some of the time, but never all of the public all of the time. For, as any experienced public relations practitioner will confirm, the best corporate behaviour is always the most profitable behaviour.

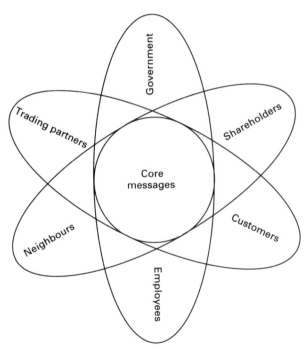

Figure 1.2 The organization must have a defined personality. Though it projects different elements, according to the needs and interests of the specific publics, the core message remains the same for all audiences, as symbolized in the Haywood communications daisy.

STABILITY AND CONSISTENCY MATTER

In every area of its operations, any organization depends on favourable attitudes. A helpful definition of public relations is that it is the management activity responsibile for the creation of favourable attitudes among key audiences.

One quality of good management is that it is stable and consistent. These are also qualities in corporate personalities that are likely to bring success. Just as we can anticipate how someone with a developed and balanced personality will behave, we can predict how high profile corporations will handle themselves.

.... *no organization should rely on luck for success*

Would you believe a rumour that Marks & Spencer was cutting corners on product quality? Would you support a Friends of the Earth report that Procter & Gamble was polluting rivers near its factories? Would you expect to find that BMW was allowing minimal safety standards in its plants? Would you listen to a claim that Electrolux was undertaking illegal share dealing? If not, then you are making a judgement about how you would expect these companies to behave. Your judgement might not be based on facts, but on your perception of the character or personality of the organizations.

The attitudes that any organization adopts towards key issues must be both responsible and consistent. These attitudes not only derive *from* the style of the organization, they help create that style.

Well-organized managements do not rely on chance to shape this business style. They discuss and define the business personality. For example, does the organization strive after uniform efficiency above all else? Or is the flexibility of the company, accommodating diverse views and approaches, of more importance? Is the primary responsibility to the shareholders, the employees, the customers or the community? Does the organization believe in its social responsibility or is profit the only factor in making a decision?

Is big beautiful or small smart? The way the organization behaves— indeed, the way some key individuals within the organization behave—will shape the reputation. As noted, perhaps the most satisfactory practical definition of public relations is that it is the professional management of the corporate reputation.

KNOW YOUR OWN COMPANY

The public relations practitioner must know his organization and ensure that it speaks with one voice—possibly different components of the message can be presented to different audiences but, overall, it must always be the same, consistent message. Harold Burson, speaking at a conference of the Public Relations Society of America, explained that he felt the organization needed to have a single voice, globally—in every country:

> The corporation must have a single voice internally to all business units, at all echelons, at all locations and a single voice in every form of communication—not limited to what's said to the media. It's what's said in consumer advertising, to employees, to share-holders and the investment community, to legislators and regula-tors. Every large company has many missions; but the company must learn to speak with one voice.
>
> Technology has forced the issue. Today's news media are glo-

bally pervasive. News is disseminated with the speed of light transcending national boundaries. What's on the satellite is available to anyone willing to spend a few hundred dollars for a dish. Corporations no longer have the luxury of treating their far-flung overseas investments as compartmentalized fiefdoms protected by national borders. News in one country, at one obscure location, is news wherever the country has operations.

Financial markets, now global for larger listed companies, are demanding a single timely data base on which to make evaluations. Employees, the world over, want to identify with common values, to be treated equally without country-to-country discrimination. Customers are rapidly developing a common level of sophistication.

Do all employees know their own company's attitudes to, say, equal opportunities, the environment, third world trade relations, suppliers, shareholders, trade unions, consumer watchdogs, and so on? How should the many officers, managers, employees, agents and trading partners know how to behave unless they understand and support the aims of the organization?

There can be many different styles of corporation—just as there is scope for a diversity of individuals who can all contribute in their own ways to a better society. There is a place for the brisk, cool efficiency of IBM or the more mellow Philips, for example. A strong personality will serve a company well but does not need to be universally acceptable; for the company that tries to please everyone may end up with a compromise which may be so colourless it will please no one. Too much compromise may give the organization the distinction, individuality (and success) of the Ford Edsel or Red Barrel beer!

Public relations is at last becoming appreciated as an important factor in the success of any organization. Today, decision-makers recognize that the public relations stance of their organization is much more important than mere publicity. It is all part of what makes Unilever like Unilever and 3M like 3M—*real* companies with deep, real personalities.

NEW ENTRANTS WILL WIN RESPONSIBILITY

Of course, public relations can be undertaken by amateurs or professionals. The public relations industry worldwide is making efforts to train professionals able to take on the most senior levels of responsibility. This new generation of highly educated, ambitious entrants to the profession will expect to share corporate responsibility in the boardroom. They will expect to earn their place alongside the other established professionals at the board table—engineers, accountants, lawyers. Good public relations people will want to prove their value by their creativity, their contribution to improved efficiency, greater commercial success, industrial expansion and better human relations.

This book is intended to help and encourage both the professional practitioner and public relations career entrant whose ambition aims him or her at the top. It is also intended to be a practical guide to the non-public relations manager in industry who will need an appreciation of what good public relations can achieve to ensure the success of his organization. I should point out that my use of the male gender does not imply a deliberate discrimination between the sexes, but is simply for simplicity! Indeed, I have been fortunate to earn my living for over half a lifetime in one of the very few *really* egalitarian businesses!

The first chapters look at some of the theory, though in a strictly practical way. Later, the book explores the areas where public relations can contribute, the type of techniques that might be applied and how to manage the function.

See you in the corporate corridors!

Figure 2.1 The new BP logo was developed following a year-long corporate image study. From this information, a number of options were developed and tested before the design was finalized. Photograph by British Petroleum.

TWO

THE CORPORATE PERSONALITY

HOW TO GET GOODWILL WORKING FOR YOU

An effective organization pays careful attention to goodwill. This asset can have considerable value. Well-known brand names can be worth billions! The value that attaches to brand names is not only of benefit to the managers of the corporation who can capitalize on these assets to grow their businesses. Such financial pragmatism is of importance to the public relations professional—for the development and protection of the brand ceases to be just a laudable aim, it becomes a commercial necessity. Indeed, such has the world changed that even the communications professionals find their reputation has a price-tag attached. For example, Hill & Knowlton and J. Walter Thompson went into the WPP balance sheet with a value of £175 million when they were first acquired.

The goodwill related to the brand as a result of investment, promotion and fair trading methods has a measurable value. Goodwill applies, of course, not just to brand names but to any organized enterprise, and of all the professional managers, the public relations adviser, potentially, has the greatest influence in this area. It is essential that all the activities of the public relations professional are carried out within the framework of an agreed corporate personality. If one is not defined, he must tackle this before all other activity. The business personality is separate from the individual personality—however closely the one reflects the other.

As it is with a corner sweetshop so it is with all organizations—from high technology research specialists to multinational consumer groups. Indeed, the same principle of corporate personality applies to non-profit organizations such as voluntary groups, religious bodies, professional associations, charities, governments—and even nations.

However, whilst the aura, image or personality of the corner shop can be closely related to the owner, this is not so simple with the larger organization. Of course, some multinational corporations grew within one lifetime and so reflect the personality of the founder and driving force, for example, Ford and Fiat, Adidas and Krupp, Ferrari and Philips, Woolworth and Benetton.

FORD WOULD REJECT HENRY TODAY

But even these companies have to adapt and modify as successive generations of independent executives take control. The corporate personality must develop to reflect the style of the top management—and the business climate of the times.

It is probable that the first Henry Ford would be unemployable in the present Ford environment. Certainly, the late Leonard Pool, the founder of Air Products & Chemicals Incorporated, once admitted that he was not sufficiently well educated to pass the latter-day selection procedures in his multibillion dollar world leader.

Today, the corporate personality is more likely to reflect the style of a management *team* rather than an individual. And as the work of the public relations specialist is so closely involved in developing reputation, then he must take an active part in defining and projecting this personality.

Organizations develop through generating the support of the many publics upon whom they depend for success; they can only succeed through combining their own internal direction and the external public consent to the policies and actions they pursue. As George Washington said, in a different context but of even greater relevance today, 'With public opinion on our side, you can do anything; without it, nothing'.

SALES ASSISTANTS SHAPE ATTITUDES

Too often, the managers of an organization allow the corporate communications policy to develop by chance. Sometimes the result will be healthy and harmonious, if the circumstances have been fortunate; but, sometimes, the result will be that the organization will have a blurred or inconsistent personality. The public relations specialist must help management to agree on the personality the corporation wishes to develop and the public relations programme that will project this.

Obviously, the personality of the corporation is shaped by many factors. These include the personalities of the people within the organization—but not necessarily only those at the top. For example, a survey carried out on behalf of one major European industrial company showed that the personnel who had the most influence upon the customers' attitudes were the lorry drivers.

Similarly, the customers' attitude towards Quik-fit or Woolworth is more likely to be shaped by the sales assistant than some financial baron at head office.

The style of management of the company will influence the behaviour of all levels of personnel. If management is intelligently managing its resources, then it will define a personnel policy that attracts the type of people compatible with this spirit; such recruits will support the objectives of the organization. Consequently, all employees will create an environment that is consistent with this top level view of the organization. Management all the way down the line will tend to recruit even the most junior members of the team who are consistent with the type of operation. This will ensure, for example, that the C&A or Radio Shack sales staff reflect the style of the board and the company.

WHY IBM IS NOT 3M

In the industrial example earlier, without any conscious instruction or direction, the lorry drivers reflected the personality that had been defined at top management level.

That concept is logical and practical. We can see the effectiveness of its operation with companies like Johnson & Johnson in the retail sector or Unisys in the business area or Ciba-Geigy in the industrial sector.

Equally, we can see examples of where this concept has not been understood. Failure to coordinate the aspiration and the reality can make a nonsense of even the most expensive media campaign. How often is the advertising let down by the service delivered to the customer? For example, what relationship was there between the British Rail once portrayed in television commercials—'We're getting there'—and the one the public used?

As in this case, the failure is not in the campaign nor in the actual operations of the organization. It is usually a failure to relate these two aspects of the same business. Many creative advertising campaigns have failed to be effective because they have been conceived by people too remote from the world where the consumer lives. For example, the television campaign may portray the smile, the gloss and efficiency of the high street fast food operation while the consumer too often sees the reality—litter, ill-cleaned premises and the off-hand manners of ill-trained and poorly-motivated staff. Frequently, the great concept does not easily translate across borders or cultures—the immaculate McDonald image in the US, for example, required major efforts to achieve the same success in the UK, where service standards are not so high. The service concept was not then natural to British youngsters recruited to staff the franchises.

PUBLIC RELATIONS MUST SHAPE ADVERTISING

The failure is sometimes in the follow-through. The most successful campaigns are those that project a truth that is as 'close to reality' as possible. The public relations adviser needs to be constantly measuring the proposals against the reality to look for areas of incongruity. He must take part in all the main marketing and advertising planning discussions.

The public relations professional would do well to avoid the use of the outdated concept of 'image'. This is really more appropriate to those organizations where public relations is a peripheral activity. (Often the spirit of the brief from those companies who use words like image is to ... 'put a little gloss on the reality'.)

Image is a reflection, an impression which may be a little too polished, a little too perfect. Far better, is the concept of the real corporate 'personality'. Even if it shows a few warts, it will be more endearing—certainly more acceptable than the super-smooth polished face that would be presented by an 'image'. True public relations is more than skin deep.

An effective promotional campaign must coordinate all the elements that contribute to the corporation personality. It seems simple and obvious, in theory. However, in practice, it can be very difficult. Often the level of management responsible for creating the promotional campaign does not have control over the parts of the organization that have direct impact upon the public. For example, some companies still run television campaigns without showing them to their own employees. This was also the criticism of one famous campaign developed for Mrs Thatcher's Conservative party by Saatchi & Saatchi; it was not shown in advance to the party's own members of parliament. It was slick and powerful but, ultimately, superficial as it was not based on the communications principles. It may be no coincidence that the advertising guru was later replaced by a public relations consultant.

PROFIT FIGHTS CONSCIENCE

Commercial companies exist to make a profit. But few companies exist *only* to make a profit. There are companies to whom profit is the primary objective. But even these companies balance profit against the responsibility they have towards the people on whom they depend for success, for example, their own employees or customers. Today's profit can be gained at the expense of tomorrow's. For example, this year's balance sheet might look better if the company does not improve employment conditions; but next year it could lose many of its better people. Similarly, today's margin could be improved if product quality is cut, but that could lose tomorrow's customers.

These important business decisions could make the difference between success or failure. It is a matter of management judgement for the company to strike the right balance and this decision has important public relations implications.

Of course, behaving responsibly may be a question of social conscience or astute business—and often a mixture of both. The Kentucky Fried Chicken chain may encourage its franchise holders to provide litter bins and ensure that their staff collect any dropped boxes because they believe it matters to be tidy. Or it could just be that they recognize that litter is offensive to most people. The distinctive red and white boxes, which would pinpoint the culprit so accurately, might discourage potential customers—even cause problems with community groups or local authorities.

There are *some* business decisions which are taken on the basis of conscience, regardless of the commercial implications. For example, an advertising agency may decline to handle a distillery. A bank may not wish to have a subsidiary in a sensitive political sector of the globe.

ONLY GOLFERS SPONSOR GOLF

Consider the general social responsibility of a company and the role of public relations in assessing the important factors. There is a risk that the social responsibility (or the 'conscience') of the company will vary according to the director or manager involved in each policy decision.

There are very few charity golf days sponsored by companies where the enthusiast behind this sponsorship is not himself a keen golfer. Similarly, many companies support charities not only through financial donations but through the less obvious but, sometimes, far more expensive allocation of company manpower, time and resources. Should this activity be on the basis of supporting the charity most favoured by the chief executive? Or should this community activity be a considered step taken by the organization to reinvest in society?

It is essential that all such activities are measured against a realistic yardstick. This can only be done if the company thinks about its social responsibility and makes decisions on the stance it wishes to adopt. As with all other aspects of the corporate personality, the organization must avoid corporate schizophrenia.

A policy established and agreed at the top will permeate through all levels of management. Social responsibility can become accepted as a positive aspect of the company and will be supported through the organization. The public relations professional will stimulate this discussion so that the options and alternatives are argued through and an acceptable policy developed to which all management will feel committed.

BUSINESS SHOULD FACE SOCIAL DISTRESS

In the UK, companies like Boots, Sainsbury, United Biscuits, IBM and Peter Black all have an active policy on social responsibility. Lord Sieff, a distinguished past-chairman of Marks & Spencer, one of the consistent stars of UK high street retailing, argued the case for the responsibilities placed on business leaders.

> To achieve a successful free enterprise sector, top management must implement a policy of good human relations with all employees. We who trade in the high streets cannot be isolated from the social distress of the back streets. Full, frank two-way communication, open management, and, above all, respect for the contribution people can make, given encouragement—these are the foundations of an effective policy of good human relations which cost time, effort and money.

Marks & Spencer is not alone in recognizing that good relations pay. 'We have a stable staff, ready acceptance to change, high productivity and good profits in which we all share—shareholders, staff, retired staff and the community.'

It can be no coincidence that Marks & Spencer has one of the most highly regarded corporate personalities in retailing. This has been achieved

	1971 %	Strongly/tend to agree 1973 %	1975 %	1982 %	1986 %	1989 %
A company that has a good reputation would not sell poor products	68	65	65	65	68	62
Old-established companies make the best products	52	52	51	51	55	39
I never buy products made by a company I have not heard of	33	37	33	39	35	32
New brands on the market are usually an improvement over old-established brands	33	27	37	25	31	28

Source: MORI

Chart 2.1 The importance of a good reputation (Great Britain). The better known the company, the more favourably it tends to be regarded. Reputation can be of measurable value if it encourages consumers to have confidence in your products. Amongst the findings of a survey conducted by Market & Opinion Research International was how consistently the public believed that a company with a good reputation would not sell poor products. Robert Worcester, MORI managing director, adds that the percentage of a housewives' sample prepared to try a new frozen food from 'a large food company' rose from 47 per cent to 61 per cent when the range was described as being launched by Heinz. A good reputation pays in direct sales results.

in a company that has evolved considerably over the years and which has a formal structure dependent on the skills and ability of many people. The corporate personality is not the projection of one individual. Indeed, this company has stated that its entire staff are members of its public relations department.

ORGANIZATIONS CAN ONLY COMMUNICATE IN THE LANGUAGE THEIR PUBLICS CHOOSE

'Tell 'em like it is,' sounds like good advice but it is only of limited help. Of course, the organization must tell the truth, handle the bad news with the same integrity that it does the good. Honesty can be the only policy. But candour and honesty are not the same as bluntness and indifference. The receiver, not the transmitter, decides the language of communication. If the recipients of the message do not understand it or misinterpret it, then that is not *communication*, for that requires two-way understanding.

Too many corporations indulge in the equivalent of raising their voice when the message does not seem to be getting through. And nowhere is this more prevalent or counter-productive than in the growing area of inter-national marketing. Kamran Kashani, professor of marketing at IMEDE, the international management school in Switzerland, has identified some of the pitfalls in a study of global marketing practices in Europe and the United States. More companies are taking advantage of their size or geographic scope to build their competitive advantage. But without careful attention to organizational considerations and both internal and external communi-cations, then even the best global strategy can falter.

In a later chapter, we look at some successes but as these are still outnumbered by the failures, let us consider one case where a logical and considered international policy failed because those who were expected to carry it through did not accept the concept. Telling 'em like it is, antagonized rather than enthused.

Some years ago, Parker Pen, under a new management team decided to go international. Policy-making was centralized in the head office in the US, much autonomy was removed from local operations in over 150 countries around the world, one central advertising agency was appointed, the product line was cut by 80 per cent and new models aimed at lower-priced market sectors were introduced. Local managers were unhappy at not being involved in such global marketing decisions. They objected vigorously and, within two years, the top management team was forced to resign and a decentralized system was reintroduced

The lessons to be learned from this disaster are that those who imple-ment the policy need to be involved in its formulation—or, at the very least, in the opportunity to appraise it before it is introduced. Where such decisions may reduce autonomy, then managers need to accept the reasons and be offered greater accountability within the new framework. Above all, effective two-way communications that examine the local implications of international policy are essential. This will always demand an understanding of the attitudes, the culture and the ways of doing business that apply to those managers and the broader publics upon whom the corporation will depend for success.

THREE
OBJECTIVES

CREATIVITY NEEDS DISCIPLINE

Public relations may be flexible, organic, responsive and creative. It may well be handled effectively by some of the most talented people—the need for creativity must never be used as the excuse for a lack of discipline. It is essential that public relations is as well planned as any other activity of the organization. It must be working to agreed and understood objectives.

It is important to differentiate between aims and objectives. Frequently in public relations these are used interchangeably. An aim is a direction in which progress is to be made. However, an objective is a *specific* point which is to be reached. Where possible, the public relations activity should be working to quantified objectives rather than broad aims.

As an illustration, an aim for a marketing public relations programme could be to improve brand awareness; this would not be an objective, as it stands. This does not mean that it has no value. Aims may not always need to be defined as objectives, but this is likely to become necessary as the sophistication of the public relations activity develops.

A small company introducing a new product might be quite happy to have simple public relations aims. If, for example, there is no awareness of the brand in the market place then *any* effort that will increase the brand awareness is likely to be of *some* value. It is also going to be relatively easy to see whether an improvement has been achieved. If at the beginning of the campaign no one is aware of the brand and at the end quite a number of people in the trade are talking about it; editorial enquiries are coming through; the product is being asked for at the point of purchase, and so on—then it is reasonable to conclude that some valuable improvement has been achieved.

On the other hand, how do you develop from that position? How do you assess the cost-effectiveness of the activity? How will you measure how much you have recently improved in future? What budget will you allocate for what level of improvement?

Start with aims ...

Therefore, in the second or subsequent years, the company is likely to find that its public relations is far more effective if it is working to objectives rather than aims. The essential factor in writing an objective is to put in a factor that can be measured. This might not be a complete measure but it must be something which would give some indication of satisfactory performance.

... move to objectives

If we continue with the brand awareness example, then it would require quantified research before the campaign to measure the level of brand awareness, and a similar study at the end of the activity to check the change. In practice, of course, this could be very expensive and could well represent a significant proportion of the total promotional budget. It could also be unnecessary—a fair indicator of the effectiveness of the public relations effort in meeting this objective can be constructed without going to the extent of a statistically-validated answer.

A modest high street test may show that only one in ten purchasers of a particular product could spontaneously mention your brand. The objective might be agreed to raise this to, say, three in ten—or whatever seems necessary for the company to achieve the commercial targets it is setting.

In practice, the advice of a professional researcher in putting together an acceptable measure for these objectives is necessary. However, the principles can be fairly simple and should be understood by the public relations adviser planning the campaign.

Your company produces paint brushes for the do-it-yourself market. How many purchasers of paint brushes, when asked, will mention your name as being a leading brand? It may be possible that there will not be enough, unprompted, to produce a meaningful measure, particularly when yours is a new brand in the market. Therefore, how many, when shown a list of paint brush manufacturers (in other words, a prompted test) will recognize your brand? A modest survey based on this principle could be carried out through interviews at point-of-purchase, within a selection of stores chosen to represent a fair balance of typical paint brush outlets.

Obviously, care must be taken to eliminate any biasing factors. A famous greenhouse company once constructed a disastrous campaign, based upon limited research carried out in the home town where their head office was located. They had forgotten that virtually everyone they were likely to interview would have a friend or relative that worked at the company. Public awareness was substantially higher than would have been the case in a city the other side of the country.

BE SURE TO INVESTIGATE THE RIGHT PROBLEM

As well as personal interviews, this type of basic research can sometimes be undertaken through telephone interviews, and post. Researchers will tell you it is important to avoid assumptions. Quite often, the public relations adviser will be asked to remedy the wrong problem.

As an illustration, it is often invaluable for a supplier to know which companies come first to mind when a buyer is looking for a particular product—in our case, say, in the industrial or business-to-business sector. One established way to evaluate this is to place a key question in the centre of a broader questionnaire and this may be phrased along the lines '... name five companies who manufacture this product from which you would consider requesting a quotation'. The answer to this question will not only indicate how many people are *aware* of the company in this market sector, but also how they *rate* in comparison with the competitors.

It can be very important to establish both awareness and competitive position *before* drafting the public relations objectives. My consultancy was once asked by a large company—the largest in the UK in its particular sector—to help improve the performance of the salesforce in converting enquiries into business. Upon investigation, it seemed that the salesforce was probably no worse than those of the competition. Yet, the problem remained that the company was not succeeding in obtaining enough of the business for which it was eminently suited.

It seemed possible that the company was too cautious and conservative in its presentation to the market; some preliminary interviews suggested that the company did not have the level of awareness that it believed its long history in the business must have created. Many of the buyers in this business were people below the age of 30; a hundred-year history did not carry much weight with them.

A limited and informal survey among potential buyers of these services was undertaken. Thirty buyers were given the specification for three different projects, each of which would have been attractive business for the client. The potential buyers were asked to nominate three companies—on the basis of quality, but regardless of price—they might consider asking to quote for these three projects.

Clearly, such a limited survey has no statistical validity. However, it was significant that the client was named as first choice on only two of the ninety possible occasions and as a second or third choice in less than half a dozen other cases. It demonstrated beyond any doubt that there was a far greater potential to increase the number of the occasions on which the company was being invited to present for business, rather than concentrating solely on the conversion rate.

COMING LAST MAY NOT BE STATISTICALLY VALID, BUT...

In this example it would have taken a very substantial effort to improve the conversion rate above the existing level—possibly including radical steps unacceptable to the company, such as changing the sales team. In contrast, there was potential for the company to increase the number of opportunities of being asked to quote for the business by a factor of ten or more. This obviously gave a very clear indication of where the public relations effort should be directed—into raising the market awareness of the company and the services that it offered. The direct effort to improve the sales effectiveness should be a second, though important, priority.

The importance of working to quantified objectives is that they can be used as the yardstick for measure at the end of each campaign to assess the success in performance. Where public relations is a new activity with a company, it is sometimes acceptable for the initial aims to be expressed as opportunities. As mentioned earlier, these can be refined and developed into quantified objectives over a period of years.

To quote an actual example, the aims for a public relations campaign for a manufacturer of home improvement products included:

1. To project an aura of credibility and professionalism for the company.
2. To develop a higher profile and improved product awareness at both national and local levels.
3. To attract and recruit high calibre sales representatives.
4. To create and instill within the existing salesforce a common purpose, team spirit and enthusiasm.
5. To encourage the salesforce to increase the level of sales calls in each working day.
6. To generate the maximum number of reader enquiries to be followed up by the salesforce.
7. To project the company as a responsible, ethical organization and a fair and honest trader.

It helps in the writing of the corporate public relations objectives if the organization has a clearly defined and agreed policy. For example, the Swiss chemicals manufacturing company, Ciba-Geigy, believes that its business is to serve people in society. The company is one of an increasing number today which has a set of published principles which are intended to act as guidelines. These cover responsibilities to special interests and the need for employee participation, the provision of satisfactory working conditions and the interests of both shareholders and customers.

When Sir Paul Girolami became chairman of British pharmaceuticals giant, Glaxo, he identified in precise terms the direction the group would be taking in the future, summarized as ... 'researching, producing and marketing profitably ethical prescription medicines for mankind'. This sharpened the focus of group activities and led to the company pulling together some of its subsidiaries and disposing of others that did not fit this vision.

At the other end of the scale, the smaller but long-established Kalamazoo company had lost direction; its paper-based systems had largely been overtaken by electronic office technologies. A new management team audited both internal and external communications and, from this, developed a new identity. Central to the new marketing thrust was a redefinition of the corporate aims, which included an overview statement ... 'to exploit profitably the company's opportunity to provide total business solutions of the highest quality for small and medium-sized organizations'. Such a policy obviously had an impact not just on communications but on product development, sales and other aspects of marketing.

GET MANAGEMENT TO AGREE

One helpful procedure to be followed in writing objectives is to start by getting management's agreement on the broad aims of the public relations activity. Then each aim can be converted into an objective with some measure written in which will give an indication of how well it is being achieved. These objectives need to be closely related to the sales, marketing and other commercial objectives of the company.

Take the third aim, above, related to recruitment. This might be converted into an objective by redrafting as 'to project the success, rewards and opportunities (enjoyed by the present sales personnel) to potential sales applicants and raise the response to recruitment advertisements by 50 per cent, over the year'.

Or consider a more complex position. It may well be a *sales* objective to increase distribution of the product from 20 per cent of retail outlets to 35 per cent. However, this could not be a fair *public relations* objective. Converting this commercial objective into public relations terms *is* practical, though. Depending on the industry, it might become: 'to raise awareness of our products among trade buyers from A per cent to B per cent', or 'to ensure that editorial coverage of our products is seen and noted by 55 per cent', or 'to ensure that 45 per cent of potential stockists attend regional product presentations', or 'to present the campaign video to 75 per cent of all potential retailers above a certain size'...

Before an integrated and comprehensive public relations programme can be developed, objectives have to be prepared relating to all key audiences and not just in the sales area, used in this example. These draft objectives must then be discussed across all operating divisions within the organization. It is not sufficient for the head of personnel to be approving objectives relating *only* to his personnel activities. If this were the case, then it would be impossible to balance the proportion of the effort dedicated to personnel support with the other requirements of the programme. Therefore, it is important that the personnel chief is aware of the objectives that relate to production, finance, marketing and all other aspects of the organization's activities—and vice versa.

RELATE ETHICAL AIMS TO COMMERCIAL OBJECTIVES

It is advisable that the proposed objectives should be approved at a board meeting and endorsed at the very highest level by the chief executive officer of the company. This board approval might be necessary once a year—or whenever a major change in direction of the public relations activity is necessitated.

Part of the aim of getting public relations objectives endorsed at the senior level is to make every operating division manager appreciate his own responsibilities in this area. Public relations must be seen to be closely related to the realities of commercial life—public relations can improve the calibre of recruits, help cut down absenteeism, support the share price, see the company through a tricky phase, help cope with consumer criticisms, influence proposed legislation affecting the organization, establish a reputation for fair dealing (which has sometimes proved strong enough to be used as evidence in legal proceedings).

ISSUES ANALYSIS SHOWS HOW TO PLAN FOR THE FUTURE

Issues analysis has direct relevance to public relations planning. The idea is to look at all those issues which might have an impact on the organization. These will usually be external forces operating in the trading or community environment.

As an illustration, let us take a company manufacturing electrical motors and selling these in the UK and international markets. Suppose a key customer for these is the nuclear industry? How will shareholders, employees and suppliers react to the company supplying products into a sector where there is such sensitivity?

Let us look at another issue facing our hypothetical company. The company has been seriously evaluating concentrating domestic manufacturing on larger motors and factoring a range of small motors made in, say, China. If it followed this policy what would be public reaction to this and would it be necessary to declare that these were Chinese-made? What would be the reaction of shareholders, community leaders, suppliers and customers if this change meant the closure of the small factory at Corby.

With the issues analysis approach, attention is focused on the external issues which may well have an impact on the company and, therefore, the way the company will need to accommodate or counter these. What is the issue? How might it affect the organization? What is our stance on this? What are the existing external attitudes? Whom do we wish to influence? What new attitudes do we wish to develop? How can we achieve this? What are the messages we need to project? When will these changes be produced? How will they be monitored and measured?

The final objectives for the organization need to take account of the public relations needs over, say, the next 3 years. The current activity needs to have objectives that are specific: successive years may only require these to be drafted as broader aims. This longer look at the company can also look beyond the 3-year period to try to identify trends that might prove significant to the organization. In particular, those issues that might develop over the next few years need to be discussed and evaluated: possible action to cope with these issues needs to be discussed.

Some organizations like to run an audit of the issues that are likely to affect their activities. This can often be run parallel to the periodic review of their crisis planning procedures. There can be some logic in this as certain issues—such as safety, industrial relations, shifts in public opinion and the actions of pressure groups—can produce crises which create special communications demands. However, it is important to consider not just the negative issues (which may create problems) but those that offer opportunities. Therefore, a schedule of the corporate public relations is likely to include:

1. Quantified objectives for year one and, possibly, two.
2. Detailed aims for years two and three.
3. Outline aims to cover those issues predicted to arise during, say, years two to five.
4. Broad aims to cover alternative issues that might arise beyond year five.

Although some of the examples quoted relate to commercial organizations the same principles apply to non-profit bodies. If attitudes matter to the organization, then activity and communications must be managed to create the most favourable attitudes possible.

WRITING AND AGREEING OBJECTIVES

Outlining the organization's aims

1. Who are the publics that matter to the organization?
2. What are the attitudes of these individuals and groups?
3. How are we communicating with them at present?
4. What processes exist for coordinating the existing communications efforts?
5. Who is responsible for each communication channel?
6. How do divisional managers wish their audiences to see the organization?
7. Where do we see the organization being in two, three, or more years' time?
8. What issues may develop to affect our direction or our communications policies?
9. Do we have a statement of corporate policy against which each communication activity can be checked?
10. Can this be presented in a way that clearly identifies the organization we are and how we wish to project ourselves?

Developing aims into objectives

11. Can we list all the audiences of importance?
12. How can we rate these in priority, for example, the proportion of budget-effort related to each?
13. Do we know the attitudes of each group?
14. Is there research available or do we need to undertake attitude research?
15. Can such research be undertaken within existing resources or do we need professional assistance?
16. Can we draft public relations objectives to support agreed sales, marketing, personnel, financial and other objectives?
17. What quantifiable measures can be incorporated into each objective, for example, media coverage or awareness?
18. Will these enable us to measure success at the end of the campaign?
19. What is the timescale over which we will measure the level of success?
20. Can we relate any improvement to the cost of achieving this and the value to the organization?
21. Have we agreed the procedures for monitoring both the progress towards the objectives and external factors that might affect these, for example, competitive activities?

Preparing the schedule of objectives

22. Are there any significant inconsistencies in the public relations objectives intended to support different divisions' activities?

23. Can these be resolved by mutual agreement with the divisional heads?
24. Does the draft schedule reflect all the input from these divisional heads?
25. Have we put a weighting against each area to reflect the proportion of public relations resource to be allocated?
26. Is it realistic to expect operating managers and staffs to agree and support these objectives?
27. Have we discussed whether we plan to keep these objectives confidential?
28. Who has authority to undertake communications activities?
29. What are the communications reporting lines to the public relations adviser and have these been discussed and agreed?

Getting corporate agreement

30. Have we circulated the draft objectives and asked for reactions from divisional heads?
31. Is it possible to incorporate such suggestions without a radical rewrite?
32. If not, are the comments:

    (a) Acceptable and need incorporating.
    (b) Not acceptable and need discussing with the contributor?

33. Can the final version now be presented for board approval?
34. If accepted, how is it to be presented to managers and staff?
35. Do we propose to publish this or treat it as a confidential policy document?
36. Have we advised all managers of this decision and their own responsibilities?
37. Which external bodies need to receive this, for example, our advertising agency?
38. Do we have the feedback systems to measure:

    (a) Acceptance of these objectives at all levels.
    (b) Reactions that might refine and improve these.
    (c) Support for achieving these from all operating managers.
    (d) The audience reactions to assess success?

39. Have we board agreement to present campaign results and revisions to objectives in, say, 12 or 24 months time?
40. Can the organization's budget and resource allocated to public relations be related to the success in achieving these objectives?
41. When developing public relations solutions have we considered a simple analysis technique such as the who, what, why, where, when and how formula?

- who—the publics or audiences,
- what—the messages to be conveyed,
- why—the aims or objectives,
- where—the channels to reach the diverse groups,
- when—the schedule, time-scale or critical path,
- and how—the techniques to be deployed,
- and how (much)—the budget or resource,
- and how (effective)—the monitoring or measurement.

FOUR

AUDIENCES

PUBLIC RELATIONS MUST MAINTAIN CREDIBILITY

It should be relatively simple for any organization to decide which groups of people are important to its success. This analysis can pay enormous dividends by concentrating the communications effort on areas that matter; it can pay particular dividends in times of crisis. Sir Gordon Borrie, director general of the British consumer watchdog body, the Office of Fair Trading and a distinguished lawyer, has commented that he sees public relations as an exercise in diplomacy: 'putting the facts and viewpoint of the client to whatever "jury" is appropriate—government, the buying public, shareholders, a committee of enquiry, Members of Parliament'.

Important groups of people can be overlooked when all is going smoothly. But when the going gets tough, their goodwill may be essential. However, this is also the least effective time to appeal to them: the employee who receives proper information when industrial harmony reigns may be more sympathetic when potential disputes arise: the factory neighbour you tell about next year's plant rebuilding may be more tolerant of the noise and dust than if the only information he gets is because of his protest over the work already begun!

Many boards of directors only realize the total power wielded by their shareholders when the company faces a takeover. It may be a little late to appeal to their loyalty, if the company has paid the minimum attention to communicating with this group of vital (but often silent) company supporters. Hasty advertisements in the financial media are an unconvincing way of building loyalty. This method can also be expensive in comparison with a planned programme of communications which would show the company really cared about shareholder opinion.

This communications investment principle applies throughout any effective public relations plan. Perhaps good public relations is a little like car maintenance—it costs time and money when you don't seem to need it, but saves the expense and embarrassment of a major breakdown that, sooner or later, hits those who skip on this precautionary investment.

DISILLUSION CAN CREATE MAJOR PROBLEMS

As we have established, it is a basic rule of good communications that it is only effective if it is working both ways. Much aggressive behaviour in industrial relations is due to the frustration caused among employees by managements who do not make enough effort to listen.

Recently, a respected public company in the UK engineering sector was not convinced of the need to keep shopfloor production personnel fully informed about financial policies and performance. In this, it was consistent with many manufacturing companies of the time. The policies of the company were never properly explained to the workforce, though communications with shareholders and city interests were very active. On occasions, the stories in city pages (and particularly in the *Financial Times*) relating to order levels, investment and prospects did not seem compatible with what the workers could observe from their shopfloor vantage.

Eventually, some of the workers bought shares and began attending shareholder meetings. At one well-reported agm, this small group voted overwhelmingly against every resolution proposed. The immediate reaction of the directors responsible at the time was to organize a vote by poll to outweigh the handful of shares represented by these independent-minded employee-shareholders.

Naturally, such a ploy provided no real solution to the frustration felt by the workforce, who turned to more direct methods of registering their concern and confusion. Pickets at a later meeting created picture stories in a number of newspapers. Eventually, the company was forced to make more substantial efforts to improve communications, including financial bulletins, employee-shareholder meetings and an employee report.

It was too late: the damage had been done. The lack of confidence was considered by some observers to be a key factor in making the company vulnerable to the takeover that eventually followed. This resulted in a complete reshaping of the company, the removal of virtually the whole board and the loss of many jobs.

GOODWILL IS A MEASURABLE ASSET

The important lesson for the public relations adviser is not only to identify the audiences that matter but to handle public relations on a planned basis so that a good reputation can be built.

Goodwill can only be developed where there is support for the aims of the organization. Support follows understanding which follows knowledge. And, as we all appreciate, knowledge comes from information. The failure to provide the proper information at the proper time is not just unfortunate. It can be disastrous and, ultimately, can cause the collapse of the organization.

Some managers may consider this exercise of identifying key audiences as being too obvious; yet many experienced public relations advisers believe that one of the most common failings of management is to have clearly identified *who matters*. And the groups that can make or break the organization may not all be obvious.

WHO ARE THE CUSTOMERS?

Let us consider an example. Marketing wisdom suggests that the customers are the most important audience for any company. But exactly who are these customers? Are we considering prospective customers or existing customers? Many companies know that their best potential customers *are* existing customers. The person who buys one book or record, usually buys many. The householder who buys a carpet may also buy a washing machine or lawn mower. Yet some companies make little attempt to develop communications with these existing customers.

Sometimes, products and services can be sold to potential customers where the business was lost the first time round. Enquiries that are *not* converted into sales may well produce results at a later stage—particularly if the company and its sales personnel work hard at creating a favourable impression.

Is this so obvious? If so, why do so many companies fail to communicate with their existing customers? Why do so many companies fail to communicate with enquirers who did not happen to buy *at that particular time*? How often have you bought a product which demonstrated you were 'in the market' but never received any follow-up of any sort? It happens all the time. Why has the public relations manager or adviser failed to help the sales personnel identify this as an important and profitable task?

One manufacturer of high quality, reproduction oak furniture advertised these products in full colour in the upmarket women's and home interest publications. Over a period of time the company had invested substantially in this activity. The advertising had generated a good level of enquiry. Yet, for some time, these enquiries were not collated, recorded or put together to form the basis of a mailing list. These enquiries were from people who had been sufficiently impressed at some stage to have asked for more information. They got the information ... but that was all.

People who buy furniture do not just buy one item. Nor do they just buy furniture once. Through their whole lifetime they remain prospective purchasers of furniture. Yet the executive responsible at that time for dealing with these reader enquiries had a very simple system for updating his files. When his drawer was full, he threw some out from the bottom to make space for more at the top.

UNDERSTAND BUYERS, SPECIFIERS AND USERS

So every company knows its customers ... but are customers the people who buy the products or who *specify* the products? With many engineering items, the specifier is of vital importance, while the buyer may be concerned more with the details of the purchasing decision.

Conversely, some business systems are so sophisticated they can never be introduced in the company if the board of management are not convinced—regardless of how enthusiastic the specialist specifier might be. Good examples here include electronic switchboards, telecommunications and data-processing equipment. For many years, Ericsson, GEC, IBM, ITT, Olivetti, Philips, Plessey and all the major companies in those most sophisticated markets, made sure that they presented the technical information properly to the specialist telecommunications managers. At the same time, they recognized that the big orders were picked up where the data or telecommunications manager was making a recommendation to a board that understood the system being presented.

Some of these companies were very successful at communications at the top level and moved into prestige sponsorship, VIP facility visits, seminars and corporate public relations. It is one reason why the UK publications, *Chief Executive, Management Today, The Director* and others became so important in this, and many other, business development campaigns. It also explains why the technical page of the *Financial Times* or the *Sunday Times* business section are so well read in boardrooms. And why companies who understand communications realize that coverage of their products and services in these areas is essential if they are to persuade business leaders and not just line-managers.

Consider another angle to establishing who is the customer. Is it simply the person in the company who orders the goods or services and pays the bill? Or might it be the actual *user* of the product? As an illustration, how important is the driver's view of cab comfort to the purchasing decision for lorries? Does the secretary influence the sale of the word processor? In both cases, the sales effort (and therefore the public relations) must cover these decision-influencers.

THE REAL CUSTOMERS MAY BE THE SALES TEAM

However, there can be other important intermediaries between the company and the product users. Distributors, wholesalers and agents are all important audiences. Some companies go as far as considering that their sales personnel are really the company's key customers. The public relations specialist needs to explore all these aspects with the sales and marketing experts. But there are other audiences which are of considerable importance to the organization.

Audiences can be divided into marketing and non-marketing sectors. The audiences in the non-marketing sectors can have a considerable influence upon the marketing success of the organization. Some of these audiences are not normally reached by conventional marketing means—or other communications. For example, these potentially important audiences can include the employees, the shareholders, the competitors, suppliers, factory neighbours, local and national government, trade associations, industry bodies, environmental and political pressure groups.

In many cases, individuals may be members of more than one audience. For example, someone may be both a shareholder *and* a customer. The interest in two different sectors may be in conflict—as a customer, he may be concerned about buying at the lowest possible price, while as a shareholder he may be keen on seeing his company maintaining and justifying high market prices. Similarly, the employee may well be a factory neighbour: during the day, he may be very keen on seeing the company busy and active, at night he may be less happy with the lorries coming and going ... and fellow-workers parking outside his front door.

IDENTIFY THE LONG-TERM PROBLEM ... AND OPPORTUNITY

Organizations sometimes try to appeal simultaneously to incompatible audiences—or try to use public relations as camouflage. This can be short-sighted and dangerous.

Cigarette manufacturers prosper through stimulating a hazardous and addictive habit, yet they attempt to endear themselves to the community by subsidizing healthy, open air sports. The two are inconsistent and the public may not be so gullible that it cannot see that this is the case.

COORDINATE THE MESSAGES TO THE AUDIENCES

It is, of course, the responsibility of public relations to maintain favourable attitudes among key audiences; this must be planned to support the effectiveness of the marketing activities which also have a major impact on many of the public relations audiences. It is essential that the public relations and marketing efforts are closely coordinated. It may seem obvious but this is often *not* the case. For example, a new product launch will suffer if the advertising appears at the same time as the factories go on strike. A high technology development will not be so appreciated if there is parallel editorial coverage, perhaps stimulated by a pressure group, which discusses the possible harmful effects of the development upon the environment or the health of the workers. Failure to recognize the importance of some influential groups can create problems.

Cyclamates were knocked out of the US market as a result of some questionable research, later largely discredited. But, by then, it was too late; the media had run the scare stories. The manufacturers and the industry had been too slow to respond. They had been found guilty in the cruel court of public opinion before they had even presented the case for the defence! Similarly, plans for the acceptance of the irradiation of food in the UK were greeted with hostility, orchestrated by a handful of self-appointed experts, because of a government ill-equipped to communicate the real facts and the consumer benefits to a suspicious public.

The marketing effectiveness of many companies can be seriously reduced because of inadequate attention to shareholder relations. In one recent case, a major capital goods manufacturer was being taken over by another public company. Both the industrial and financial relations were handled with equal ineptitude. There was a vigorous argument between the respective chief executives which was widely reported in the city pages—and which inevitably spilled over into the trade press. At one stage, the chairman of the company publicly queried whether the acquisition could continue to trade independently. This made headline news in the trade publications and seriously undermined the marketing effort. The salespeople of the competitors of both companies were very soon visiting prospects armed with these press cuttings. These raised a question mark over the ability of either company to deliver products; it was not surprising that some specifiers stopped specifying.

Competitors' salespeople know how to use bad newscuttings. The moral is that any company's activity outside the marketing sector can substantially influence marketing performance. It is a public relations responsibility to ensure that all sectors of the company that face up to external audiences, appreciate the importance of control and coordination.

PUBLICS MAKE JUDGEMENTS FROM GOOD NEWS ... AND BAD

Professional public relations can overcome many of these problems, particularly those which stem from the failure to understand the significance of attitudes among the defined audiences. With many products and services, attitudes can have a bigger influence on the decision to buy than price, quality or delivery.

Similarly, attitudes have a big influence on all other audiences. Some years ago, an educational survey looked at the attitudes of graduates who were considering moving into industry and asked them to rate the career opportunities offered by a number of leading manufacturers.

At the time of the survey, Ford came well down the list behind such organizations as BASF and ICI. Yet, in many respects the facilities offered to graduates by Ford were among the highest available. The reason for this apparent anomaly was identified by the researchers. The survey was carried out at a time when Ford had been experiencing some industrial relations problems which had been of considerable news interest. This had influenced this important group making decisions about careers.

When the personnel and public relations team are dealing with industrial relations matters, it is important to remember the broader impact on other audiences—in this case, prospective employees. The manager responsible for the public relations function has to convince senior management colleagues of the importance of recognizing the information needs of key audiences; these often outride their direct responsibility—the public relations chief needs to be aware of the impact of personnel policies on share price, the finance director needs to consider the impact of company results on salesforce morale, for example.

The central factor in all cases is that information intended for one specialist audience can reach all other groups. As this dissemination of information is through public relations channels, it is obviously a public relations responsibility to assess the impact of such information and advise on the timing and manner of handling the dissemination to the broader audiences. In other words, the personnel chief may rightly wish to retain responsibility for communicating with employees: however, he has to accept that the public relations chief will need to handle other audiences. Under no circumstances can important information be allowed to reach important audiences via uncontrolled or second-hand channels.

Of course, in more sophisticated organizations, the public relations specialist will be involved in formulating policy and advising executives on all aspects of organizational communications. He will need to get management agreement on the groups that matter and some assessment of priority. It will be necessary to measure the existing attitudes, then plan and implement programmes designed to develop optimum attitudes towards the organization.

CONSIDER EACH INFORMATION GROUP SEPARATELY

A communications audit will not only appraise the effectiveness of any existing communications. It will also identify those individuals and groups of individuals critical to the organization's success. Let us look at this step by step: identifying the audiences; locating priorities; measuring attitudes; evaluating communications opportunities; reinforcing company credibility.

Start by listing all publics or audiences that appear to be important. Try to be specific—not just 'customers' but, for example, 'retailers' or, better still, 'the managers of independent retailers in primary high street sites with premises of a retail area not less than 5000 sq. ft', or whatever may be appropriate. This initial listing may well identify several different sectors within each audience group—within the broader retailers' category, or within, say, employees (management, supervisory, shop floor, delivery personnel and so on).

Produce this draft list, initially, in alphabetical order to avoid any weighting towards any department. Circulate it to directors, division or departmental heads, as appropriate, asking them to notify any omissions.

Interview each main division or department head to establish the importance of each group; the scope of existing communications; present attitudes (if known); unexploited communications opportunities; existing channels of communication (e.g. professional bodies or trade associations, works committees or social clubs and so on); future activities that might be of interest or could affect these groups; activities within each management discipline that could affect other company audiences (e.g. possible personnel changes that could create news which would influence customers), and so on. From the interviews, the public relations adviser will be able to confirm the important audiences and, equally important, potential communications channels and likely information requirements.

ASK YOUR COLLEAGUES . . . WHO MATTERS?

How do you establish the communication priorities to give some weighting to the public relations efforts to reach the different audiences? Whichever the technique agreed, it is essential to try to establish some priority that will be accepted by all directors or divisional heads. (They need to accept that only a realistic proportion of the efforts can be directed towards the special requirements of the audiences within their own sector.)

However, this balancing of the effort will help reinforce to each divisional head the responsibility that *all* managers have for good communications; the public relations specialist should be seen as an adviser and planner, helping to coordinate the very diverse communications activities undertaken by all lively organizations. The public relations manager is *not* responsible for all communications, any more than the finance director is responsible for all money matters and, therefore, collects the money for lunches in the canteen.

The vital question to ask in trying to decide the importance of the various audiences is . . . how dependent is the organization on their goodwill?

For example, it may mean that they can be separated into categories; their goodwill towards the organization is critical; contributory; helpful; or simply desirable. (This last category might include those groups towards whom the organization feels a responsibility, but which have limited or long term commercial influence—local charities might be an example. This should not mean the organization makes no effort to generate favourable atttudes in these sectors, but that they may not warrant *exclusive* communications efforts and may be grouped with other community publics.)

IDENTIFY THE PRESSURE POINTS ... AND THEIR INFLUENCE

However, some minority groups may well require special attention. If the organization is working in a sensitive area such as defence, chemicals, tobacco, pharmaceuticals or political research, it is essential that any pressure groups are identified. However, most organizations would be wise to keep the influence of pressure groups in perspective. In many cases, their power is limited to the amount of media attention they can create; an effective handling of public issues by the organization will keep their influence in balance.

Suppose your company manufactures potentially toxic chemicals; then the Friends of the Earth might be an extremely important group, requiring special handling. However, if you use plastic packaging for your own products, then the measurement of this pressure group's importance relates more to public concern about plastic packaging (or lack of it) than it does to the attitudes that Friends of the Earth may have on the subject. Indeed, public concern has encouraged many companies to launch plastics recycling schemes.

For while many organizations underestimate the influence of some groups, many overestimate the power of others that simply have the ability to make media noise. Often this media noise relates more to the inability of the organization to handle criticism than it does to the merits of the pressure group's case. Consumer protection bodies, trade union leaders, TV pundits, are often examples of observers with more bark than bite.

In judo, the skill would be knowing when to turn away from trouble; when to make peace with your opponent; when to bend with your protagonist and use his weight to throw him over your shoulder; and when to smack your assailant in the face. Public relations is often like communications judo.

In the analysis of the key audiences, these factors matter. The efforts that can be expended on coping with a spurious watchdog may be better spent on a group of people who *really* matter. In many cases, pressure groups

....public relations is like communications judo

can only apply pressure because of the negligence of the companies they oppose. If the organization cares, it has worked to establish its reputation and keeps open the channels of communications, then it will be less likely to be asked to explain itself to any self-appointed inquisitor.

Some US companies have become oversensitive to the unauthenticated criticism of doubtful consumer protectionists or the spurious social audits of bodies more concerned with controlling enterprise than creating wealth. The more cooperative and compliant the organizations became, the stiffer the demands on them.

In some cases, better attention to being good citizens and better care about their social responsibility would have enabled these corporations to have politely but firmly told these inquisitors to play elsewhere. The moral is that if you have done your homework and kept your slate clean then you can afford to tell the busybodies to take a running jump.

ACTIVITY MUST NOT BE CONFUSED WITH RESULTS

From the assessment discussions with senior colleagues, the public relations manager will be able to give some weighting to those audiences. This will be reflected in the balance of the programmes to be planned and implemented. To calculate this balance, it is helpful to give a numerical weighting to each group. The final calendar of activity will reflect these ratings.

The weighting may not always be the same as the priority. For example, some contingency situations may require the diversion of effort into a particular sector, for a period—an example might be an increased emphasis on personnel relations at the time of an industrial dispute, or more weight behind trade relations when a new competitor enters the market. (Of course, good planning will hold contingencies to the minimum. The 'unexpected' can often be redefined, unfortunately, as 'unexpected by management'!)

The attitudes reflected by the audiences may influence the amount of effort to be applied in each sector. An undersubscribed share issue could be an embarrassing and expensive way of finding out that the city and shareholder relations require attention, for example. As every experienced manager knows, activity must not be confused with results.

It is essential to check attitudes among the more important groups. This effort should not be confused with monitoring the results, which is covered in some detail in another chapter.

The objective is to audit the communications and the audiences' needs to establish that a sound programme is being planned. This should obviously be structured in parallel with any intended monitoring of the effectiveness. The audit should cover these points: this is how the organization is perceived, this is how we would like it to be seen, this is the activity we will undertake to achieve this change in attitude and, finally, this is how we will asess our success in achieving this objective.

BROADEN THE COMMUNICATIONS TARGET

If you know the audiences and how they perceive the organization, how can you identify the opportunities to influence them? Later, we will be looking at the elements that could be part of a planned programme. At this stage, consider how these efforts might be structured. Certain audiences will be so important they will need direct communications channels established. These often exist because their needs are so obvious. Others may require only existing activities to be adapted to reach them. A third group might require efforts of a special nature, tailored for their requirements.

Some of the audiences may not be sufficiently important to warrant a substantial commitment of time or budget. However, it can be advisable to consider methods of covering these sectors so that the company does not appear indifferent or discourteous. This can often be achieved with simple leaflets, documents or notes. Sometimes standard letters, established on a word processor, can be specifically prepared to handle certain categories of enquiries—retired employees, prospective employees, teachers, students, researchers, and so on.

Communications to a low priority sector can often be improved by directing other communications activity towards them rather than the cost and manpower investment in creating completely separate efforts. Invite the leader of the city council to the agm, mail the annual report to suppliers, get existing employees to deliver invitations to the factory open day to pensioners, and so on. It only requires a little imagination.

PUBLIC RELATIONS IS THE ROUTE MAP TO DISCIPLINED SUCCESS

From these elements, the actual calendar of activity can be constructed. The most effective public relations campaigns are based usually upon a detailed programme of activity. Of course, there will be contingencies (and opportunities) that may not be pre-planned. But it is always better to adapt the programme to accommodate them, rather than flying solely by the seat of the pants. To stretch the metaphor, the aviator uses a map to get from A to B, but can always change course if he hits a storm.

All the elements in the final campaign must be coordinated and they must project a consistent corporate personality. This does not mean projecting the *same* perspective: if the personality is to be real and rounded, it is logical that different aspects will be shown to different audiences. This is exactly the same as the different aspects of the individual's personality that may be revealed to different groups—colleagues at work, friends in the club, children at home.

These efforts are designed to close the credibility gap. Consequently, to see if the influence on these audiences has been effective, the attitudes need to be monitored and re-measured. This will also enable objectives and the activity to be adjusted as the programme progresses.

The public relations specialist will not know if the activity has worked unless he has an agreed method of measuring this. (This aspect is covered in some detail in Chapter 28 on research.) Equally important, he will not be able to convince anyone else of the success in influencing key audiences without this evidence.

But the finest measure of the effectiveness of the relations with all the audiences which relate to the organizations will be the smoothness of its operations. Sensitive management producing good policies, well communicated, will create favourable attitudes and the best possible environment within which the organization operates. And this success will stem from a

AUDIENCES	ATTITUDES				
	Critical	Contributory	Helpful	Desirable	TOTALS
Employees					
Managers	17				
Production		11			
Sales team	12				40
Customers					
Wholesalers			5		
Retailers		8			
End-users	22				35
Corporate					
Shareholders		7			
Government			4		
Suppliers				2	13
Community					
Recruits		6			
Neighbours			5		
Educationalists				1	12
TOTALS	51	32	14	3	100%

Chart 4.1 When key audiences have been agreed, some weighting can be given to the level of the professional public relations resource to be allocated to developing relations in each of these sectors. This might later be related to time or budget. In this simple example, a percentage weighting has been used. This could be translated into the time available for each activity. For example, assuming one public relations specialist with 250 days per year available, he or she would spend 5 on supplier relations and 55 on consumer relations each year.

clear appreciation of the publics that control that success of the organization.

AGREEING THE COMMUNICATIONS AUDIENCES

Drafting the preliminary list

1. Does our previous activity give us an indication of audiences that matter to the organization?
2. Can we ask directors or divisional heads to list those audiences they consider important?
3. Have we asked them to break these down into practical sub-groups, for example, customers into wholesalers, retailers and so on?

4. Is it possible to identify the prime sector within each group, for example, MPs with an airport in their constituencies?
5. Have we double-checked these listings with those managers in each division who may be closer to the key audiences?
6. Can we identify groups that could be of relevance if certain issues developed or emergencies arose, for example, Friends of the Earth?
7. Have we identified those groups whose support might be taken for granted, for example, family shareholders, the charity founders?
8. Are there publics that might represent more than one group, for example, shareholder/customers or employee/neighbours?
9. Would there be any potential conflict in information they might receive from different sources, for example, annual report/house journal, local newspaper/factory poster?
10. Has the organization experienced any problems or difficulties that might suggest influential groups that need greater consideration?
11. Have we asked our colleagues with communications functions (advertising, marketing, personnel, for example), to give their views?
12. Which audiences might be reached by direct communications and which by indirect communications, for example, the house journal or local radio station?
13. Can any of these audiences be grouped together for communications purposes, for example, civic leaders and local businessmen?
14. Have we established the means to monitor the attitudes of these audiences, for example, by providing feedback channels such as reply questionnaires or discussion groups?
15. Are there existing communications channels that reach any of these audiences?
16. Can we identify other existing channels that have not yet been used, for example, trade associations, local business groups, professional bodies?

Producing the coordinated audience profile

17. Can we now draft these audiences into a comprehensive list, possibly in non-priority alphabetical order?
18. Is it possible to divide these into groups and sub-groups for ease of planning, for example, internal, marketing, community audiences?
19. Can we give each an importance rating, for example, where goodwill is essential, or contributory, or helpful, or desirable?
20. What weighting relating to the allocation of resource can we put against each group, for example, a numerical factor from 1 to 10?
21. Can we now check this back against the public relations objectives and potential issues that will need handling?

Agreeing the audience plan

22. Have we interviewed divisional or departmental heads to obtain their views on relative importance?
23. Are the emergency situations covered which, in the short term, might have priority over the deployment of resources, for example, with employees at times of industrial action?
24. Has this final listing with weightings been circulated to divisional heads and approved?
25. Is there a feedback system so that the public relations adviser is alerted to any change in these communications audiences?

FIVE

MANAGING THE REPUTATION

THE CORPORATE STANCE IS VITAL

Some organizations discuss whether they should have public relations or not: they have no option. An organization has no choice whether to 'have' public relations. All organizations are communicating with all audiences that are of importance to them, whether they like it or not; all are listening (or not listening) to the reactions of key publics to their activities.

The decision is not whether to have public relations, but whether these relations will be handled in a planned, organized manner . . . or allowed to be accidental, haphazard and possibly inconsistent. It is a fact that, in the absence of evidence to the contrary, an organization is what it *says* it is . . . or what it *shows* itself to be.

Some organizations allow their reputation to evolve naturally. Others allow their publics to decide—perhaps create—their personality profile. Others, particularly those participating in the commercial sector, make positive decisions about what they stand for, how they will behave, how they wish to be seen—all facets of the corporate personality.

Some companies simply state what they are and then organize themselves to live up to their self-styled standards. Rolls-Royce advertising used to describe its vehicles as 'the best car in the world'. The Philips electronics group talked about 'simply years ahead'. For a major corporate UK television campaign, ICI called itself the 'pathfinders'. Each set a target for performance for all aspects of the organization. Such statements can be rather bland unless backed by a more substantial mission statement. Management needs to be careful about whom they entrust with the preparation of such slogans. Too many are created in consultancies or advertising agencies by writers with only a superficial understanding of the businesses they are advising.

(When I was a writer in agencies, there were a number of buzz-words regularly used in various permutations to indicate the excellence of the client in their business sector, however esoteric. I am embarrassed to be the author of 'pacemakers in industrial gases' and 'world leaders in grassland technology', both in use some 20 years later and to this day, as far as I know. It would be good to feel the world has moved on, but just one edition of the *Wall Street Journal* or the *Financial Times* will prove that banality is still thriving in corporate advertising.)

Every organization is making a positive statement about itself in everything that it does and everywhere it is seen, not just when speaking publicly or when exposed to the glare of the media. Every telephone call, every vehicle, every letterhead, every comment by members of the staff, every advertisement, every poster, everything that carries the company name is making a statement about the organization.

Does it matter? And do these aspects have an influence? There are at least three main levels at which persuasive communications work and it would help to look at these.

UNDERSTAND THE DIFFERENCE BETWEEN INFORMATION, OPINION, ATTITUDE

Information is obviously an essential element in any communication programme. Information helps shape opinion. But information is only *one* element and not necessarily the most important. However, few communications programmes can do much unless they have a hard core of information—few valuable opinions can be built unless they are on the basis of clearly understood fact.

An opinion may be held with conviction, but it may or may not be true. For example, an employee may have an opinion that the company does not consider staff views when making decisions. If that is true, then the company has a problem. If it is *not* true, then it may be a relatively simple matter to provide information to enable the employee to change views. For example, the company might need to explain the processes involved in consulting its employee or how employee views can affect decisions taken by the company.

However, if this employee were to feel that the company is a poor organization to work for, then the management has a *real* problem, because that view will be an attitude. *No amount of information alone will change an attitude*.

This simplification is not always true. Bad news (negative information) can change attitudes—for example, an industrial accident can create public concern over products or processes, as we have seen in Europe over chemical spillages into the Rhine. Yet good news (positive information) alone will not reverse this perception. Favourable attitudes are not created so simply. *You must be a good company because your annual report says so!*

An attitude reflects a position or stance adopted by someone. This may be shaped by the influence of comments and other peoples' opinions, as well as direct observation. Sometimes attitudes can be developed over many years—your attitude towards Renault, for example, or Belgium or conservation; attitudes can also be created almost within seconds—as we saw, for example, with Union Carbide at Bhopal or Exxon in Alaska.

Surveys consistently prove that attitudes do not always relate to the facts. Was Watergate the worst blunder of Nixon's administration? Are the Irish *really* stupid and the Italians cowardly? In European Parliamentary circles they tell the story of the European heaven and the European hell. In the European heaven, the French are the chefs, the Germans the administrators, the British the police and the Italians the lovers. In the European hell, the Italians are the police, the French the administrators, the Germans the lovers and the British the chefs!

A more serious but parallel illustration of these deeply-held perceptions has been demonstrated by leading opinion researchers, MORI. Bob Worcester's teams researched the European nations' perceptions of each other in relation to such areas as productivity, exports, product quality, industrial relations and so on. The relative placings of each nation varied significantly from country to country—reflecting, perhaps, more the attitudes of the viewer than the realities of the situation.

If public opinion can oust a president or bring the East German or Polish people on to the streets, it can make an awful mess of any business communications plan—however well-intentioned.

Now this illustrates a most important point: actions are sometimes the uncontrolled element in many communications programmes. After all, it is what *happened* at Bhopal, in the shipyards of Poland, the jungles of Vietnam and the streets of Belfast and not what was *said* that so dramatically influenced public opinion and created such powerful attitudes towards these issues.

This is equally true for organizations. It is not just what they say but what they do, or are reported to do, that is of importance. There must be no disparity between what the organization says and what it does.

The importance of attitude

Why should an organization spend time, money and effort in creating favourable attitudes? Because attitudes are a major factor in influencing decisions.

Attitude is the biggest single factor in influencing any decision. Shareholders' attitudes towards the company will help influence whether they invest or not—just as powerfully as the security of the investment or the financial return they will get. Attitudes will help decide whether people work for the company—just as certainly as the conditions of employment and rates of pay. Attitudes will be a significant factor in convincing people to contribute time or money to a charitable cause—just as much as how persuasively they are asked.

Above all, attitudes will help sell the product . . . whether that product is a community group, a football match or a motor car. If you are not convinced, then consider this. Would you buy a Libyan watch?

Why not? Suppose the price is right? Quality, delivery, service, everything is right. You don't believe it? The sales person says so. The advertising says so. But it is going to take a lot more than their information to change your attitude. Right now, for all I know, the Libyans could be putting out the right messages about Libyan watches. But are you receiving them? Even if you are receiving them, are you believing them?

Accentuate the positive

If communication is to be effective, the business communicator needs to consider the stance from which his organization is speaking. It is not only what is said and to whom that matters . . . but where is this message coming from and when?

As a simple example, the public would view with caution information about the pharmaceutical industry that comes from the country's largest drugs producer. Also, they will have a different attitude towards information that comes to them as part of a continuing debate on the issue—in comparison to the information that may be published to answer a public criticism or which follows a mishap with one of the drugs.

A popular way to express this is that prevention is better than cure, or attack can be better than defence. But the public relations adviser needs to be careful about entering into the attack. The short-term benefits can look good but the long-term situation can become a disaster.

Take the actual case of the yellow fats market in Europe. The development of mass-selling margarines was achieved with the support of public relations and advertising which increasingly stressed the claimed health benefits of vegetable oils. In particular, the margarines that were high in polyunsaturated fats took an aggressive stand on the health issue. Van den Berghs, the largest manufacturer in the UK market, ran the Flora project for heart disease prevention for many years. They issued literature and information to millions of consumers and throughout the medical profession. Some other brands undertook equally aggressive promotional campaigns. The obvious subject of this attack was the butter industry, where sales declined, at one stage, at a significant 5 per cent per annum in Britain alone.

The butter industry mounted a substantial advertising campaign to counter these arguments. It showed that butter was a simple, natural product but margarines were processed, treated and handled in factories more like chemical plants. The public relations support for this campaign also went on the attack with news material claiming the fat scare was running out of steam. Over three million booklets were distributed to homes and the Butter Information Council sponsored a cardiology conference on alternative coronary heart disease risk factors.

This public health battle did not expand the overall market. It succeeded in creating media hostility and considerable public confusion. In the end, the two sides of the controversy defeated each other.

The public relations specialist should remember the old advice to *accentuate the positive*. And, if this is the technique to achieve your objective, why antagonize the opposition? You could both be the losers in the end.

THE RECEIVER IS THE MESSAGE

Let us look at what is *communication*. Marshall McLuhan got it wrong. The *receiver* is the message. Not the medium and not the sender. Because the receiver selects those messages he wants to hear and those he wants to accept.

No message can be sent until the acceptance of it has been set up. After all, Marconi would hardly have had much success in inventing the transmitter if he had not invented the radio receiver! Similarly, in human communications, the audience must be tuned to receive the message *before* it is transmitted. The essential factor for effective communications is empathy; any programme should be based on listening before speaking—and it must be structured to achieve real two-way communications.

The company plans its message, but whether it communicates depends on whether the audience want to know or want to believe the information . . . or trust the source. People *automatically* and instantly decide whether they should trust the source. They have very different attitudes to those messages which are *in the family* and those from strangers.

When your head ofice in Detroit or Geneva tells those folks in Manchester or Adelaide the good news, do they *receive* it as good news—or with caution, even suspicion? It may depend on whether they see the messenger as being in the family. It is worth working on building reliable and regularly-used channels of communication which eventually will become trusted.

Effective *family* communications has been one of the reasons for the Japanese success in their trade colonisation of the world. Although their culture is alien to many of the people with whom they work, they make considerable efforts to recruit the best quality of management that they can find in each country where they operate. They brief them thoroughly on all aspects of corporate activity and use them as their channels of communi-

.cation. Local management like to be involved and consulted; in turn they become respected and trusted by their colleagues in their own countries.

LOGIC IS NOT COMMUNICATION

It takes more, much more, than logic for effective communications. For, however clear, precise, accurate, truthful and factual the message may be, it may still not be communicating. The managing director of the German engineering subsidiary of a large American corporation called the whole staff of 100 in one division into the canteen to explain the implications of a new investment plan. It was part of his passion for face-to-face communications. However, he was not very good at it. One hundred interested, curious, anticipatory expressions faced him. And he began: 'I don't want any of you to worry about your jobs.'

The statement was truthful, factual and well-intentioned. The result was disaster. Instantly, one hundred enthusiastic people became worried about their jobs. The more-able immediately began to consider alternative employment. The less-able became suspicious, cautious, uncooperative.

The truth is not enough. The facts are not always relevant. Logic can be of limited value. The personnel director of a major construction company had to explain cut-backs to a group of clerical staff. One queried the chairman's new Rolls-Royce. 'He bought that', explained the hapless negotiator, 'because it's a good investment. It goes up in value faster than inflation.'

The facts may have been correct. It may be logical but everyone at the meeting knew it was a lame excuse. The chairman bought a Rolls-Royce because he wanted one. Investment was just the justification. The personnel director might have been better to discard the logical but unbelievable tack and have adopted the bolder, positive approach, 'The chairman has a new Rolls-Royce because it represents the best in motor engineering. It says about cars what we believe about our buildings. It projects our confidence in our success, when he is out acting as ambassador. He works hard, he's earned it. He deserves it and enjoys it. We would too if we had achieved what he had.'

GOOD COMMUNICATION NEEDS EMOTION

Do you remember the theory of relativity? Perhaps you don't. Perhaps you should, for it has had a profound effect on science and an enormous impact on the whole world around us. Do you remember the films you went to as a teenager, perhaps the songs, the plots, the gags? Perhaps you do. Perhaps you should, for they had a profound effect on your lifestyle and a minimal real impact on the whole world around us.

The moral is not that Einstein should have put more gags in his theory. But that emotion appeals more than logic. Mercedes and SAS are not just good employers of people because of some finely polished employment policies. They are good because they care deeply and this commitment comes through within minutes of discussion with any of their personnel. Does the care, the commitment, the passion come through when *your* colleagues talk about your organization? If not, why not? It is worth working on.

AUDIENCES ARE PEOPLE

If communication is concerned about receiving, then we must all accept that we are weak, superficial, human characters and we receive messages in an illogical and emotive way. It might not be good enough for Einstein but it is the only way for audiences of ordinary folk.

But there is still a danger here. What are these audiences? Who are these folk? And are they so ordinary? Each one of us is an individual person who will react in an individual way. Consider this. You go to a football match and there are 50 000 or 100 000 people around you. Yet that crowd is composed entirely of individuals like you. Indeed, it's certainly composed of individuals who are *not* like you. They probably have no more in common than the millions of people across Europe who at the same time may be fishing from the bank of rivers and lakes. Yet no one would ever call those millions of fishermen a crowd ... or an audience.

Never underestimate the intelligence of the audience, they say. And never overestimate their knowledge. For—so goes the theory—most general audiences are composed of lay folk with no specialized knowledge. But that, too, is wrong. Almost every member of every audience is a specialist, with deep, specialized knowledge of their particular subject.

EVERYONE KNOWS MORE THAN YOU

An unthinking manager in a well-known public company began a talk to a visiting group of investment analysts with the words: 'I don't know how many of you got beyond basic physics, but micro-electronics is a bit specialist, so stop me if you get lost following the drift . . .'.

He meant well but failed miserably in communicating. He succeeded in getting everyone he was addressing to switch off their receivers. Why? How could an intelligent, experienced person get it so wrong? An audience is not a single body, it is composed of individuals. People must always talk to individuals. And the phrase 'I don't know how many of you' makes it clear he sees the group as all being the same. That was his first gaff.

But it gets worse. 'Basic physics' may be a joke, but it is an insult to an audience many of whom had arts degrees and professional qualifications. 'A bit specialist' suggests the speaker is the rare one of intellect, not his audience. In fact, no one is going to 'stop me if you get lost following the drift'.

The 'communicating' manager should have built a bridge, established his regard for the visitors and led them gently into his area. He might have begun: 'I appreciate your work is vital to our industry (*recognition is a hundred times better than the warmest welcome*) and forgive my limited financial knowledge. However, behind the complexities of your profession (*gentle compliment this*) I am sure there are some basic simple rules and the same is true of my own craft (*appealing modesty!*), micro-electronics. If you haven't had the opportunity of spending 20 years in this business, (*to explain why the speaker knows a little more than the guests*) let me outline some points you might find of interest ...'.

Five minutes working on his introduction might have made the first manager a million times better at communicating.

CONFLICT IS NATURAL

In some circles, it is fashionable to consider the behaviour of people in terms of conditioned reflex. Indeed, there is even a theory that much of our behaviour is inherited instinct, in exactly the same way as the migration of birds or the web-spinning ability of spiders.

The human species evolved over thousands, hundreds of thousands, even millions of years. To put this into perspective, there would certainly be no measurable difference in intelligence between modern men and women and the ancient Egyptians. We may have more accumulated experience, we may have more information, we may have more records and methods of transmitting this data, but we do *not* have any more intelligence.

This period of time which we can call history, and in which we have completely changed the face of the world, is but a tiny moment by comparison with the evolution of our species. If you were to consider the period since our remote predecessor appeared on this earth as, say, a day, then primitive man would have appeared around 6 o'clock in the evening. And while for us the clock is chiming midnight, our ancient Egyptian cousins were building their pyramids *just 30 seconds before midnight*.

Our species was developed to live in a far more primitive world where, superficially, different factors for success and survival existed. Today, we all carry with us those same instincts, although civilization has taught us to control and direct them. Public demonstrations around the world have become accepted as a reflection of the views of the people, although they are rarely democratic and often are a direct show of strength, even when no physical violence occurs. However, in controlling and directing our instincts we do not need to suppress them. Conflict, today, can certainly be considered as natural and can be productive when directed into the proper channels.

As a simple example, industrial, business or political disputes are generally thought to be negative and destructive. However, they can be viewed as an extremely effective way of resolving different points of view. They do not normally involve any direct force or violence. They do not appear to have any lasting effects on relations between groups. Indeed, some of the most extreme disagreements can produce a high degree of satisfaction, mutual respect and understanding between both sides.

Though this is not yet proven, a factor of immediate practical assistance is the understanding that conflict is a natural state and a healthy step towards the resolution of different points of view. Disputes can present us with some of the best opportunities for lively, effective two-way communication. Yet how often do organizations miss the opportunity? How many company communications programmes are bland, as if we were all in perfect unity and accord?

The public relations manager need not necessarily be terrified of conflict, but accept it as a natural aspect of human relations; we all have a continuing role to play in the resolution of conflict. To quote Howard Moody, director of Scottish Enterprise: ... 'Tension can be a valuable contributory factor in management, so long as it is constructive and not destructive tension'.

The communicator plays a vital role if he has a two-way programme which enables views to be expressed both ways. Conflicts can be resolved in a civilized atmosphere—rather than suppressed to the point where conflict can break out in a less acceptable form. Constructive tension can sharpen relationships, introduce healthy competition and bring out the best in people by challenging their accepted views.

BE SENSITIVE TO THE COMMUNICATION ENVIRONMENT

There is another important factor which must be considered in all communications programmes and that is the communication environment. Within our own family, our own community, our own town, perhaps even our own county and our own country, we understand these conventions so well that we barely give them a second thought. The problems arise when we are communicating across geographic or social barriers. Local traditions can be very strong and can distort communications. As Norm Leaper, president of the International Association of Business Communicators, has said, cultural ignorance can hurt when doing business in a foreign environment. For example, in some countries of the world white is the colour of mourning, not black. So that could make nonsense of your corporate identity.

The Bank of London in South America used to be called by its initials BOLSA until someone pointed out that that was the name of a different sort of trading establishment where bankers do not go—at least not during banking hours! For generations, the Russians were paranoid about the West because they have been invaded and ravaged by Ghengis Khan, Napoleon and Hitler.

Rolls-Royce nearly launched the Silver Mist, which in Germany would have given Mercedes a laugh, where 'mist' is something you might use to fertilize your roses. Products that have been considered for international sales have carried names that were innocuous in their original language but hilarious in English—such as the chocolate called Plopp, the toilet paper called Krapp and the sweets called Sor-Bits.

A telephone call to make a business appointment in Japan can be considered rude. Business discussions in Italy always wait until the second meeting. On a social level, Europeans know that you never call Germans by their first name; they don't like it. Never invite a Frenchman to a social event without his wife. Americans should not be upset if they are not invited home by English colleagues: it's not the custom. Such social traditions help create the communication convention which you break at your peril.

In the US, the working breakfast is common but it is not a normal concept on other continents. Indeed, in Japan, the deal is more likely to be cemented in a late night bar or club.

Superficial airport guides to local cultures and customs may not be too helpful, other than to act as a warning that, as they say in Norfolk in England, 'they do different'. If possible read a specific local cultural handbook. Or, bettter still, get a local manager to advise you. However, to illustrate the dangers, it might be cautionary to look at some of the more obvious differences.

For example, do not expect to do much business in Riyadh on a Friday, for that is their Sabbath, while, in Tel Aviv, it is Saturday and, in the UK, Sunday; though only a tiny proportion of Brits are actively religious, it is virtually impossible to do business on this family day. A visiting chief who tries to set up a meeting on a Sunday may create much unspoken resentment.

The simplest rule is, if in doubt, simply be careful and polite. Of course, it is wise to be aware of the most obvious gaffs. Do not swat a fly in front of a Hindu, for he may feel it could be the reincarnation of a departed relative. As a Thai thinks the head is holy and the feet unholy, watch that you do not cross your legs and point your foot at his head, for he will be very insulted. Do not expect an Arab to be delighted at the family snaps with your wife or daughter in a bikini; he will merely be embarrassed. Arabs only eat with their right hand and would expect you to behave similarly. Do not include lamb on your carefully-chosen menu for your Japenese guests; they may be unable to eat it as it makes them feel ill.

Other countries also have different ways of doing business. In the Middle East, for example, do not be surprised if other people join your meeting for parts of the discussion, unintroduced. In Japan, it always seems to take a whole team to discuss everything. In both cases, do not object for they will be reviewing your case together later.

Body language also does not translate at all. In some countries in Europe, forming your thumb and forefinger into a circle means OK but in others it is a very rude gesture. An Iranian will be saying 'no' when he briskly nods his head and not 'yes'. Your Arab counterpart will use a bewildering complexity of hand signs that are meaningless to virtually anyone except another Arab. As some signs mean different things in different countries, the simple rule has to be to use none—including your own familiar ones—unless you are 100 per cent sure of their meaning.

The changing scene can make or break

The universal product sounds like the marketing dream, but it can cause problems. The world is becoming sensitive to universal uniformity. The multinational society is changing to the micronational society. Nationalism is acceptable. Small is beautiful. Ethnic and cultural differences are accentuated. And not just across countries but, almost, from city to city, village to village, street to street.

As third world nations grow out of the cultural-adolescence of aping Western customs they may reject heavily-promoted, foreign-oriented, locally-unsympathetic life styles and products. What role in this possible scenario should the public relations professional play? He should be monitoring the position, talking to opinion leaders, researching attitudes and advising management.

Brewers across the world learned, to their cost, that their uniformity policy did not work. Today, hotels groups are questioning the validity of the universal corporate style and off-the-shelf design. Will the Hilton or Ramada in Cologne always be the same as those in Milan? Hotels that reflect local ways are showing a strong resurgence and the large groups are moving to more local flavour in architecture, design, science and food. High street stores are learning the same lessons. They continue to listen to the market environment; this is constantly changing and no company should rely on a formula simply because it has brought them success to date. As the eyes and ears of the company (and not just its voice), the public relations executive has a key role to play. He will be aware more than most of his fellow managers of public attitudes, perception and demands that his organization needs to anticipate. Although a sensitivity to market needs is vital for every organization, it is in retailing that the changes are often the most noticeable, for they affect us all.

Today's market is now the world

It must be certain that tomorrow's shops will be as different from today's as these are from the ones our parents patronized. Despite the common background, US or French stores are a world removed from UK concepts.

When Habitat opened in the United States, the concept worked but had to be adapted. Initially, the store, trading under the name Conran, projected itself as being of European origin but soon developed its own US identity. For example, the range of glassware had to be changed for the British products were not nearly big enough for US tastes. Knock-down furniture, designed for self-assembly, was a completely new concept, but the company stuck with this as they felt it an idea worth establishing. Duvets hardly existed but again these were successful when they were re-launched in the United States as comforters.

The harmonization of Europe has created an acceleration in the translation of retailing concepts from one country to another. The major transatlantic moves—both ways—are already familiar. Other sectors that are picking the best experience from wide-spread international operations in such regions as Europe, North America and Asia include home electronics, business systems, financial services, religious marketing, community planning, charities and even government services; other organizational sectors will follow the concept of selecting the most innovative practice and testing its application, suitably adapted, across other nations. All such developments provide challenges for the public relations professional who increasingly will be expected to advise his management on the opportunities within their own competitive markets. Few people in public relations will be able to afford a solely national perspective or they will get fenced in their own backyards by aggressive and imaginative competitors, many of these being new into the market. Let us consider another important communications guideline. Everybody cares, but nobody cares as much as you do! Perhaps it is right that you are projecting your company as a thoughtful, caring organization, involved in the community and with a strongly developed sense of responsibility. Your company may believe it and you must believe it. The community may not.

What is acceptable in one business environment may not be acceptable in another. Indeed, what is acceptable in one time may not be acceptable now. World events have a powerful influence. For example, not many people now go to fancydress parties in Texas, dressed as Arabs. A comic British character Ali Jamjar was created to promote a glass recycling scheme; he was banned from one city, through the efforts of a minority ethnic council group, on the grounds of racialism. Black Georgia politicians succeeded in getting the Southern rebel anthem 'Dixie' banned from official state events because of its historical connections.

Nor could a company today carry out the simple altruistic and well meaning exercise that it did in the 'thirties. The founder of Mayers, the US sausage company, distributed free sausages to the poor during the depression and that was accepted as being a generous and well meaning gesture. Who would dare do it today?

The message to the communicator today is to know the communications conventions within which you are working.

PEOPLE ARE HUNGRY FOR INFORMATION

Information is as essential to the human spirit as exercise is to the human body. This requirement for information is not just a desire but is a deep felt need. People need to know the news . . . and particularly the bad news. As we know, there is no such thing as a vacuum in information. Merely because the news is bad, is not a good enough reason for withholding it.

For we all know that rumour, gossip and speculation are always worse than the real news. Managers with communications responsibility must try to handle the bad news as positively as the good news. If the organization does this effectively, the good news will have more impact and the organization will be trusted, even when it has to handle an unpleasant, sensitive situation.

Someone's good news, in one part of the globe, can become someone's bad news across the world. An investment in one country may mean a cutback in another. Automation in one may mean redundancies in another. Today, news is international and instant. It is no good putting out the story today from London or Toronto and thinking tomorrow about the situation in New Zealand or Brazil.

One multinational corporation developed a system for communicating major policy simultaneously around the world through telex from their Paris head office; this meant that the telex operators were better informed than management. The workforce in one African plant walked out over one policy decision, before the general manager had any idea what all the fuss was about.

One useful principle to avoid leaks is to shorten the lead time on information. As early as possible after the decision is made, let people know. Always tell your *own* people before you tell the world at large. If the news is bad, the principles still apply. Handle it boldly and honestly. At best you reduce the impact. And often you score points for honesty and courage.

An obvious example of the truth of this is the credibility that the BBC generated for itself during the Second World War by being prepared to broadcast the bad news as well as the good. Similarly, some international corporations you believe—Shell or KLM, for example—others you may not. Consistency is convincing. Any organization is likely to be better understood if it has a consistent stance. Schizophrenia is no more attractive in corporations than it is in people.

It may be right for IBM to project itself as large and efficient—though its very efficiency may run the danger of it coming over as a cold organization. Equally, your local garage may well come over as being friendly but they will find it difficult (and unnecessary) to convince you that they are innovators in motor engineering. Horses for courses.

PEOPLE TALKING IS THE BEST FORM OF COMMUNICATION

Which communications techniques are we using today? Whatever the corporation or organization, the communications areas seem to have broken themselves down into three main categories.

These are face-to-face, audio-visual and printed media. Perhaps the most powerful is still the traditional face-to-face communication. This is an organic method of communications. It is two-way, it provides feedback; and the shape of the communication can grow and develop according to the input of the receiver as well as the sender.

Face-to-face communication can be one to one, or one to a thousand, but the same essential principles apply. A good speaker, even with the largest of audiences can (and must) create the impression that he is talking to just one person. However, while this method is very powerful, it is not normally very cost-effective because of the limitations on the number of people that can be reached. Some commercial organizations like Mobil use this technique to great effect, with senior executives regularly talking to key groups.

Audio-visual techniques have emotion

Audio-visual communications methods have developed in recent years. These present a kind of face-to-face communication, although of a second-hand nature. Standards need to be very high. We are all educated by the television, cinema and radio to expect the highest level of communications. Audio-visual techniques have emotion.

Deciding which technique to use can be a very important point. A sensitive or emotional issue can often be put over best by audio-visual means. However, even today, such techniques are still limited by the hardware—size, complexity and associated problems. But the biggest handicap with audio-visual means of communication is the fact that all of them are ephemeral—the message does not exist as hard copy. While it is possible to give people video tapes, for example, there is no guarantee they will be used and, if they are to be used, then access to special hardware is necessary. Neither audio nor video tapes have the immediacy or accessibility of the printed message. A further limitation of audio and video can be that the audience has to be taken through the whole message, all at the same speed, regardless of the interest of individuals in certain sections, or their ability to absorb the information. There is only a limited ability to linger, to reread, to ponder, to flip the dull bits—and no such opportunity at all if the material is presented to a group *en masse*.

This highlights one of the strengths of the third main group of communications techniques—printed material.

Paperless communication is a myth

The printed media have conviction. We have all been educated to believe what we read, perhaps even more than we believe what we hear or see on film or television. Journalists in print tend to have a higher regard for accuracy. Every mistake, error or misinterpretation can be studied at length, passed from hand to hand, commented on—and even produced in court as evidence!

While video recording has made the electronic moving image a little more permanent, it has not substantially altered this argument. The strength of the printed medium is its conviction, but it does have incidental benefits: many facets of the subject can be covered; the reader has the opportunity to select; he can skim or ignore items and he can return as much as he likes to any section.

The sheer volume of information that can be covered in print is out of all proportion to that achievable on, for example, the broadcast media. One page of an average popular daily newspaper alone would make a radio news bulletin of at least 20 minutes if read, word-for-word.

Now, if you look at a communications problem where it is necessary to balance the requirements against these three options—face-to-face, audio-visual and print—it becomes far easier to select the techniques that should be applied.

Let us take, as an example, a plant closure. An audio-visual technique may well be the ideal method to tell as many people as possible as fast as possible (perhaps even simultaneously) of the broad implications of the plan. It can also be an excellent way of putting over the sincerity of the management and the thought that they are applying to the solving of the inevitable problems. The reason being that *real* people are presenting a *real* story.

However, they are not able to respond to the mood generated by the presentation or to deal with discussion. Therefore, some form of face-to-face communication will be necessary. This might be meetings addressed by members of the management which would allow for questions and answers. These might be planned to follow the audio-visual presentation.

However, if both techniques are used effectively, everyone who has been informed will go away with the messages *only in their head*. The head is a very unreliable receptacle for anything complex. If members of the audience are required to recall a message, they may get it confused. If they are required to relay it to someone else, they may get it distorted.

Therefore, the complete communications programme will require some form of printed material. This will be able to put the facts in plain, incontrovertible form and explore all aspects of the subject. Thus the recipient will be able to study the details at leisure, or look at any particular points, or pass it on to other interested parties. He also has something that is almost certainly truthful and accurate: no organization is going to risk confusion or misunderstanding in their printed communication.

For these reasons, the printed media will survive, regardless of the development of audio-visual and other forms of electronic information communication. Our printed material of the future may well be *transmitted* electronically, but at some stage it will end up in people's hands as hard copy, in a printed form. Paperless communication is a myth.

In summary, the useful communications guidelines to remember are:

1. No organization can decide whether to have public relations or not.
2. Unless proven otherwise, the organization creates its own credibility.
3. Every aspect of the organization reflects its personality.
4. Information creates knowledge.
5. Knowledge helps shape opinion.
6. Opinions may only be loosely related to the truth.
7. Attitudes are the single most important factor in most decisions.
8. Information alone is not effective in changing attitude.
9. Communications at times of pressure are less credible.
10. Be wary of creating an unnecessary news challenge.
11. The message is what the receiver receives.
12. Effective communication is based on listening before speaking.
13. Logic is not always effective in influencing opinion.
14. Good communication needs emotion.
15. Audiences are collections of individuals.
16. Every individual is a specialist in some field.
17. There are few instinctively good communicators.
18. Conflict can create communications opportunities.
19. Be sensitive to the cultural and social ethos.
20. Be prepared to change as the environment changes.
21. People need to know—even the bad news.
22. There is no such thing as an information vacuum.
23. Rumour, gossip and speculation will fill any communication void.
24. Be consistent in all communications.
25. Select the optimum mix of techniques to suit the messages and the audiences.

THE FUTURE IS OURS ... NOT THEIRS

If you are concerned about the future, if you are uncertain about the shape of communication to come ... be reassured. It is largely speculation for all of us. Do not be fooled into thinking that the experts know exactly what is going to happen. They never have and they never will.

If you have any doubt, then consider those ludicrous science fiction films which were made only a decade or two ago. Or the famous Astronomer Royal in Britain who as recently as the late 'fifties proclaimed vigorously that man would never walk on the moon—or the head of the US patents department who proposed to close it at the turn of the century because, as he believed, there was nothing worthwhile left to invent!

However, there is one very sobering thought. Tomorrow everything will be different. And if that is true, then it means that however careful, conscientious, successful and efficient we may be, *everything* we are doing today is wrong.

PLANNING COMMUNICATIONS ON A SOUND BASE

There are some basic communications principles that need to be appreciated by everyone in the organization who has a relationship with any of the key audiences—in other words, everyone! The public relations adviser should ensure these points are understood and supported throughout the organization. This checklist can make a helpful start for an article in the house journal, the introduction to the corporate public relations plan or talks by the public relations adviser to his or her colleagues.

1. Does everyone from the chief executive down understand there is no choice over whether the organization has public relations or not?
2. Are they all committed to organized, disciplined, sustained and controlled public relations?
2. Will they support the public relations adviser to achieve this aim and ensure their own communications are consistent?
4. Is there a distinct difference between what the organization says and what it does?
5. Are there gaps between how the audiences see the organization and the way it would like to be seen?
6. Do we have a clear and defined corporate personality that everyone (including the public relations team) is responsible for projecting?
7. Can this personality be reviewed and developed as the organization progresses?
8. Is our stance properly reflected in everything the organization says and does, from phone calls to advertising?

9. Do the managers appreciate:
    (a) information changes knowledge,
    (b) opinions may not be based on fact,
    (c) attitudes are critical to success,
    (d) no amount of information changes attitudes,
    (e) favourable attitudes can take years to build,
    (f) ... and minutes to destroy,
    (g) public opinion is a most powerful force?
10. Do they understand that attitudes are the single most important factor in most decisions?
11. Do we always act to avoid any information vacuum which might allow rumour, gossip and speculation to grow?
12. Is all our promotional effort concentrated on stressing the positive and eliminating the negative?
13. Do we always carefully judge the consequences of fighting a communications battle whether, for example, with competitors or the unions?
14. Are we effectively evaluating the public relations alternatives to confrontation?
15. Do we never undertake such a challenge unless we are certain we can win?
16. Is it our policy to communicate regularly and consistently and not just when the circumstances demand?
17. Does every public relations activity we undertake have a feedback channel so we can monitor attitudes and communications effectiveness?
18. Do our messages bear any relation to what people want to know?
19. Have we always behaved in such a way as to build our reputation so we can be trusted?
20. Are we sure, therefore, that the receiver is tuned in to the messages we are transmitting?
21. Does our communication have emotion because we care deeply about our organization?
22. Do we always remember that audiences are people and not numbers?
23. Is every company message checked for accuracy, truth and relevance to our corporate objectives?
24. Are we setting the highest possible standards and communicating as we would be communicated unto ... in other words, no patronizing, stalling or waffle?
25. Do we, therefore, respect the people with whom we are trying to establish two-way communications?
26. Is every manager conscious of his communications responsibilities and does he take these seriously?
27. Do I (the public relations adviser) always follow my own rules and earn the respect of my management colleagues?
28. Does the organization use the positive aspects of conflict to help build bridges and resolve disputes?

29. Are we sensitive to the current state and trends within the communications environment?

30. When we are communicating with people who do not have the same social or cultural environment, is there a procedure for getting advice and guidance from someone who knows? If so:
    (a) what language do they use?
    (b) do we have local, trusted colleagues to assist?
    (c) how will we back-up the verbal messages?
    (d) what local factors should we consider?
    (e) are there customs/traditions of which we should take note?
    (f) how best can we get meaningful feedback on our views?
    (g) is there a way they can have input to shaping policy?
    (h) how can we assess the acceptance/rejection of our messages?
    (j) what follow-up action should we consider?

31. Can we adapt our style, our services or products to suit the requirements of such people?

32. Are we ready to handle the bad news as positively as we do the good news?

33. Do we always try to communicate sooner rather than later, particularly when we are in trouble?

34. Do our senior managers understand that one function of public relations is to initiate changes in policy to help prevent the recurrence of bad news?

35. In other words, does everyone, right up to the chief executive, appreciate we have to be well-behaved to be well-reported and well-respected?

36. Are we proud of our identity and display it proudly, clearly, consistently, wherever we can?

37. Is it our policy to focus as much of our communications efforts on creating opportunities for people talking?

38. Do we understand that other means of communication are substitutes forced on us by time, by scale or by other circumstances?

39. Have we adequately explored the respective roles of face-to-face, audio-visual, print, broadcast and other communications techniques?

40. Are our programmes using each technique to its best advantage and in complementary ways?

SIX

PLANNED ACTION

AGREEING THE BACKGROUND TO THE CAMPAIGN

There are a number of central elements in the planning of public relations, all discussed in more detail separately; these include defining the objectives, identifying the audiences, appraising their present awareness and attitudes, agreeing the messages to be projected, allocating the resources (in both financial and manpower terms), planning the activity, carrying this through, measuring its effectiveness and making any necessary changes to planned follow-on activity.

One technique which can help establish clearly the present position is to undertake a communications audit. This surveys the important audiences, methods of communicating with them, the effectiveness of these communications channels and where they can be improved – or gaps filled.

A method for establishing the size of the task is to combine this communications audit with the compilation of a corporate reputation 'balance sheet'. The aim behind this helpful procedure is to clearly establish those factors which have an influence on the perceptions of the organization among the target audiences. For example, good products, excellent service reputation and major investment in research may be plus factors to be built upon. An unstable management record, foreign ownership, or recent redundancies may be minus factors to be counteracted. Remember that all activity undertaken in the public relations programme is designed to build and develop the reputation of the organization, its management and the products and services it offers—in other words, managing the corporate reputation.

HOW TO HANDLE THE FUNCTION

Once an organization has established that it has a public relations need, there may be a number of options open on how this can be covered. The three main methods are: the nomination and training of an existing executive to handle the public relations responsibilities; the appointment of professional public relations staff; the appointment of a consultancy. Sometimes the ideal solution may involve a combination of more than one of these three options.

One of the major factors in deciding which route to pursue will be the level of commitment to public relations that the organization will adopt. A company operating in a competitive market, under public scrutiny, possibly operating in sensitive areas, will find public relations absolutely fundamental to trading success. Therefore, it is likely to have to use skilled, professional executives—whether staff or consultancy or mixture of both.

Some organizations (such as companies with a near-monopoly situation, statutory bodies, professional associations and some government authorities) may feel that they can relegate public relations to a lower level of importance. (A similarly limited role for public relations also tends to be shown in those organizations where the function is defined by giving the executives such titles as press officer or, even more restricting, information officer. Clearly, a press officer is responsible for only part of a broad public relations function: press relations, however effectively operated, can only be *part* of public relations.)

Of course, many organizations have to rely on voluntary or untrained assistance in public relations, because of the limits on their budget. This may well be the case with voluntary groups, churches, small charities, local arts societies, and so on. However, even in such cases, there is usually a public relations professional within the society or community who has an interest in the particular cause and who can be persuaded to lend his expertise in a voluntary capacity. Similarly, many consultancies will accept one or two worthwhile campaigns, often on a cost-only basis.

Pick the best resource

Possibly the least satisfactory method of handling public relations is to allocate the responsibility to a non-specialist executive. A limitation on the size of the budget is not always a legitimate reason for not tackling public relations properly.

Frequently, the reason why the budget is not available is that the management do not rate the importance of the public relations function highly enough. If the management can argue that they do not *need* a significant public relations resource, then this may be an acceptable point for debate. However, the contention that they cannot *afford* a proper resource is very questionable. Effective public relations, ultimately, costs no more than poor public relations; the returns from an investment in public relations are usually so significant that a company has to be spending a very substantial amount of money before it reaches the point of diminishing returns.

Do not accept low budgets

'Margins are so narrow/our profits are so tiny/our budgets are so tight . . . that we cannot afford public relations expenditure.' These comments are nearly always a reflection of the low priority given to the function. If in doubt, try applying the same principle to the need to provide desks for the office workers or chairs for the secretaries.

Companies heat and light work areas not just because it is a statutory requirement, but because, demonstrably, people work better under these circumstances. It was not always the case; in Dickens' time, office workers paid for their own coal! Management in those days claimed they could not afford decent working conditions. It reflected their view of the importance of their staff's requirements—in the same way that some of today's managers claim they cannot afford public relations! A good reputation is essential for most organizations and effective public relations can be the best way to achieve this.

Select the best person for the job

If a non-specialist executive *has* to be used to handle the public relations function, make sure that the candidates have the right temperament, the right brief, the right commitment and the right training.

Temperament It would be helpful if he is articulate, responsive, energetic and has plenty of initiative. Courage is one of the essential elements for running any effective public relations campaign; the practitioner will frequently have to make his own decisions and be able to stand by them.

Commitment It is better to have a willing volunteer than a conscript. The nominated executive should be someone who is open and direct and believes in the importance of good communications. He must also be a strong supporter of the aims of the organization.

Brief It is only fair to the executive that he should have clear guidelines on what is expected to be achieved. The writing of the objectives is, perhaps, even *more* important where the public relations is being handled by non-professionals. Whoever is nominated for this responsibility must report in at the highest possible level. Ideally, the manager should not have to combine public relations with other responsibilities.

Training In selecting the ideal candidate, his level of skills may not be the most important factor. An effective public relations practitioner must have the right attitudes and motivation but may have no more than normal writing and language skills. However, such an executive will need training. This might take advantage of courses offered by professional institutes, trade bodies and commercial training organizations (see useful addresses, listed at the back of this book). Training courses are also valuable in exposing the practitioner to other executives undertaking comparable work for other organizations.

HOW TO SELECT PROFESSIONAL STAFF

A certain level of commitment by the organization to the function may require the appointment of professional specialists. The comparative costs of employing staff public relations personnel or using a consultancy work out to within 10 or 20 per cent of each other. Therefore, it is likely to be other factors which influence the final decision.

Consider the calibre of the person that you require. Your analysis of the public relations requirements should enable you to write a profile of the ideal candidate. This is important—not simply to ensure that you appoint the right person but to decide whether it is practical for you to offer *career prospects* to such a person. It may not be sensible to offer someone a job that they will grow out of within a year or two . . . and be forced to leave because there is no prospect for personal advancement.

When the organization has identified the level of staff professionally suitable, it is helpful to consider some basic factors relating to selection. Some people in the communications industry have little experience in selecting staff. If possible, use the professional skills of a personnel colleague or a recruitment agency. Remember that some candidates may have presentation and interview skills that are better than their public relations competence! You will need to be objective and cautious. However, when considering candidates for vacancies, it is very easy to become so concerned with the job to be filled that you forget you are dealing with people with their own feelings, perspectives and interests.

Even if you have to reject 9 out of 10 or 999 out of 1000, remember that every interview will give you an opportunity to enthuse, encourage and motivate each applicant. It is possible to turn down a candidate without the person feeling rejected. Your care and consideration can create a good experience which will help them tackle the job search ordeal. Every applicant should be dealt with promptly, efficiently and with the maximum of courtesy possible. It is important not to allow any unnecessary delay, particularly if you have to advise them that they are not successful. At the end of the selection process, every applicant should feel warmly towards you and be a friend of your organization.

That is plain common kindness. However, on a practical level, if these people are looking for positions in the world of business communications, you will find it surprising how many you will come across later during the course of your career. Some may later turn out to be your client or even your boss!

Five years on, do you want to be greeted at a public relations conference by someone who reminds you of how discourteously you treated them? Or would you prefer to meet a colleague who will smile (perhaps even a little ruefully) but thank you for the advice that helped set them on the right path? As noted earlier, doing what is right results in doing what is profitable. Everyone you ever interview for a job should become an ambassador for your organization.

Recruit the right person

At the selection stage, decide, not only whether you can recruit the right person, but whether you can provide the necessary career opportunities and fulfilment. If your industry and market tends to be a little conservative, you may feel that you require a solid, stable practitioner, who will be likely to stay with the organization for some years.

If you are in a fast-moving industry, working in a complex market, you may need a more aggressive and, possibly, creative personality. It can be more difficult to attract a younger, ambitious high-flyer unless he can see an attractive career future. In contrast, it can be fulfilling for a certain type of temperament to work within one environment, in one industry—while this can be extremely frustrating to the more volatile temperament.

Watch the high-flyer

It may *not* be an ideal answer to opt for someone talented but younger than your preferred age. The risk may be that the person will simply use your position as a stepping-stone to better things. Much of your training, induction and familiarization will have been wasted. Your colleagues will be frustrated. The public relations function will be devalued. The fault could be yours for selecting a high-flyer for a routine job.

It may be an alternative policy to decide whether the in-house staff or consultancy method would be best for your situation. Many companies find that they achieve the best by a combination of these two skills. For example, the staff adviser can be a very senior, highly-respected diplomat who works with the smallest of head office staff. Consultancy resources can be used for specific public relations campaigns or in special areas identified by the staff executive, or in an advisory capacity.

It is interesting to compare this ideal situation with the reality. A survey by the Public Relations Society of America among senior executives of 500 of the largest companies in the US established that public relations was accepted as a necessary function in the corporate organization. Practitioners were considered good spokesmen for the organization and effective at supplying the necessary range of communications skills. However, practitioners were not generally invited to become part of decision-making groups. This was because they were not considered to have sufficient qualifications and useful experience in the management function itself. Whether this is true is less important than this perception of public relations practitioners among such an influential group of senior managers. In the UK, a study by the Public Relations Consultants Association showed that nearly 90 per cent of *The Times* top 1000 companies retained consultancies—though very few had public relations represented at board level, except under exceptional circumstances such as during an emergency or a takeover. Indeed, public relations professionals were likely to be the last consulted, even on marketing decisions.

Obviously, good public relations can only be developed by respected professionals with a proper mandate for the job, working with the confidence of the highest levels of management of the organization, reporting to the chief executive. This demands that public relations must ultimately be the responsibility of a main board director reporting to the chief executive. Otherwise, key audiences may well deduce that the company does not care about its appearance in other peoples' eyes.

Get the best person to head the public relations division

With the trend towards smaller staff public relations departments, organizations must be certain that they have the best possible person for the top public relations staff job. The responsibilities of the public relations director are very demanding. For the general business manager or aspiring public relations practitioner it may be helpful to identify some of the key characteristics that are likely to make a successful public relations director.

The top professional must be effective as a manager. The emphasis will be on achieving results. He will be able to get things done through his own colleagues and departmental resources. In addition, he will be able to work effectively with his colleagues in other professional areas within the organization. In his own department, he will have an ability to recruit, train, motivate, develop, organize and control the skilled people necessary to complete an integrated public relations function.

The ideal public relations director will fully understand the broadest aspects of public relations, rather than being a specialist in some aspects of the work or certain industries. It will be essential that he has sufficient depth and knowledge to identify problems and solutions in all sectors. An all-round staff practitioner will not be a public relations professional if his expertise is limited to, say, marketing support or financial relations or parliamentary affairs.

The public relations director must be able to make a contribution to the overall *direction* of the organization for which he works. The difference between a director and a manager is much more than a job title. The director must be able to manage, but also must be able to contribute to the longer-term direction of the organization: be able to set public relations objectives and develop strategies to achieve these and identify priorities and create policies. He should be able to create the public relations environment for the organization within which all corporate activity will take place.

In addition, a complete public relations professional at director level should be able to contribute to board policies on the future of the organization. He should bring a high degree of knowledge, experience and practical skill to all management decisions that have public relations implications.

BUY CONSULTANCY AS YOU NEED IT

Consultancies can offer a range of expertise. The company can choose the consultancy to suit the projects in hand and buy the services almost 'by the metre'. The best way to handle the public relations activity may not be staff personnel or a consultancy: it may be a combination of these resources.

Public relations consultancies range from one-man outfits to international organizations. The first decision the manager has to make is what type of consultancy he requires. For example:

1. Do we need special experience of our industry?
2. Do we require a national service solely, or international representation and, if so, in which markets?
3. Do we have special public relations requirements, e.g. in parliamentary, industrial, environmental areas, or do we need general public relations?
4. Is the consultancy to be responsible just for advice or advice and implementation, with or without an internal public relations operation?

Make a shortlist

Having agreed the nature of the public relations programme, produce a list of public relations consultancies which appear to be able to offer the services required. To produce a shortlist you may:

1. Approach the public relations managers of companies whose public relations work you admire and which is not competitive with your own.
2. Discuss your aims with key journalists and discover which consultancies offer them an effective service.

3. Talk to a relevant professional communications body to prepare a shortlist of members appropriate to your objectives.
4. Check in established directories for public relations organizations with appropriate expertise.

Time and money will be spent by both your organization and the consultancies before the final choice is made. Therefore it is advisable to reduce your list of possible consultancies to perhaps half a dozen before approaching them direct.

Look at their existing client list. In Britain, this might be the *PRCA Year Book, Hollis* or *Advertisers' Annual* and eliminate any that have competing clients, or are working in an unrelated specialized field. Check on the ownership of your prospective public relations advisers. It may be to your advantage (or disadvantage) if they are members of an international group, or subsidiaries of an advertising agency. It may be important to know that the directors have been in business for two or twenty years, that the consultancy has two or twenty directors.

Put the first enquiry into writing

Now is the time to approach the prospective consultancies. This always should be in writing. This preliminary letter should invite the consultancy to write to you with details of its expertise and service. Your letter should be addressed to the managing director, though it is fair to expect that the reply may be from a director more relevant to your organization.

Outline your business interests, your broadest promotional aims and the fact that you are approaching a number of consultancies. Ruthlessly eliminate all those who do not reply or are excessively slow and any whose letters are not up to an acceptable business standard. (If they cannot project themselves, they will hardly be able to project your organization.) Do not eliminate those whose experience or skills do not appear to match your needs: this may not be a fair test at this stage and the public relations consultancy may be dealing with many enquiries, such as yours, without the benefit of your knowledge of the potential.

From this response, you will have perhaps 3 or 4 consultancies you would wish to invite to visit you for further discussions. Reply with a suggested date for a meeting and clarify your requirements—for example, you would like to see examples of their work, discuss your public relations aims in more detail, meet the executive they consider may be suitable to your work. Above all, give every consultancy the same information and the same opportunity; however, if one asks more perceptive questions, then this could be a critical factor. There is no need to provide this extra information to the others who are less enquiring.

With one prospective plc client, a small consultancy with special expertise spent days in research, including time on the road with the salesforce. From this, they revised the client's broad brief and produced a substantial and closer-focused document. They were astonished when the client gave copies of this to their competitors, all of whom realized they had been on the wrong track. Perhaps because of this embarrassment, the client appointed an international competitor with a name, but to whom the business was less critical—another nice name on the client list. Sadly, this consultancy was going through an unstable time and badly let them down within six months. The client was taken over by the backdoor, largely because of its ineffective communications; the whole of the board was fired. Is it unreasonable to think that the outcome might have been different if only the plc had had the courage to make the bold choice instead of opting for what seemed the safe selection?

So, what procedure to follow at the preliminary interview to be sure you are setting the correct course for the ultimate right choice? Conduct this as seriously as a personal job interview. (An appraisal form where you can note responses is helpful when it comes to comparing the strength of the cases presented to you.) Avoid any lunch or drinks appointments unless you extend the same opportunity to every contender. Be prepared to expand on the brief you put in your letter. And assess the response to this—particularly the questions the firm asks.

The conclusion of this interview should be a suggestion that you visit their premises—assuming that this preliminary interview will have eliminated one or two of your prospect consultancies. Be fair in giving the consultancies you wish to visit a brief on what you wish to achieve—for example, meeting the team, assessing their facilities, looking at client work and so on. Allow each consultancy a fair choice of dates to ensure they can meet your needs. Advise them who will be attending this meeting from your organization. Again, only accept a meeting running over lunch or dinner if this opportunity is given to each public relations company.

Visit the consultancy

If you have given the shortlisted consultancies a fair brief then you will be able to assess their response by direct comparison. Factors to be considered include:

- their research into your organization,
- the physical resources available,
- the expertise of the team offered,
- the success of other client campaigns,

- the degree of probing into your claims,
- their perception and understanding of your aims,
- the empathy between you and their executives,
- the intelligence of the suggestions they make.

Do not expect the consultancy to present a programme to you nor field a particular account executive. It is more important to decide whether they have the skills to contribute to your organization's public relations aims than to be too concerned with details of staffing. By now your shortlist should be down to two or three.

Ask for recommendations not proposals

Write to the consultancies you have visited. Those you have eliminated should be told so and, politely, why. Now, you should be able to give them a written brief expanding your aims. You should clarify the reporting situation—to whom do they report, when and how. Those you have selected for further discussion should be invited to write a report on how they believe they could assist your organization. It is also fair to explain to them the position of your selection—'you are now in our last three consultancies under consideration'.

However, do not expect full proposals. These take considerable time to prepare and require a deeper knowledge of your organization than would be reasonable to expect at this stage. Give each consultancy an opportunity to revisit your offices with the executives they wish to put on your account. Invite your key colleagues who will be involved in public relations to attend this meeting.

Ask the representatives of each consultancy to discuss their report and any recommendations they have. Points to discuss should include creativity of their work, suitability of the executive, the back-up team, ancillary services (print, design, house journals, exhibitions, for example), calibre and reputation of existing clients, the reporting and control procedures, fee structure.

Ask for budget calculations

When selecting a consultancy, it is important to relate your size and needs to their size and services. It may not be ideal for you to be either their largest or smallest client. If you are too big they may become nervous of jeopardizing the business and so soft-pedal on their advice: equally you may become wary of moving the account if they do not perform for fear of creating redundancies. Conversely, if your account is too small you may not get the level of service you wish—or feel able to crack the whip, when necessary.

There are three main methods of fee charging practised by most consultancies. All are based on hourly charges for executive time. The most popular method of calculating fees is on a fixed monthly retainer (representing y hours at £x). The other common methods are fees billed monthly according to hours (or days): and a basic fee charged for an agreed programme plus increments for additional work. Additional projects or costs above an agreed level should normally be quoted and approved in advance of commissioning.

Consultancies also tackle projects on an *ad hoc* basis where they quote for an identified activity. This tends to be expensive and the least satisfactory way to build relationships between consultancy and staff personnel. It can be helpful though to support staff public relations departments at times of particular need for additional manpower or special expertise.

Do not judge solely on the hourly rate; an average executive at £x may be a poorer buy than a senior man at £$2x$—alternatively you may not want £$2x$ an hour charges for writing a simple appointment story. Ask the consultancies to prepare a budget—or recommendations on the breakdown of your own suggested budget. This will need to cover fee, operating costs, press conferences, print, photography and any other items which will involve significant work and expenditure. Avoid an open-ended fee system and agree a level of expenditure you would allow without prior consultation. Clarify how their invoices will relate to the activity reporting procedure.

Choose the consultancy with proven ability

Ask each consultancy to give you three or four client executives with whom you can discuss their public relations service. Talk to key journalists or members of other key audiences to check whether they have any experience of your preferred consultancies. Discuss the consultancies with colleagues who attend the presentation.

If you do feel you need more detailed proposals, then it is only fair to agree some fee with your final shortlist of two or three consultancies. This may be nominal, but nothing less than £1000 would be acceptable. This will also help avoid problems should more than one candidate consultancy come up with similar ideas; this fee can be negotiated to cover such an eventuality. (At this stage, do not be surprised if they want confirmation of your budget and the names of their competitor consultancies. Both are fair requests which should be answered.)

Finally ... choose. Write to the chosen consultancy and ask them to attend a final meeting to confirm working arrangements and financial matters. At this stage, you may well agree a fee for a limited period, say three months, so they can prepare full recommendations; alternatively you could pay them to prepare full proposals and costings; or you can agree an estimate of the work load for the first year, perhaps with an option to review at six months.

Ask them to write with these details and acknowledge this. (Some consultancies will offer a contract rather than simply letters of agreement. In either case, these should be checked with your company secretary or legal adviser. Copies should also go to your financial director and accounts department.) Write to the unsuccessful consultancies, thanking them for their efforts and explaining the reasons for your choice.

Arrange your first working meeting and open up your heart!

GET THE CONSULTANCY AND THE CLIENT ON THE SAME SIDE

Sounds obvious doesn't it? But it is still possible to hear organizations talk about their consultancy as if they were the enemy—and not a vital part of their resource to help them succeed in a tough, competitive world. Some consultancies talk about their clients as if they were involved in a constant battle of wits with them. And perhaps they are, too often.

Certainly, both sides of this relationship are often in confrontation, in an insecure, fragile relationship that benefits neither party. It is rarely all faults on one side, so here are a few suggestions for both consultancy staff and clients on how to get the best out of the cooperation. The relationship is rarely between one person on each side, as suggested here for simplicity; both parties usually have a team. But, nonetheless, the relationship *does* depend on goodwill and understanding between individuals.

Some advice to clients ...

Let your consultant act as a consultant As you employed your consultant, ask for and listen to his advice. If he is any good (and why would you be employing him if he were not?) he has some expertise. Public relations is not plain good sense; it is a fairly sophisticated craft and an amalgam of many skills. When he says what will and what will not work, it may just be because he has experienced it before. Little is more irritating (or unfair) than to suggest that your consultant can offer nothing but his own commonsense. If that is all he has to offer, then get your advice cheaper from the-man-in-the-street.

Always try to tell your consultant what might be happening *before* it happens. He will appreciate having an input into the policy-making process and his commitment and advice will be all the stronger for that. Also create opportunities for him to present his view at the top of the company.

Play by fair and declared rules It is supposed to be a partnership, so treat your consultant as a colleague and not a disposable 'supplier'. If he accepts an arms-length status you are not necessarily proving you are the boss. He may just be accepting the position until something better comes along.

Remember the objectives when commenting on or appraising the work. If the aim was, for example, improving trade relations, do not moan about the poor consumer coverage. And, if your own colleagues try to change the rules as a method of criticizing the consultant, have the courage to defend him—even against the chairman. There's nothing wrong with changing the public relations requirements, but remember to discuss these with your consultant before you start measuring his work by these new criteria. And make sure all your own management team understand and agree the brief, before the programme or project starts.

Praise and criticize first-hand—and with equal candour If he does a good job, have the sense to tell him, preferably in writing. You will be amazed at the effect this can have. Such a letter gets circulated within the consultancy, pinned on notice boards and mentioned at internal meetings. Everyone starts to feel warmly about you and all the best people in the consultancy will want to work on an account where the client is appreciative. Equally, if you have a beef, make it plain, direct and verbal. Who needs a griping letter the day after a friendly meeting? There is absolutely no need to record complaints in writing unless they are not being rectified. And, if that is the case, the relationship may have already broken down too far. And if *that* is the case, it is a failure on your part, either in selection or management.

Never try to make a triumph out of firing the consultancy, for everyone will know it's a foul-up and you will win no glory. Do you know the client who fired six consultancies in ten years? Everyone in the consultancy business does and he is not respected for his management capabilities!

Give him scope and a fair deal Allow your consultant the scope for creativity. Do not suggest that 'this is worth a news story' when there could be six other better ways of achieving the objective. You should be asking him to solve problems and take advantage of opportunities, not simply to handle communications activity you have decided. Otherwise you might as well do it yourself.

Make sure your account is profitable to the consultancy. Have the confidence to enter into a long-term relationship so both sides can develop the activity. Expect value for money but do not expect miracles for pennies. 'We have decided to spend £4 million on the television campaign. What can you do to support this massive new product launch? Mind, we've got no budget.'

Above all, if you do not like his advice, stand back and try to see if it is wise and fair. If so, accept it. If not, explain why it is not acceptable and give him the chance to think again. Never, ever threaten to take the business away if you do not like the advice. That's how cynicism creeps into the relationship.

... and for the consultant

Let your client be the client Do not tell your client how to run his business. It is unlikely that even if you worked together for 20 years that you could do a better job than him. Your role is to advise on public relations and there are few things more annoying to the client than to have a superficial view on an area where some specialized experience is essential.

When he gives you a brief, ask questions. He may not expect flip, off-the-cuff answers and will accept that a little consideration may improve the quality of the advice. Understand that the client is an expert in *his* field ... that is why you are supposed to be working together as a complimentary team.

Above all, do make sure you listen to the client. After all, you learn nothing when you are talking, only when listening.

Make sure he understands your capabilities If he treats you like a press oficer, maybe he has forgotten you are a public relations consultant ... or maybe you have forgotten to demonstrate your capabilities in the advisory area. Show him examples of your consultancy's work on behalf of other clients. Always keep looking for those problems where you can provide a solution and ease his workload. This will enhance your work on his behalf, make the account more valuable and win more credibility with your client and his colleagues.

Present regularly your consultancy skills to the client and his colleagues; if not, do not be surprised if he turns somewhere else for advice that you could have offered. Do not complain if this happens. It is your fault. And if he is commissioning work that he knows you could handle, find out why before presenting your case to him.

Take the praise and act on the criticisms—with equal enthusiasm Do not gloat over the few kind words, but, even more important, build the confidence between you so that he can have a moan without you throwing a 'moody'. Who needs a prima donna as a colleague? If you get it wrong, tell him, apologize, then get it right and make sure the mistake never happens again. Always thank your client for criticisms ... he is doing you a favour, giving you a chance to get it right.

Your client is human, with normal strengths and frailties. Do not expect him to be a superman. He has the same worries as anyone about the mortgage, home and family and is usually an ordinary chap trying to do the best he can. Win his confidence and take some of the worry out of his work. Never criticize him in front of your colleagues or allow them to rubbish him, or his company. If they do not like him, that is their problem. They can always go out and get business from people they do like. (Though it is a curious fact that people who disparage clients rarely seem to have any of their own. I wonder why?)

Build a long-term relationship Your client has his own career. Remember the work you are undertaking on behalf of the company is part of his broader responsibilities, so make it successful and never try to take the credit. Everyone will appreciate what you have done without you needing to be petty. Support your client with his colleagues. No one likes disloyalty. If you cannot agree with the policy he proposes, tell him first privately so that he knows how to handle the situation. Remember no one ever *really* agrees to disagree—it is a polite way of describing a breakdown in personal communications.

Help your client develop his responsibilities and you will have a friend for life. One day, if he moves on, you should find yourself with two clients in place of one.

Get the relationship wrong and you are wasting precious resources and opportunities. Get it right and you will enjoy not only success but the satisfaction that comes from doing a job well ... you may also build some friendships that will last your whole career.

Look at the international consultancy options

The options available today if the public relations executive decides to use consultancy internationally are considerably improved and will continue to get better. Many of the principles noted here will still apply to selecting a consultancy to support your organization's operations in any country of the world. (It may be helpful to read these brief notes alongside the suggestions in Chapter 8, which cover the planning of the programme, including its international dimensions.)

In many countries, the local public relations consultancy industry (alongside public relations in general) has grown significantly in recent years. For example, it is now possible to appoint a professional general consultancy (and even specialist ones in such developed business areas as property, leisure, chemicals, financial services, pharmaceuticals, shareholder and government relations) across the whole of North America, Western Europe, Australasia and much of the Pacific rim. The Mediterranean, Middle East, Africa and South American regions are also beginning to develop their own home-grown industries—a process likely to accelerate over the coming decades.

The selection of a consultancy has also been simplified through the growth of the networks in the 1970s and 1980s. These fall into three broad categories: the organically-grown companies which have set up offices in those areas where they identified there was a client need or opportunity for growth (such as Burson-Marstellar); those that have developed coverage by acquiring existing companies where they wanted to be represented and welding these into an international organization (such as Shandwick); and those partnerships formed by independent consultancies banding together into a formal international network (such as Worldcom).

How should you choose between these options? Clearly, on the basis of the quality of service that can be delivered to your organization at point of need. It might be helpful to look at some views on the respective merits of these three different styles of international consultancy:

1. Burson-Marstellar chairman, Harold Burson, originator of some of the best practices in modern international public relations, says: 'An organization that has grown organically over the years has a character, strength and style that shines through in all its work. We believe we are able to offer clients the best service because we are able to offer an organization staffed and managed by local nationals, delivering a service that is up to our standards worldwide.'
2. Newer on the scene, but with an impressive achievement in building one of the world's largest public relations companies, particularly through strategic acquisitions in the 1980s, is chairman of Shandwick, Peter Gummer; 'By identifying the best companies in each of those markets where we wanted to be represented, we believe we have the best of both worlds. We have nationals on the ground who have won their credibility through growing their own businesses in their own countries, yet backed by the resources and cooperation possible within the global structure we operate.'
3. Heading the largest of the partnerships of independently-owned consultancies, which also moved into challenge the big four in the late 1980s, is Washington public affairs veteran, founder-chairman of Worldcom Incorporated, John Adams; 'Our partners are chosen because they are the best independents in each country around the world. They are staffed and run by locals who know their markets; it is this independence that is their strength. They cooperate so effectively because the future success of every Worldcom partner depends upon this key international dimension.'

Each of these organizations—and many others with international capabilities—are contributing to the development of ever higher standards in public relations. Whichever option you choose, use a disciplined selection procedure when making your appointments and select the best public relations partners to meet the needs of your organization.

When choosing consultancy away from your 'home territory', consider carefully the views of your own local management where they have the knowledge or expertise. Involve them in the selection process. It can often be wise to compare the purely local operation with the services offered by each of the three main types of network. If one of the structured networks can offer an equally high service across all your main markets then it could offer substantial advantages in control, coordination, standards and performance appraisal.

Any Company Limited   Order
No. **1022**

From   To

Date

Client/division   Project No

Description

Price agreed

Despatch to

Signed on behalf of

Date required   **Any Company Limited**

Registered office:
VAT Registered No.

Copyright of all work accepted by you and described or resulting from this order is assigned to
Any Company Limited and any material or artwork becomes the property of the aforementioned company

Figure 6.1 The public relations adviser needs to control the ordering of services from outside suppliers. An order form is recommended. This should be used for all projects even where it has to be a confirmation of an urgent telephone order. Suppliers should be advised that all invoices submitted must quote an order number. The order form can also prevent any problems arising over issues relating to copyright.

ORGANIZING THE PUBLIC RELATIONS RESOURCE

Establishing the function

1. Have we agreed audiences, objectives and programme?
2. What level of workload is needed to meet these requirements?
3. Can we identify the manpower and the budget necessary to carry out this level of public relations activity?
4. Have we agreed an adequate resource in terms of staff, access, seniority and budget to enable the public relations executive to undertake the function?
5. Is management aware of the steps we propose to take to provide this public relations resource, its scope and its limitations?
6. Have we agreed the balance between advisory and implementation responsibilities?
7. Are these to be carried out by the same executive or different personnel, for example, advice from a staff colleague, implementation from a consultancy or vice versa?
8. Can we decide which option will best suit our needs:
   staff executive—existing,
   staff executive—recruited,
   consultancy?

Using an existing executive

9. Do we need a full-time staff executive or can public relations become part of the responsibility of an existing manager?
10. If so, how do we train him to carry out these responsibilities:
    through external courses,
    by appointing a professional trainer,
    by assigning him to a consultancy or public relations department for a training period?
11. Have we written a job specification and identified the temperament and other characteristics our executive will need?
12. Does our nominated candidate have the right temperament and commitment to make this operation successful?
13. Has this executive been properly briefed, including responsibilities, reporting procedures and deployment of the public relations resource?
14. Have we agreed and established monitoring procedures to record performance and cost-effectiveness of the activity?

Recruiting professional staff

15. Have we taken the steps outlined in questions 11 to 14?
16. What level of training support, if any, will this new member of the team require?

17. Can we provide a career development path for this calibre of executive and have we explained this to him?
18. Is management clear on the need to involve and listen to an independent professional adviser?
19. How will the organization measure the effectiveness of the executive and deploy commensurate resources in successive years?

Appointing a consultancy

20. Will the consultancy provide advisory and implementation services, solely or in liaison with staff personnel?
21. To whom will the consultancy report and have we agreed control procedures?
22. By what criteria will their success be measured and how will this be related to the agreed budget?
23. What levels of expenditure will the consultancy be able to commit before needing specific clearance?
24. Has a proper agreement been drawn up covering such areas as notice, budgets, approvals, payment procedures, staffing responsibilities and liaison?
25. Have we looked through the following selection checklist to ensure we have picked the best organization for our needs?

Selecting a consultancy

The following notes give a guideline to one method of getting the right consultancy working for the organization. These points should be read in conjunction with the recommendations on choosing a consultancy which go into more detail. Remember, it is not difficult to separate good consultancies from bad: however, it is not easy to get the right one for the job in hand.

Expertise Identify special skills or resources needed:
(a) International resource,
(b) Marketing support,
(c) Community relations,
(d) Parliamentary affairs,
(e) Financial relations,
(f) Other.

Requirements Decide factors that are important to the organization:
(a) Particular industry experience,
(b) Advisory and/or implementation,
(c) Local and/or national location,
(d) Regional offices,
(e) Other.

Possible consultancies Prepare a list of candidate consultancies from:
(a) Nominations by relevant journalists,
(b) Suggestions from other public relations executives,
(c) Recommendations by professional bodies,
(d) Listings in directories such as *Hollis, Advertisers' Annual*, etc,
(e) The Public Relations Register or similar search organizations.
Eliminate any not suitable.

Initial enquiry Write to shortlisted consultancies asking for:
(a) Background details,
(b) Resources and special skills,
(c) Current clients and activities,
(d) Appointment to visit.

Preliminary discussion Give each shortlisted consultancy a brief on the organization and why public relations is required. Visit each to ascertain:
(a) Their depth of research,
(b) Office and staff facilities,
(c) The team's expertise offered,
(d) Campaign effectiveness for other clients,
(e) Their perception of the public relations problem.

Second interview Invite each consultancy still considered suitable to visit the organization with the consultancy team to meet the client executives. Invite them to present:
(a) Observations on the problem,
(b) Examples of work,
(c) Methods of charging,
(d) Possible account team.

Final presentation If proposals are required, negotiate an agreed fee for each consultancy. This meeting should be at the consultancy and should cover:
(a) Public relations objectives defined,
(b) Audiences and messages,
(c) Techniques to be deployed,
(d) Consultancy resource offered,
(e) Budget and resource required from client,
(f) Monitoring and control procedures,
(g) Financial and liaison terms.

Selection The client should now:
(a) Confirm details with selected consultancy,
(b) Promptly and politely advise others,
(c) Arrange final planning meeting,

(d) Set a review date to check progress,
(e) Agree internal/external announcement.

The client and consultancy working together

26. Are the objectives clear and agreed by both parties?
27. What will be the balance between the advisory and implementation functions?
28. How do consultant and client discuss options before the policy is decided?
29. Can joint presentations be made regularly to the board for their input?
30. What is the procedure for handling complaints and criticisms?
31. Are there other activities in communications that could be developed together?
32. Is the agreement fair to both parties and allowing for a long-term relationship?
33. How is the programme to be reviewed and developed?
34. Are we allocating reasonable resources and agreeing respective responsibilities?
35. Have we gained the support of all colleagues for the proposed campaign?

Selecting partners for international support

36. Do our local managers have views and experiences that might be helpful?
37. How best can we involve them in the selection process?
38. Would we be best served by selecting consultancies individually, market by market?
39. Should we include the three main types of network as options in our selection process and which are represented in which of our relevant regions?
40. Have we set up a selection procedure as suggested for 'home' consultancy and as reviewed in Chapter 8 on programme planning?

The communications audit and reputation balance sheet

41. What are internal/external perceptions of the organization?
42. How effective are existing channels of communication?
43. Are any audiences not covered or poorly informed?
44. Can existing channels be developed?
45. Are there feedback opportunities for all publics?
46. Which elements of the organization create favourable/unfavourable impressions?

47. Can these be appraised and logged as plus and minus factors?
48. Have we produced this analysis as a corporate reputation balance sheet for consideration by management?
49. What steps can we take to improve communications and the reputation balance?
50. How can we measure any resulting improvement?

SEVEN

BUDGET ALLOCATION

CALCULATE REALISTIC FIGURES FOR THE CAMPAIGN

You gets what you pays for. There is no such thing as cheap public relations. It is either good or it is not. Fortunately, planning for public relations activity is reasonably straightforward. Most problems over deciding the budget can be traced to uncertainty over the objectives. If these are clear, then the programme to achieve them can be realistically planned.

The resource to achieve the successful completion of the plan will determine the budget. Is this reasonable in relation to turnover or what it is necessary to achieve? If it is not, then management has to review the priority allocated to public relations, the techniques being considered or go right back to re-evaluate the objectives: it is rarely reasonable to cut a realistic budget by more than 10 per cent or so without affecting success.

The major element in any public relations programme is likely to be the cost of the personnel involved—the salaries of staff or the executive fees of consultancies which, allowing for overheads and profit, are likely to be very similar. Compared with advertising (where the executive element of the budget in any campaign might be 10 per cent or less), the manpower element in a comparable public relations campaign, is likely to be 50 per cent or more.

There is no case for cutting back expenditure on manpower in professional areas that will be fundamental to the success of the organization. It is a simple rule: always go for the best possible. For example, it might take a £100 000 worth of manpower to handle your £1 000 000 advertising budget. There may be some scope for economy on the £900 000, if that is what you have to spend to reach your audience. However, a cut-back in the £100 000 achieved by using lower calibre personnel may mean that the £900 000 will be utilized less efficiently; the loss the organization will suffer will be out of all proportion to the small overall percentage economy.

At the other end of the spectrum, your £100 000 public relations budget may contain £60 000 of manpower. A good public relations operator will make a substantial difference to the success of the activity, primarily because of the quality of advice he will be able to offer. Frequently, this advisory element may not require major operating budgets. However, should the agreed public relations objectives show that there is a need for a substantial programme of activities, this could involve a far more significant total sum than the advisory activity.

SEPARATE ADVISORY AND IMPLEMENTATION BUDGETS

The budget for the public relations activity should make allowance for the separate costs required for the advisory aspects and for the implementation of any recommended campaign. The budget will also need to identify that part which relates to manpower (whether consultancy or in-house personnel) and that part which is to cover operating and other costs. Ideally, an annual budget for a programme should have separate totals to cover the advisory time, the executive fee for implementation, the operating costs or expenses, photography, plus expenditure on any activity such as print, sponsorship, seminars and so on.

A budget agreed for a programme to be handled by a consultancy might look like this:

> Advisory fee to cover public relations consultancy, director and executive time in giving advice, planning, attending the monthly meeting and preparing necessary reports and recommendations on action to be taken, calculated at AAA executive days per month at £BBB
>
> £CCC
>
> Executive time to implement the agreed plan as detailed in report DDD, including director supervision and necessary client liaison, calculated at EEE days per month at £FFF
>
> £GGG
>
> Operating costs to cover printing and distributing news material, media entertainment, travel, hotel and out-of-pocket expenses, fax, long distance telephone calls and other costs authorized by the client
>
> Allow £HHH
>
> Photography including coverage of activity in the campaign, news pictures, transparencies and colour prints for record purpose where agreed, prints for library and media use
>
> Allow £JJJ

Project activity as discussed and agreed, covering, for example, research, studies, publications, sponsorship, seminars, radio tapes, media training as appropriate.

Allow £KKK

Secretariat costs associated with maintaining files, records and running the agreed public information service

£LLL

If a consultancy is handling this programme, the budget may well allow for expenses recharged direct and production costs which will be subject to a handling charge. In broad terms, where the consultancy has the legal and financial responsibility for work undertaken on behalf of the client, an agreed percentage may be added to suppliers' invoices. Often this is 17.65 per cent (equivalent to 15 per cent of the gross). On *ad hoc* or project work outside the normal programme, costs would normally be subject to separate quotations.

In the UK, the Public Relations Consultants Association publishes guidelines on drawing up an agreement between an organization and a consultancy. (As well as financial matters, it is important to agree on legal points such as responsibility for complying with the Trade Descriptions Acts and other relevant UK and European legislation, ownership of copyright and so on. The illustrated order form—see p. 81—includes a recommended phrase to ensure that copyright is vested in the consultancy commissioning the work.)

PLANNING AND COSTING NEED PROFESSIONAL SKILL

The size of the budget necessary for the public relations campaign may be decided in one of two ways: the public relations objectives may be agreed and a costed programme of activity drawn up to achieve these; alternatively, a sum may be allocated according to an agreed formula and a plan of activity drawn up within the scale that this budget will allow. The costing of the programme to meet agreed objectives requires considerable professional skill. The public relations adviser should insist that both of these areas are undertaken only by experienced professionals.

There are some useful yardsticks for an organization to use to begin to consider an allocation for public relations. These provide the starting point for management to consider whether they can (or should) appoint their own public relations staff or call in outside consultants to advise them. If you are the appointed manager responsible for the public relations function, these guidelines will help ensure that management allocates to your department an intelligent resource to implement your advice.

Perhaps the most common method (the least helpful) is to take last year's figure and add an element to compensate for inflation or market increase/decrease. (Or, sometimes, knock a bit off, if times are hard!) Any company following that method presumably would still have a budget for shoeing the horses!

The next method (and somewhat more helpful) is to calculate the budget on a fixed formula basis. A broad figure for promotion or marketing services is allocated and this is broken down into, say, public relations, advertising and sales promotion.

It is quite usual for companies who consider (understandably but mistakenly) that public relations is purely a marketing function to allocate an overall marketing budget from which the public relations effort is funded. This marketing allowance may be a fixed percentage of turnover, which would most usually fall in the range of from 2 per cent to 10 per cent, though sometimes it can be up to 20 per cent. Few organizations could justify spending less than 5 per cent; this might be considered the normal minimum for a marketing budget, of which, up to half might be directly spent on promotional activity. The balance will be the marketing management, manpower, establishment costs and so on. The greater the emphasis on mass-media expenditure the larger the proportion that will be spent on promotion. In some consumer companies, the costs of the marketing functions might be as low as 20 per cent of total budget.

In all calculations of marketing expenditure it is essential to compare like with like. Is product development part of marketing: are research, the cost of the sales force, distribution and so on? For simplicity, the figures outlined in this chapter cover marketing as the management function including market research, planning, product management and promotion but not physical product development and testing, nor the cost of the salesforce and distribution.

SOME FACTORS MAKE PUBLIC RELATIONS EASIER OR MORE DIFFICULT

The broader the audience to reach, the larger the budget that is likely to be required. Similarly, other factors such as the strength of the competition, the importance of the branding of the product, where the product or service falls on the commodity/luxury scale and other market influences will all weight the proportion to be spent.

An interesting method of calculating promotional budgets is to relate these to the sales or marketing job that has to be achieved. Although the example quoted here is a commercial product introduction, the same principles apply to the non-commercial sector. To work through an example using the Haywood formula, a company budgets for a sales increase and calculates the promotional effort as part of the selling cost. This proportion would normally fall between 10 per cent and 25 per cent to achieve the best of anticipated sales, with the lower figure being for industrial companies and the higher figure being for consumer products—where not only may the margins be higher, but the size of audience to reach may be broader. For example, a company looking to increase sales of an engineering product by half a million pounds might allocate 10 per cent or £50 000 to promotion. Whilst a grocery leader introducing a packaged food with first year budgeted sales of £10 000 000 might need to allocate 20 per cent or £2 000 000 to get the product accepted.

The proportion of the marketing budget which should be allocated to the manpower element of promotion can vary widely. A £1 million consumer spend could be administered by one relatively junior brand manager in his early twenties. In contrast, a leading industrial marketing company may require a marketing staff of a dozen senior people.

It is useful to try to identify some broad ratio between advertising and public relations expenditure. Experience shows that less than 15 per cent of the total promotional budget being spent on public relations will not be getting the best value from the budget; with smaller budgets or more specialized markets the minimum proportion will rise. For example, an industrial marketing company will probably need to spend upwards of 30 per cent on the public relations area. With some smaller companies and those with a high degree of specialization in their products or services, this figure might rise to virtually 100 per cent.

FIND OUT THE COMPETITIVE SPEND

It can be useful in deciding the potential budget to look directly at competition: this provides some indication of the public relations resource against which you have to compete. The most obvious method to assess the competitor's budget is to ask! Many progressive managers are quite open about these things. However, weigh the disadvantage of asking: if they tell you, equally, you will be obliged to reciprocate with the comparable information!

There are a number of indirect methods of estimating competitors' expenditure. Check on the people in the marketing, advertising and public relations departments. As a rough guide, marketing salaries (excluding sales personnel) might total between 0.25 per cent and 0.75 per cent of total turnover, depending on the marketing factors outlined earlier. And marketing salaries might be between 10 per cent and 30 per cent of the marketing budget (again excluding sales costs).

Check on the company's agencies and consultancies. Many publish client lists and it may be possible to calculate how an individual budget might relate to their overall billing.

In Britain, the blue book (*Advertisers' Annual*) has useful information on agencies and clients, while *Hollis* and the *PRCA Year Book* cover the same information relating to consultancies. Media Expenditure Analysis Ltd publishes the media expenditure and an intelligent estimate of the proportion this may be of the total budget can be made. (Remember that MEAL data is calculated at rate card and the space/time may have been bought below this rate. Media specialists can advise on converting such figures into likely *actual* expenditure.)

Sometimes trade press reports—particular of sales conferences and campaign launches—will provide some further information: so open a competitive press cuttings service. The advertising and marketing publications often report account changes in some detail. (Treat the figures with caution; it is not unknown for the winner's claimed budget to have an extra zero on the end!)

CONSIDER THE ACTIVITY-COSTING METHOD

As outlined earlier, the alternative is to approach the calculation from the opposite end—decide what has to be done and then cost this activity. Remember that measurable objectives do not only apply in the marketing and sales support areas. As an illustration, an organization might be concerned about the rate of turnover of personnel. If this problem relates to factors that could be influenced by improved communications, it might be realistic to consider public relations to help solve the problem. The objective might be to deploy public relations to reduce the annual turnover from 30 per cent (considered normal in some high technology companies) to a more reasonable 15 per cent.

If this company employs 1000 people, then this reduction in recruitment, training and disruption costs could be £200 000 per annum. It might be reasonable to allocate say 50 per cent of this initially to the public relations effort, perhaps reducing to 20 per cent in the second and successive years. This would give the public relations team a specific potential budget if they can convince management of the action they could take to improve this position: equally, it gives management a very specific measure against which to evaluate the effectiveness of the public relations campaign.

Similar cost-benefit calculations can be made relating to such situations as improving safety awareness, factory relocations, recruitment, productivity achievements, industrial relations, environmental improvements and many others. Where there is no quantitative commercial factor—though it may be surprising how few areas there are where this *cannot* be made to apply—the activity-costing method must be used.

QUANTIFIED OBJECTIVES WORK IN ALL PUBLIC RELATIONS AREAS

Take a public company that considers it is not well known enough in city circles. It may establish an objective among these lines: 'within two years we want to move from being known by one in five city financial advisers on the construction industry as a manufacturer of bricks to being recognized by at least two in three as the pacemaker in our industry'.

Such an objective really combines the subjective views of the company and a very specific method of measuring achievement. But how much should be spent to achieve it? That question is not difficult, nor is the answer. Management should set such a brief to the public relations adviser. He will evaluate the possibility of achieving this and, if viable, the techniques that might need to be applied. These are then costed—the programme of media relations, the seminars, briefing sessions, special reports, upgrading the agm, possible sponsorships, the factory visits, the chairman's lunches and so on. The total will cover the costs of the executive time (or consultancy fees) plus other expenditure.

It is up to management to decide if this is a realistic figure ... and, then, whether it is worth spending this sum to achieve this objective. Ill-directed public relations normally arises not from the difficulty of the task, but from the vague aims that some organizations accept. If management can be encouraged to set a specific brief then the public relations adviser can develop a practical programme to achieve specific results.

If the public relations objectives can be defined, the public relations to achieve it can be planned; if the objectives cannot be written down, then *no* activity is worth considering.

ASSESS THE PLUS AND MINUS INFLUENCES

There is still another method to calculate the budget. This has the advantage that it combines aspects of many of the methods outlined earlier—this is the weighted calculation.

In simple terms, all of the objectives to be achieved are rated in importance and the proportion of the public relations management and financial resource are allocated to these (as explained in Chapter 4 on audiences). Those factors which will be helpful or unhelpful to achieving the public relations objective need to be listed and given some weighting.

Let us consider a case—the introduction of a consumer durable product—and work it through the possible calculations.

Turnover percentage The company will turnover, say, £50 million in this budget year. Say 5 per cent of this will be allocated to marketing support, which is equivalent to £2.5 million. Some 75 per cent of this will be spent on promotional activity, which gives £1 875 000.

Sales increase proportion This is a new product with a first-year sales target of £5 million. It might be reasonable to allocate 10 per cent of this to first-year promotional launch costs, which would be £500 000. (This is equivalent to around 27 per cent of the existing promotional budget: a management decision would be necessary on whether all or part of this should be *additional* budget to support the new product.)

Proportion of promotion Let us assume that 60 per cent of this sum is to be spent on media advertising, 15 per cent on promotions, merchandising and dealer incentives, with 25 per cent on public relations. This would give a base public relations budget of £125 000—equivalent to 2.5 per cent of anticipated first-year sales.

Activity costing At this stage, a programme of possible activity to launch and support the new product for the final year should be planned. This should be costed and, again, compared with the £125 000 provisional budget.

Weighting calculation The aim is to adjust the allowance to compensate for known market factors that might make the job easier or more difficult. These factors need to be listed and divided into those that will be helpful and those that will be unhelpful. Some numerical weighting needs to be given to this. For the purposes of this simple example, a weighting factor on the scale of 1 to 10 is given to each according to the assessment of how much each provides help or hindrance to the sales objective.

Helpful factors	Rating	Unhelpful factors	Rating
Strength of brand name	6	Competitive position	7
Quality of sales support	4	Market resistance	6
Advertising effectiveness	7	Market share target	9
News value of product	10	Timescale for success	6
Company reputation	3	Educational requirement	4
TOTAL	30	TOTAL	32

If the two totals had been the same, then the helpful and unhelpful factors would have balanced out—there would have been no market need to adjust the budget.

However, in this hypothetical example, the negative factors outweigh the positive by 2 points—that is, an average of 2 on the original scale of 10. Converting this into a weighting might suggest that the budget needs to be increased by 20 per cent to compensate for the perceived market difficulties.

If this logic is followed then an outline budget of £150 000 (£125 000 + 20 per cent) would be allocated. This should be taken as no more than a starting point ... it may not be a totally accurate method of calculation but, balanced with experience, it can be far more helpful than the traditional stab in the dark! It should be pointed out that this method has no scientific basis and even the mathematics is not unarguable.

All calculations and assumptions must be recorded. This will prove invaluable when analysing the results at the end of the campaign. This information will also help to allocate the budget more accurately for successive years. The public relations adviser will be able to develop a reasonably accurate calculating model to suit the needs of his organization, its market and competitive position. The public relations professional will achieve more credibility with his colleagues if he works at developing a disciplined approach to costs, results and effectiveness. This involves more than controlling the public relations budget.

CALCULATING THE BUDGET

1. How does the public relations activity relate to the corporate plan and the scope of the task to be undertaken?
2. Have the objectives of public relations, the audiences, messages and activity been outlined?
3. Has this activity been related to the strategy of marketing and other key areas the public relations will support?
4. Is there any intelligence relating to competitive public relations activity and expenditure?
5. Is a strict system of budgetary control in operation that will allow the progress of expenditure to be checked?
6. Has the executive responsible for public relations the budget authority necessary to run the activity?
7. Can expenditure be separated and related to each aspect of the public relations campaign, for example, through a worksheet system, covering:

staff salaries	exhibitions
employment costs	conferences and seminars
overheads and expenses	research and evaluation
consultancy fees	media relations
operating costs	media training
photography	trade relations
house journals	personnel, community
print and production	public affairs
sponsorship	financial relations
	... and others?

8. Have we related the public relations expenditure to total organization turnover to check it is realistic?
9. What proportion of the total promotional expenditure will be allocated to the public relations budget and is this additional to corporate public relations funds?
10. Are there separate budgets for advisory services and implementation activity, for corporate and marketing public relations and so on?
11. Is each budget related to the value to the company in goodwill and credibility if the objective is achieved?
12. Has each activity been examined by the activity-costing method to ensure a good return will be achieved on the public relations investment?
13. Have we evaluated all the alternatives to the activity agreed within the budget?
14. In new public relations areas, have we adjusted the budget using some weighting calculation related to the potential ease/difficulty of the task?
15. Are acceptable systems in operation to monitor cost-efficiency of activity and allow adjustment to the campaign?

SECTION
THREE

Figure 8.1 The European Parliament is of central importance. It is a consensus body, unlike the UK and some other European national assemblies; although there are groupings of allied MEPs, there is no confrontational position between 'government' and 'opposition'.

EIGHT

THE PROGRAMME

CREATE A SCHEDULE OF ACTIVITY

Public relations is planned, continuous and is built upon two-way communications. Only when the activity is coordinated to achieve both long-term and short-term attitude objectives can it be considered a programme. In contrast, a campaign is planned activity to achieve specific shorter term objectives; sometimes a series of campaigns form the central part of the longer-term programme.

An analysis of the audiences the organization is trying to reach will have given some indication of the public relations requirements. Often it is possible to identify aspects of common interest between separate audiences; it may be that factory neighbours, environmental groups and local authorities all have an interest in a reduction of noise, traffic or fumes related to a production plant. Plans can be developed to monitor the attitudes and communicate accordingly with these groups, possibly simultaneously.

Nor is it always necessary to use separate channels of communication to reach each separate audience. For example, the company's external newspaper can be mailed to opinion leaders, key customers and trading partners. A series of factory visits can be organized to cover the needs of prospective employees, shareholders, financial advisers, suppliers and many others. As we noted earlier, the agm, the company report, the open days and new product literature can all perform a useful communications function with publics *other* than the primary target audience.

From the list of audiences, the public relations adviser will develop a range of options covering potential activities. This should be developed into a schedule of activity which might, initially, list the suggestions so that these can be related to the resource available. What *could* and what *should* be undertaken may be different.

PLAN THE ACTIVITIES

A typical listing for a manufacturing company producing components for the electronics industry might read:

> **Audiences:** customers, suppliers, shareholders, financial analysts, professional advisers (bankers, lawyers, solicitors etc) trade associations and professional bodies, officials of relevant government departments, local MPs, MEPs, community leaders and local authority executives, government export departments, the European Commission and Parliament, international distributors and agents, employees, graduates and professional prospective employees, educational, social and community groups.

The draft campaign schedule might identify the following items:

> **Candidate activities:** media relations covering company news stories, a major company profile in the key trade publications, exclusive interview/facility visits for selected end-user publications, an anniversary lunch for employees and families; a briefing document for MEPs constituency and other MPs; VIP facility visits for suppliers, opinion leaders and international trading partners; an open day at the factory for community leaders and neighbours; an annual report and half-yearly results statement plus interim briefings for shareholders, bankers, financial analysts; a national conference for the salesforce; sponsorship of the local youth five-a-side tournament and a travel scholarship endowed at the technical college of higher education to contribute to the community relations; participation in the main national exhibition to support the sales effort; a parliamentary dinner for national account customers; a press launch for the new product range to give sales support and generate enquiries; a company external newspaper to generate awareness among key customers, etc.

Remember that many of these audiences exist within every country where the company is trading and special communications activities relevant to their needs must be planned. Such 'home' audiences in each operating region will be in addition to those special groups that need to be considered in *international* communications, such as the top global management of the organization, the governments, trade associations and professional bodies in each host country, who want to know not just the local situation but your organization's international perspectives and intentions.

At this stage an approximate calculation of the time and money to undertake each of these activities should be made and an initial balance created to make best use of the budget and manpower resources, ideally, country by country. However, for this example, we are considering a programme just for the head office region.

This rough plan and budget might indicate whether it is practical to issue one key company news story every week, every month, or simply a couple of times a year—or whether the company newspaper could be handled three or four times a year. Too low an activity level may not create credibility, too high might produce saturation or start invoking the law of diminishing returns.

In practical terms, a small organization may not be able to cope with more than one VIP party of visitors per month. A larger company may be able to handle this, say, on every working Friday. If the company is working in a sector where there is only one key trade journal, then a major feature once a year may be realistic. Yet in a diverse market sector such as agriculture, manufacturing or groceries, there may be sufficient publications reaching key audiences to allow a major feature every month.

Decisions on time-scales will enable a broad schedule to be converted into a calendar and a timed programme. The organization is investing money and resources in attitude maintenance amongst key audiences to create the ideal operating environment. This investment has to be on a continuous basis and the results will be cumulative over a period of time.

Regular attention to this important task will result in a steadily improving position. Neglect will result in deterioration. In practice, the deterioration may be rapid because the shift in attitudes will not happen in a vacuum. The market situation, competitive activity, gossip, rumour and old-fashioned apathy may well push reputations down faster than the organization was able to build them up. A reputation can take years to build, but can be destroyed overnight.

ASSESS THE PROGRAMME BALANCE

It is useful to apply an oblique measurement to determine whether the balance is right in the proposed level of activity. Go back to the original audiences and look at the percentage of the effort that would be justified in influencing these. For example, your company may say that sales support is worth 60 per cent of the effort and all the rest has to be covered with the remaining 40 per cent. If this is agreed as a fair basis, then the amount of activity which is going to contribute to sales support should be calculated and adjusted so that it approximates to this 60 per cent of time and budget.

During the development of these ideas every member of the management team should be given the opportunity to have an input. One effective way is to have a structured brainstorm session chaired by the public relations adviser and involving all the management team. This will help generate ideas and ensure commitment among the senior executives.

Get them to agree the weightings that will be applied to the final programme. For example, it may be as important for the personnel director to appreciate that 80 per cent of the effort is going towards marketing support as it is for the marketing manager. This way, the personnel director will ensure that the maximum utilization is made of the available resource and manpower working in his area.

While the programme is taking shape, prepare a schedule of the activity so that management can see what will be happening and when. Include in this your procedures for administering the activity and monitoring its progress. Management colleagues will want to be satisfied that the programme will be efficiently managed or they will have no confidence and the public relations department will be constantly under pressure.

PLAN THE INTERNATIONAL DIMENSION

Increasingly, public relations programmes have an international dimension. Sometimes, this simply will mean communications between one organization, its operations and markets in just two or three countries. In such programmes, there is often an 'export' flavour to the communications, where the head office is very much the head office and the operations are the 'colonies'. However, you cannot really export public relations—people only communicate when real bridges are built.

However, campaigns can often be run with limited success by 'exporting' the information through international news and distribution agencies, or through briefing resident foreign correspondents of the national media in the head office country.

In the UK, the Central Office of Information is a public service that exists to project Britain worldwide. Commercial attaches in British embassies and consulates can also help. Professional, commercial services such as UNS and EIBIS also offer an excellent service. International news agencies may also be interested in the more significant news and these include Reuters and UPI.

At the other end of the spectrum, some organizations run public relations activities that are so international that they almost cease to be 'international'; they become a series of *national* campaigns tailored precisely to the expectations, needs, customs and cultures of each country, yet operating together in a harmonious, synchronized and inter-related way— within clearly understood corporate guidelines and objectives. In the commercial arena, companies like Unilever, ICI, Shell and Olivetti are among those getting close to this concept.

At whatever stage of international evolution your organization may be, there are some important basic factors necessary in the planning of supporting public relations.

The technology of communications is now so advanced that information can be instantaneously available across the globe. Today, the media is international and news boundaries have disappeared from the public relations map. Correspondents for major newspapers can feed in their copy from any place around the world for it to be set directly and in print in hours. Television items can be transmitted via satellite directly into television companies and studios, wherever the news editors require. And radio, cheaply and easily, can be almost anywhere and everywhere—so much so that we are no longer surprised to hear a live news item from places that were remote and inaccessible names in our childhood atlases. The public relations professional has to keep pace with this frantic development, which will continue through our lifetimes. Public relations offices and consultancies are setting up their own electronic links and providing sophisticated services to their companies or clients.

When planning your programme, consider which of those elements need to be international and which need to be domestic to each market. As Michael Morley of Edelman International has said, some aspects 'travel' like good wine and others do not. For example, the financial world has few international barriers. Company news cannot be adjusted or adapted to local needs, as all analysts and financial advisers are working to standards that are getting ever more unified. There is a similar trend in medicine, the environment, technology and consumer marketing.

Major news about the organization or corporation needs to be handled simultaneously around the world and the public relations adviser needs to be sure that he has the machinery for this ... for example, the electronic links, the public relations executives in overseas associate or subsidiary companies, or a network of properly briefed consultancies. The type of news that needs to be distributed immediately will include annual results, acquisitions, responses to crises and so on.

Alongside such major announcements, each operating country will require a continuing and two-way flow of information. The principles outlined on planning and selecting the resource apply to the development of the campaign within each market. The following points may be helpful:

1. Clarify the coordination responsibilities; which items need central clearance and where local public relations autonomy will operate; what are the international objectives and how do local objectives relate to these?
2. Agree authorities so that the coordinating public relations executive can control such elements as the use of corporate identities, company policy statements, or the timing of release of corporate news locally.

3. Set corporate and local budgets and resources, so that an effective job can be done on the ground. There is little point in setting grand objectives for South America, say, without recognizing the number of separate countries in that continent, the size, range of cultures, languages and attitudes. Brazil is not Texas, Peru is not Switzerland.

4. Be very clear which costings are local and which can be charged to corporate. Local companies should have their own budgets and use either staff or consultants, possibly under policy direction from the centre but responsible to local line management. When using consultancies, management must get quotations in advance for major activity unless this is clearly structured within the agreed programme and budget.

5. Use as much common material as is practical to keep unity and consistency of the messages, allowing local personnel to adapt only as necessary to local needs. Distribute the central standard material to be used by the regional operations—for example, photography, technical articles, research developments, policy statements by top management, corporate information, videos and so on.

6. Make face-to-face meetings central to each programme and remember to use visiting VIPs, as they move across regions, as a focus for news activity. Similarly, make sure your own public relations team (staff, colleagues or consultancy advisers) also meet regularly to improve coordination and understanding.

7. Establish a uniform policy for the regional public relations people to report back to the centre so that corporate management can keep up to date with what is happening to company communications around the world and react accordingly—or make adjustments to policy. The regional advisers should also report on any trends or developments to which the organization needs to give consideration and possibly adopt a stance or prepare a policy on—these might include, for example, the activities of pressure groups, shifts in the local economy, political changes, competitive activity and so on.

8. At the centre, the coordinating public relations executive should take the responsibility for preparing a precis of this information to keep top management informed. He should also be responsible for monitoring the supra-national activity that crosses national borders, for example, the EC, World Health Organisation, World Bank, International Monetary Fund and so on.

9. Finally, international public relations must be discussed in some depth and reviewed at the highest level within the organization. It should be the responsibility of the coordinating public relations executive to advise the chief executive on how this should be tackled.

PUBLIC RELATIONS IS THE UNIFYING FORCE

The aim of this planning is to ensure that management and the company provide the maximum support for the public relations objectives and the resulting public relations programme. It is equally critical to cover the presentation of the problems, solutions and the proposed plans to deal with these within the organization and at the different levels which have influence.

The public relations efforts will only be effective if they have endorsement from the top and from the operating levels. Public relations objectives must be understood and supported. The public relations function should be recognized as central to good management and able to act as a unifying force within the organization in the way it presents itself to the world. That way, a schedule of activity can become a campaign. And the campaigns can become a programme.

Activity	Days	May	June	July	Aug.	Sept.	Oct.	Nov.	Dec.	Jan.	Feb.	Mar.	Apr.
Monthly planning meeting	1	X	X	X	X	X	X	X	X	X	X	X	X
Quarterly board presentation	2			X			X			X				X
Company news releases	½	X		X		X		X		X		X		X
Management articles	2	X		X		X		X		X		X		
Survey features	2		X			X			X			X		
Management seminars	3		X						X					
Director interviews	1½	X		X		X		X		X		X		X
Parliamentary briefing	1½					X			X					
Plant open day	2						X							
Institute presentations	2						X							X
Technical papers	2						X							X
Presentation training	3	X												
Annual report	5			X										
Interim results	2												X	
Employee bulletings	2				X							X		
Contingency	½	X		X		X		X		X		X		X
Total 88 days per annum		3	8½	8	8½	7	7	9	5½	6½	8½	7	9½

Chart 8.1 The public relations programme should be planned to give as even a schedule as practical. This will help continuity and assist in planning the deployment of the public relations resource. In this example, an estimate of the time for each agreed activity has been made so that the executive manpower is available when required. This calendar is for a corporate campaign based on an actual plan. If this were handled by a consultancy, the calendar would help in agreeing the necessary fees and related costs. If this programme were run by a staff executive, the calendar shows that proportion of his or her time to be spent on corporate public relations—the balance being, perhaps, on marketing support or international relations. In both cases, the calendar provides a management control.

PLANNING THE SCHEDULE

1. Have we agreed our list of audiences, priorities, weightings and communications objectives?
2. Are the messages we wish to project about the organization consistent and agreed by top management?
3. Is it possible to arrange the audiences into helpful groupings, such as community or wholesalers?
4. Have we drawn up an outline list of potential communications techniques to inform these groups?
5. Is a brainstorming or planning session with other departmental heads helpful at this stage to develop ideas?
6. Can we calculate the likely executive time and cost to undertake each of these candidate activities?
7. How does this total relate to the available executive time and budget within the agreed public relations resource?
8. Which activities are likely to be most cost effective so that the lower-rated ones can be eliminated from the potential programme?
9. Can this schedule be adjusted so that the balance of activities reflects the communication priorities of each audience group we have already agreed?
10. Are there fixed dates in the organization calendar that need to be considered in the programme, such as founder's day or the annual general meeting?
11. Can we confirm those activities which will be needed to support these events and, therefore, will happen on fixed dates?
12. Is it possible to spread the other public relations activity across the year to achieve the best possible utilization of the public relations resources that are available, particularly management time?
13. Have we discussed this programme with divisional heads and incorporated all reasonable requests, observations and modifications?
14. Has it been presented to the board and endorsed as an operating policy by the chief executive?
15. Can we now confirm this schedule and circulate it to all executives affected by public relations planning?
16. In planning the international activity have we considered:

- in which countries will we need public relations support
- what resources already exist on-the-ground
- how do these report into local management
- should we reinforce these with local public relations staff
- or would consultancy provide a better option
- what programmes are planned locally
- how do we coordinate these with central policy

- which elements must be controlled from the centre and which can be handled as decided locally
- is there a coordinated international programme
- how do we brief all public relations partners on this
- what budgets are to be allocated/approved
- are any elements of this to be approved centrally
- when do the public relations principals need to check policy
- what feedback procedures should we have
- do these cover appraisals of trends and issues
- and how do we monitor effectiveness to improve both the local and international levels of performance?

NINE

EMPLOYEES

DO NOT CREATE INFORMATION JUNKIES

Today's employees expect 'communications'. But, even in the most sophisticated companies in the most advanced countries, too many employees are communicated 'at' rather than 'with'. Often little more than lip (or pen!) service is paid to the concept of two-way communications. Management needs to question seriously whether one-way information activity is productive. The objective of real employee communication must be to create understanding and support among employees to enable the company to operate more efficiently.

Again, some organizations behave as if they were in the publishing business and produce newspapers, reports, documents, discussion papers, films, video and slide-tape presentations *ad nauseam*. They can end up converting employees into information junkies. The bemused workers cannot make a decision unless they have a fix of more information.

With some companies, communication has almost become easier than management. It can be simpler to put out yet more information rather than to make a decision. It can be more gratifying to offer involvement than leadership. It is the responsibility of management both to manage *and* communicate; they are inseparable. Any employee misunderstandings, confusion or lack of support must be the result of management failing to communicate effectively. This responsibility cannot be delegated or abdicated.

MANAGERS MUST MANAGE

The most common example of abdication is where employee communications has been left to the unions—though less common now in the UK since the balance of union/management power has shifted, this is still the norm in many countries. This is generally worse than unsatisfactory; it is potentially disastrous. It does not take much analysis to identify that the objectives of the unions are unlikely to be the same as the objectives of the organization.

Even today, most unions are unsophisticated in their operations. Their prime responsibility will be to obtain the best terms and conditions for their members while protecting as many of their jobs as possible. These shorter term aims generally take priority over the longer-term needs of the industry.

The company may well be concerned about other factors not automatically compatible, for example, the return on investment, manpower costs, improved productivity, market-place competition, introduction of new technologies and so on. Why do some companies allow vital information relating to these changes to be communicated via the very group of people who are intent on resisting such change?

Under *no* circumstances should management information be communicated to the workforce through union channels. Equally, under no circumstances should management base decisions upon workforce information which is fed back through the same union channels. In both directions, there is a certainty of distortion to reflect the views and attitudes of the union officials who are acting as the transmitters in the communication channel.

KEEP UNIONS INFORMED

It is equally important to recognize that the unions are, themselves, an important audience. Sensible managers will ensure that they have identified the trade union officials that need to be kept informed: they will be certain that a programme of two-way communications is operating efficiently—rather than waiting until some dispute focuses attention on the *need* for improved communications.

The personnel world is not an arena to be played in by amateurs. The public relations professional will have to work extremely hard to earn respect from his personnel colleagues and ensure that there is an understanding of each other's roles at all levels.

It is vital that they work closely together. If not, there is a danger that a cautious personnel department can allow a communications vacuum to develop; this may rapidly become filled with unhelpful speculation or gossip. Alternatively, an over-enthusiastic public relations operation can create unnecessary problems for the personnel professionals, for example, through not being sensitive to all factors involved in human relations negotiations.

UNDERSTAND INFORMATION NEEDS

The employees of an organization have an information right, need *and* desire … and these are not all the same. For example, the information rights are often laid down by law. In the UK, an employee must have a contract of employment, must be advised of his rights relating to sickness, holidays, pension, safety at work and many other factors. Some companies have negotiated agreements which cover information requirements and these soon become established as 'rights'.

Across the EC and in the US there is a growing level of legislation that is identifying and defining the information rights of all employees. We are likely to see some important changes over the coming years. In particular, European legislation affecting multinationals could involve companies changing policies in countries *outside* the European community, if this affects employees in an EC country.

However, the *needs* of employees in relation to information are rather different to their legal rights. At present there may be no statutory *right* for employees to know about the anticipated development of their company; but it might be a very realistic *need* to ensure that they will understand and support any such management plans. Equally, employees might want to know how secure their jobs are, how much they will be paid in the future, what new investments are likely to be made that will materially affect their jobs and so on.

The public relations adviser will need to have a clear view and understanding of that information that has to be provided by statutory right, union negotiation or trade precedent; that which should be provided in the interest of good understanding and that which is confidential and does not have to be freely available until the time the company decides it is appropriate.

INFORMATION PERMEATES EVERYWHERE

The organization should be at the centre of its own communication network with information radiating out to the key audiences. At the same time, information should also be flowing back towards the organization. And, whether the company likes it or not, information will also be flowing between the various audiences, bypassing any official source; none of these is operating in a water-tight compartment. For example, there will be communication between factory neighbours and company shareholders; customers and suppliers; prospective employees and environmental groups. This is one reason why all information must be consistent and that the corporate personality must be reflected in all communications.

If the company has integrity, then any information (or rumour) will be checked back by employees to see whether it is credible. If the company personality is well established and the gossip unlikely, then it will be rejected immediately. If the company has no communications tradition then there will be no yardstick to check against; equally, if the company has no credibility then unfavourable gossip may be believed. In both cases, the rumour will become established as pseudo-fact.

This up and down (and sideways) communication network is particularly important to employees. The well-run organization will ensure that the communications responsibilities of each manager are fully understood and implemented. Indeed, these responsibilities should be part of each manager's job description.

It is essential that *all* communications at all levels are factual, accurate and consistent. As an illustration, it is damaging to management credibility if the first time the chairman reveals policy changes is in his foreword to the annual report; this may be picked up by shop floor shareholders but may come as news to middle managers when asked to explain. Who is managing whom? A programme relating to a substantial expansion by one consumer giant was thrown out of gear when a member of the personnel department included one short but revealing sentence in the middle of an article on employment prospects for a local newspaper survey.

The public relations adviser may recommend to management that the communications capabilities of all managers should be regularly assessed and their performance monitored (starting at the top). The casual handling of information may be viewed as inefficiency at lower management levels but may be the norm at the top, where some directors are able to make their own rules: the uninhibited freedom to handle information can be one of the headiest of corporate powers.

Too many companies disseminate information from the top and allow it to filter down without checking its progress. Equally important, the information coming back up to management may not be of the quality necessary to make proper decisions, depending on the ability of the managements in the communications chain. Some people believe that information is power. Therefore, they tend to be very careful about how much of this they give away. This covetous attitude towards information can create extremely weak points in the communications network. Any information bottleneck must be identified. One manager may be reckless, while another may be miserly with information.

Some managers act as a *one-way* communications valve, constantly transmitting but never receiving; they are all mouth and no ears. Again, it is a relatively simple process to check each manager's ability to feed back information into the communications network. Special attention should be paid to any manager who is not providing any information or whose assessments are constantly adrift. Try a test: feed in information at an open level (perhaps through a story in a local paper) and see which managers react— and how they respond.

Training will help improve communications weaknesses but the most critical point is for each manager to realize that the company *requires* him to be an effective communicator: this is not a voluntary option. Include an appraisal of each manager's communications skills and motivation in annual performance reviews. Offer management communications training courses.

GET INFORMATION MOVING IN

One effective way to help establish the principles of two-way communication is to work with each department in creating an internal communications programme. The techniques of putting information *out* are reasonably well established. The techniques for pulling it *in* are equally simple, but less well developed.

As always, one of the most effective ways of communicating is face-to-face. All managers should ensure that their communications programme includes an element of this. These do not all need to be one-to-one situations but can often be the manager talking to groups. Special attention needs to be paid to ensure that these are not simply lectures or pep-talks for the troops. Such face-to-face briefings by management need to be held regularly. Within a very large organization, *some* of these personal briefings may contain an element of prepared audio-visual material, such as a video interview with the chief executive. Even this must be presented by a senior manager able to speak authoritatively and handle discussion.

Such briefings must be accepted by executives as part of their responsibility for good management. All personnel giving briefings must be equipped with briefing notes covering agreed answers to all possible questions. It is the manager's responsibility to stimulate, note and take action on audience reactions. Response has to be worked at and managers have to be trained to encourage input and response.

Some people have a natural ability to intimidate. At one planning meeting I witnessed at a famous engineering company, a middle manager was explaining to foremen a proposed new manufacturing process. He did not put over the implications very clearly but asked for comments. One man who had not understood the brief asked an important but somewhat naïve point. The manager dismissed the query and immediately asked for more serious questions. Naturally, there was complete silence. Eventually, everyone left the room, not only confused but resentful. The new method was never successfully introduced. Years later, I was told by management that this was because of bolshie shop floor attitudes...

TRAIN MANAGERS TO LISTEN

The simplest rule in building a response network is to ensure that for every channel of management information, there is a channel for response. *Every* meeting must include a discussion section during which responses will be recognized and actioned. Every question must be recognized as a demonstration of interest. Often the seemingly irrelevant question identifies the *real* area of concern: quite often it also means that the main aspects of the presentation have been accepted.

Let us run through the introduction of the new process as handled by the poor communicating manager. He has put over the technical aspects, say, adequately. Now for reactions:

Any questions? This is not a good start. It is more a challenge, defying the group to respond, perhaps suggesting they may not be bright enough to understand. Far better would be to lead in the discussion. 'It seems to me that to make this work we might need to look at the layout of machines in shop B. How do you feel?'

This identifies a specific area and outlines an infinite range of options. If there is still some slowness in response, bring someone in known to be constructive and confident. 'Mike, you have some experience in this area. How do you feel it might work?'

Let us assume the manager has to handle a serious question: 'Mike wants to know about excess heat from the new plant. Don't worry about the conditions in the shop, the machine will be well insulated. Next question?'

If Mike's question has to be interpreted, ask *him* to do it. Simply rephrasing it suggests it was not too bright. Never put your own interpretation on why he asked. If in doubt, ask him. Always answer *every* question. A serious question requires a serious answer.

A more sympathetic response might be 'Mike has raised an important point. Of course, in the presentation, I only touched on this, but the new plant does generate more heat than the present machinery. What sort of problems do you feel this might create?' This will bring the group into the discussion.

Let us assume the serious question has been properly covered.

Next question? Again, this is not an encouraging way to handle discussion. It may even suggest that the whole exercise is just a mechanical routine. Remember the objective is to create support and understanding: to do this the real objections must be established and either satisfactorily covered or taken into consideration in amending the proposals.

A more effective way to lead from one topic to another might be ... 'That seems to have covered that factor. Everyone happy with what we've agreed? Any other points on this subject we need to consider? Fine. I've noted these ideas and we'll revise the proposal to see if we can cover your suggestions. Let's move on. There are some other important implications, for example, the late shift. How can we best plan for that do you feel?'

Eventually you will have covered all serious points. However there may be some minor points ... at least, they may seem minor to management, but can be major to the people involved. Lead into these areas.

'We seem to have covered the major aspects. But I appreciate there are some important details we need to resolve. One thing that has occurred to me is that we'll have to move the tea machine. How do you feel about that ... or any other points big or small you want to raise?'

Remember, if the tea machine problem comes up early, it has been raised because it matters to the people concerned. It *must* be properly dealt with ... remember, this also suggests that the questioner is happy about the broader implications of the plan.

The communicating manager will know how to handle discussion. It is not necessary to prolong debate about detailed problems for which management should have identified detailed solutions. Equally, it is not helpful to browbeat the group: silence tells you nothing.

This simple example is only an illustration of one small aspect of a vitally important area. The public relations adviser needs to assess the discussion management skills of managers reponsible for communicating public relations messages. Those that need development should be encouraged to attend personal communications training courses. Alternatively, a consultant could be invited into the organization to assess the levels of competence and run training sessions.

NEWSPAPERS MUST REFLECT REAL ISSUES

Similarly, every company publication, particularly the house newspaper or magazine, should arouse a reaction and response. It may mean that the reporters on the publication need to be recruited to represent the main employee groups; that the editor should be one or two steps sideways from management; that he should have a duty to establish strong links at all points within the organization and report all feelings and attitudes; maybe the publication needs to carry readership surveys, letters, columns and other direct response features. Perhaps the paper should not be a paper at all but a video or audio tape?

CAN THIS COMPANY LISTEN?

The chairman of United Biscuits each year personally visits nearly 40 plants to give a presentation on the company's trading and prospects. It creates great goodwill, understanding and commitment.

Many organizations are using video to put over management or policy information. Some companies prepare a simplified version of the annual results presented by the chairman or chief executive. A number of companies have taken this one stage further and organized a video recording of a studio discussion (sometimes chaired by an independent TV or radio commentator) where selected representatives of the employees question the chief executive. Few (although there are one or two notable exceptions) have gone as far as to record the discussion sessions that *follow* the presentation of this video: this way, the observations and comments from employees, often at distant locations, can be fed back to the chief executive. Where this has been done, it has provided the opportunity for a second discussion on issues of concern. This creates far more acceptance of the concept of a *genuine* exchange of information and views.

The fundamental issue that the effective public relations adviser has to assess is ... are we a communicating organization, will we listen and act, or do we only want our employees to be compliant and listen to what *we* want to say. It may be one way to run an organization ... but it is not *communication*.

A communicating organization is likely to be a caring organization. It will take a responsible attitude towards minority and disadvantaged groups in the community. To illustrate one aspect of this need for commercial organizations to contribute to removing barriers between groups, in the UK, the Manpower Services Commission produced a series of advertisements on the theme 'Fit for Work'. These identified that Nelson, Beethoven, Julius Caesar, Milton, Leonardo da Vinci, Sarah Bernhart, Roosevelt and Helen Keller were all disabled. The message was clear. Creative ability does not relate to physical ability.

BAD NEWS CAN BE VERY BAD NEWS

One of the practical ways of ensuring that all communications elements contribute to the whole, is for the public relations practitioner to present the agreed corporate public relations programme to the heads of department so that they have the opportunity to observe and react; eventually they will need to ensure that their own communications activities are consistent with this corporate public relations plan.

Each divisional or departmental head should have the opportunity of agreeing on their priority audiences, the communications policy, the messages and methods. It is also essential to identify the potential problem situations that might arise. The company should be prepared to handle the bad news situations as well as the good news. (These contingency procedures are covered in more detail in a separate chapter.)

In all the areas of public relations responsibility, there are few that have more priority than employee relations. In virtually all organizations, the major resource is the people working in the enterprise. But above all, the people are the only *intelligent* resource ... only people can think, can plan, can enthuse, can dream, can make things happen. The organization is as big as the ambitions of the people who make it work. David Ogilvy, the eminent advertising man, said that if you recruit people smaller than yourself you build a team of pygmies, but if you recruit people bigger than yourself you become a team of giants.

It is equally true that if you deprive people of information and treat them as of small importance, they will behave like pygmies. If you communicate properly, negotiate and treat them as important colleagues they will behave like giants.

EMPLOYEE COMMUNICATIONS

Identifying the communications needs

1. Have we identified employee information needs, for example, by surveys or management assessments?
2. Should these be considered separately for each employee sector, grade or geographical location?
3. What attitudes exist towards the organization among these groups?
4. What attitudes would the organization wish to establish and what is the gap between reality and the ideal?
5. Is any part of this difference capable of improvement through better communications?
6. Can we list all the existing communications channels that are in operation, whether company-controlled or not?
7. Are there any unofficial communications channels which might indicate a need the organization is not meeting?
8. Can we research or make an accurate assessment of the credibility of all communications methods?
9. Which of these provide a real opportunity for feedback from employees?
10. How effective are managers at monitoring reactions and assessing the attitudes of employees for whom they are responsible?

11. To what extent do managers pass back up the management communications chain the feedback from their staffs?
12. Are managers able to identify and report on information inadequacies and areas of concern relating to attitudes, before these become problems?

Assessing the communications problems

13. How do employees get the information that they need to do their respective jobs?
14. Are there any identified blockages in the management information chain?
15. Do different departments or divisions cooperate in the exchange of necessary information; in other words, are the lateral as well as the vertical links working?
16. Are there any complaints from managers about the proportion of their time spent in meetings, discussions or communications?
17. Can any specific problems be related to poor communications such as indifference, absenteeism, industrial unrest, negligent housekeeping, poor customer service, safety or quality control?
18. How well-informed are employees about company policies, product developments, competitive activity or other items necessary for them to perform efficiently?
19. Can a method be established for measuring this knowledge of developments?
20. How can this be related to attitudes and established information links to identify gaps, barriers or weaknesses?

Establishing the solutions

21. What are the costs involved (manpower plus expenditure) in the existing communications channels?
22. Which are the most effective in providing information that employees need to perform well and maintain positive attitudes?
23. Which also provide effective feedback to monitor these attitudes and, therefore, adjust the communications programme?
24. Can the cost effectiveness of each activity, therefore, be assessed and the better channels identified?
25. Have we considered and costed all the alternatives including:

company newspapers or magazines	posters or wallcharts
regular news sheets	information folders
noticeboard bulletins	induction programmes
telephone information service	regional or national conferences

news videos or films
cctv discussions
tape/slide presentations
company radio station
information seminars
local or trade press relations
local radio and TV news
new corporate identity

policy leaflets
direct-mail to home
annual reports
company history
community sponsorship
open days
facility visits?

TEN

LOCAL COMMUNITIES

BEING GOOD CITIZENS PAYS

Good community relations are important for every organization. Perhaps it is easiest to illustrate the point by looking at the interrelationship between community goodwill (or its lack) and a commercial organization's sales objectives.

Poor community relations can have commercial consequences. The managers of a chicken processing plant—ironically, a subsidiary of Sainsbury's—in a country region of Britain were frustrated to find planning permission refused for a factory extension. The public relations specialist was asked to look at the problem. He identified that planning permission had been refused because of the local authority's concern over complaints from local neighbours about an unpleasant smell. One or two neighbours were central to these complaints but the management had refused to have any dealings with these members of the public. In one case, a member of the factory night security team had been unhappily abusive to one of the complainants. What had been a small (and reasonable) complaint had become a major issue. However, it only proved of concern to the management when it created a practical problem.

The public relations professional should not have been in the position of rectifying a situation *after* the damage was done. The company had a very good story to tell: management had invested a substantial sum which would eventually eliminate the smells. However, this story had never been put over. This was rectified by holding meetings with the neighbours and a press relations campaign, beginning with a briefing for the local newspaper correspondents.

As a result, the neighbours recognized that the company was making efforts to listen and respond to their fair criticisms. Equally important, better balanced stories began to appear in the local press and these were commented on by local councillors who had been concerned about the neighbourliness of the company. After a reasonable period of time, the complainants were satisfied by the action of the company and the planning permission was ultimately granted.

An incidental benefit of the problem was that it demonstrated to an insensitive management the role of the public relations professionals in helping the company communicate effectively. It also illustrated the need to consider the public relations implications of policy, at the planning stage.

The public relations professional must ensure that procedures for dealing with complaints are agreed and operate sensitively. The company need not give disproportionate attention to every complaint. But, at the same time, it is sensible to deal with all complaints as if the caller is a campaigning journalist, an Esther Rantzen, or a consumer watchdog. Acting responsibly is not only fulfilling, it pays.

The community groups that will be of importance to each organization will vary but are likely to include professional, business and social sections. Some of the most frequent groupings are neighbours, suppliers, existing and prospective employees, community opinion leaders, professional associations, social, leisure and cultural societies, educational establishments and local authorities and departments.

As it is important to understand the attitudes which operate at factory-gate level, before trying to influence these, each needs to be considered and related to the aims and the cost effectiveness before a programme of action is planned. It is helpful to outline some of the more useful techniques that can form part of a community relations programme.

Press relations It is essential that the company has a good working relationship with local press, radio and television. A senior executive of the company needs to be made responsible for ensuring that there is an effective and continuous media relations campaign.

Visits Many groups within the local community will be interested in seeing industry at work. These visits need to be properly organized but must not be too demanding on management time or disruptive to production. Some companies have solved this problem by allocating a specific time when visits can be booked (say, every Friday afternoon) and appointing somebody to act as a guide (perhaps a retired employee).

Speakers' panel Many opportunities exist for the company to be represented by speakers at meetings of community or professional groups. This speakers' panel can represent the main facets of the company's operations. Each member can draw upon standard materials such as prepared talks, statistics, audio-visual aids, handouts and training in speaking.

Open days Major events such as the opening of a new research facility can be marked by holding an open day for employees, families and the local community. Such events can be established on an annual basis, perhaps combined with a sports day or fete.

Internal communications This specialized area includes company news-papers, bulletins, discussion groups, notice boards, internal broadcasts, telephone news services, video presentations and others. In all but the smallest company, these areas will almost certainly require at least a part-time specialist who may well be able to undertake other community activities.

Facilities At very little cost, some companies are able to make their facilities available. These might include sports fields, car parks, lecture rooms, meeting rooms, fax, telex, telephone or other administrative facilities. Many organizations involved in sports, arts, leisure, fashion or charity fields will appreciate the use of such facilities.

Sponsorship Considerable goodwill can be generated by the company con-tributing financial or administrative aid to local events, such as art exhi-bitions or festivals, charity days, local or national celebrations, such as civic days or jubilees.

Community projects Companies can adopt a particular project on which to concentrate their energies and encourage employees to participate. Suggest-ions for these nearly always come from within the company. Examples may include fund raising for a local charity, helping establish a needed local amenity such as a mobile library, old folks' club or children's nursery.

Secondment Some companies have a policy of seconding senior personnel. This can also be as refreshing as a sabbatical for the manager. In the UK, the Action Resource Centre offers expert advice in this area and will act as a broker where companies wish to second senior personnel to such community projects.

Anniversaries An important anniversary provides an opportunity to project the organization to many of the defined audiences. The anniversary can be tied together with a self-explanatory visual and verbal theme—such as ... 'a century of service'.

VIPs Most companies have relations with public figures who would like to see the organization at work. Such VIPs might include senior government officials, directors of larger customers, ambassadors from major export markets or representatives of overseas buying delegations. Employees like to meet the star of the new television campaign or the new sales film. (Often a day's visit to the works can be negotiated at the time the celebrity's contract is agreed.)

Society members Many employees will already be members of professional bodies and societies within the community. Companies should consider encouraging such involvement, possibly including administrative or financial assistance. Company facilities can be offered to support this participation.

GET MANAGEMENT TO AGREE THE PROGRAMME

If there is a need to improve communications at factory-gate level, then the programme must be as planned as any other activity. The move from the 'what should we be doing?' to the 'how the devil do we cope?' position can be disastrously rapid.

Management exists to manage, *not* to provide free and unending support for the local community. It is important that resources should be agreed in advance. In particular, a community participation budget should be established. An analysis of the policy of a number of companies shows that a reasonable figure might be 0.025 to 0.05 per cent of turnover; this is equivalent to £2500 to £5000 for a company with £10 million sales.

Alternatively a percentage of pre-tax profit can be earmarked. The largest shareholder-owned insurance company in the US, Aetna Life and Casualty has found that 2 per cent of pre-tax operating earnings provides a general guideline. As the corporation has explained, it invests this sum to help maintain the health of the society on which the well-being of Aetna depends.

What community projects should the organization support? To agree a policy, a small meeting of the interested executives needs to be called. This might well cover the personnel, public relations, marketing and administrative functions. Prior to this meeting, other executives might well be asked to advise on problems/opportunities that have occurred over, say, the last couple of years. This meeting should define the key audiences, their relative importance and the way that the organization wishes to project itself.

Once the programme has begun, the company will be building a reputation that it is receptive to requests for help, comments or ideas. A policy, therefore, has to be agreed to ensure that there are clear guidelines on what can or cannot be done. This will ensure that there is the minimum resentment caused when projects have to be turned down.

An executive needs to be appointed to be responsible for the control of the programme and its budget. Because many of the decisions will be at fundamental policy level, this responsibility must be handled by someone as senior as possible. The implementation of the programme may be undertaken by specialized executives within the personnel or public relations departments—or a public relations consultancy may be retained for advice and action in these areas.

FACTORY GATE PUBLIC RELATIONS WORKS

Many companies now have a policy of seconding managers to community projects. In the UK, Esso, National Westminster, Barclays, Midland and Lloyds banks, Rolls-Royce, ICI, Marks & Spencer, The Bank of England, the Williams Lea Group and IBM are just a few of many who have seconded managers to work on projects as varied as counselling small businesses, youth employment, probation and after-care service.

Large companies usually have a well-defined community relations policy. As an illustration, Unilever provides financial support to a range of charities and to selected projects in education, youth work, care of the elderly and disabled, medicine, scientific research, social welfare, civic and environmental issues, though the company makes no political contributions. This is in addition to its secondment programme. All local appeals for financial help are considered by a staff committee which has a charities and community projects fund at its disposal. The company has also accepted a responsibility to develop a non-commercial programme to inform and educate people about nutrition.

At the other end of the commercial spectrum, Babcock Woodall-Duckham Ltd is an industrial company selling expertise, without large manufacturing facilities. However, it still has a strong company policy of community involvement. For example, its large ground floor restaurant facility is available to the community as a weekend/evening venue for occasional voluntary community efforts. The company has on occasions sponsored local events such as the donkey derby at the local carnival and a full-scale gymnastics event at the sports centre. Administrative support was provided for a midsummer youth festival. The company has a policy to use as many local suppliers as possible. Sir John King, when he was chairman of the parent company, Babcock International Ltd, introduced a VIP luncheon in those areas where the Babcock companies operate, when he entertained community opinion leaders, including local journalists.

When plans were announced by the Kellogg Company affecting one of their British subsidiaries, the company organized a briefing for local councillors, press and officials.

Some manufacturers have processes that can cause problems with neighbours and, if mishandled, public complaints can lead to poor publicity, even demonstrations and production disruptions. UK engineering leaders, Wilmot Breedon, for example, tackled concern about heavy presses working through the night by inviting local residents into the factory to see the work in progress. They heard expert opinion on solutions and the visit allowed them to air their problems. Soundproofing solved the problems; the discussions generated goodwill and mutual understanding.

Rhone-Poulenc, the French multinational, managed a schools project to create a cleaner city, in association with the local authority in Norwich where it has one of its major European plants. Managers also supported exhibitions and open days at the local art school and, at a national level, organized the first-ever exhibition of the work of French sculptor, Bourdelle, in Britain.

The concept of good community relations is not new. Pioneering work was undertaken in Britain by such companies as Colmans and Cadburys as far back as Victorian times. In the US, considerable worker resistance to the methods of Astor, Carnegie, DuPont, Gould, Morgan, Rockefeller and others built up. The pioneering efforts of the Mutual Life Assurance Company, Ford, Westinghouse and American Bell to improve genuine communications were in contrast to the cynical gestures of some of the industrial entrepreneurs. Public relations went through an unfortunate period before emerging as an effective force for social improvement and mutual understanding. In Europe, companies like Nestlé, Volvo, Fiat and Philips pioneered bold initiatives in community relations.

Regular events in the organization's calendar can be extended to create opportunities to talk to members of the community. It is interesting to see the skill with which American corporations use public meetings to create interest. For example, their annual meetings often provide a convenient platform for a major corporate announcement or speech. US and Canadian corporations tend to reprint these and distribute them very widely. Some also have a range of meetings for non-shareholder audiences including directors and managers, plant neighbours, financial leaders, bankers, local or trade journalists, husbands and wives and many others.

PRIVATE ENTERPRISE CAN HELP PUBLIC SECTORS

A major campaign was run in the US involving a partnership of public and private interests under the theme 'WIN—Whip Inflation Now!' Although this was a public relations initiative, it represented a trend towards greater cooperation between government and private enterprise.

The significance of this development so impressed Atlantic Richfield Company that it formed a partnership with the body that represents the mayors of communities across the US, the Conference of Mayors. The aim of this arrangement was to run a series of conferences to examine how business, non-profit organizations and local government could work better together. The company sponsored a national meeting in Philadelphia, followed by a whole series of local sessions, attended by over 150 mayors of US cities and 1000 other participants.

The concept that the private sector should subsidize programmes to cover cuts made by the national government has been resisted—however, the skills and expertise that are available within private industry can help communities in such areas as engineering, economics, finance and general management. In the UK, senior directors from such companies as Marks & Spencer, Midland Bank and others have been drafted into government services to apply business methods and improve efficiency. With the pressure on public finance and the need to control costs, as well as find sources for alternative funding, business managers have more recently been acting as advisers to local authorities, charities and arts bodies, such as the Tate Gallery and the Covent Garden Opera.

Where the public relations adviser's responsibilities are international, then it becomes even more important to ensure that an effective programme of community relations is in operation at all locations where the organization has facilities. Similar techniques to those outlined above may be suitable. However, it is important to allow local management to take the initiative, supported by a local consultancy if suitable—along the lines detailed in planning the programme in Chapter 8.

Such activities involve a major investment of time and expertise. But even the smallest organization can benefit from becoming more closely involved in the community. It is not only more pleasant to be a good employer, a good neighbour, a sympathetic member of the community ... but it pays!

LOCAL COMMUNITY RELATIONS

Establishing the present position

1. Does the organization have an identified standard of behaviour as defined, for example, in corporate communications objectives?
2. Have these standards been explained to all employees with responsibility for external relations?
3. Have we checked that these are understood and supported at all levels?
4. Do we know the audiences that form the community within which we operate?
5. Can we measure or assess their attitudes towards the organization?
6. Are there areas where attitudes could be improved through better communications?

7. Do we need to concentrate on information going out and/or improve our monitoring of opinions coming in?
8. What channels of communication exist that the organization uses regularly and on a planned basis?
9. How effective are these in communications and budget terms?
10. How many of these provide opportunities for feedback and are such opportunities used?

Identifying areas for improving relations

11. Which managers have responsibility for activities that affect the community, for example, transport, personnel, waste disposal?
12. Do they have the responsibility for communications related to these organizational activities?
13. Have they been trained in the communications responsibilities of their work?
14. Are they operating to the agreed organization aims outlined earlier?
15. To whom and how do they report on matters of communications policy, monitoring of standards and the handling of those problems that have communications implications?
16. Are these responsibilities written into their job descriptions?
17. Should we run a seminar on the need for good community relations and the managers' part in this campaign?
18. Are information lines in operation that enable these managers to be properly informed about the organization's policies, actions and developments?
19. Do they communicate directly with their staffs and other key audiences *before* any indirect communication, such as local media?
20. Who is responsible for ensuring that commercial objectives are compatible with social objectives, for example, when sales demands create unsocial hours for distribution vehicles in neighbourhood streets?

Establishing the programme

21. Could a planning meeting of interested executives be organized to discuss improvements in community relations?
22. Can we canvas views throughout the organization on issues and opportunities to be evaluated by this committee?
23. Have we established a budget for this activity?
24. Who will be authorized to expend this and who will monitor the effectiveness of any action?
25. What procedures can be established to limit demands on organization resources, particularly executive time and finance?

26. Do we have facilities that could be offered for the controlled use of the community such as meeting rooms and sports fields?
27. Are there activities already undertaken that could be extended to encompass these community audiences, such as open days, product launches, annual meetings?
28. Are there community projects to which we could add our support, such as local charities, educational or professional initiatives?
29. Do we wish to consider a programme for seconding executives on a sabbatical basis to work in community areas?
30. Are we treating all our trading partners, suppliers and neighbours as fairly as we would wish them to treat us?
31. Do we take efforts to make each of our employees able to act as a public relations officer for the organization?
32. Are we concerned about customer satisfaction and long-term goodwill as much as short-term profit?
33. Have we proper proceedures for handling politely and efficiently all complaints that might be made about company products, services, operations or policies?
34. Are we concerned about protecting the environment in which we operate in terms of noise, smell, pollution, traffic and other aspects?
35. Do we consider the interests of neighbours when planning production changes, extensions, closures, resitings, shift changes, deliveries and so on?
36. Have we maintained regular and proper contact with all community opinion leaders, civic heads, MPs, MEPs and others?
37. Is the theory at the top reflected in the practice at the bottom?
38. Do we have a system for efficiently handling local media relations covering the issuing of information, handling enquiries, providing facilities and coping with emergencies?
39. Have we evaluated all alternative techniques for developing community relations including:

open days	speakers' panel
facility visits	sponsorship
community papers	secondment
project support	anniversaries?
presentations	

40. What systems exist for monitoring the effectiveness of activity and introducing any changes which might be necessary?

ELEVEN

POLITICIANS, LEGISLATORS AND OPINION LEADERS

PUBLIC AFFAIRS IS OFTEN AT THE HEART OF PUBLIC RELATIONS

Today, major organizations cannot operate to full effect without a proper understanding of the political climate at local, national and international levels. What is happening in the public arena will have a direct effect upon what can and cannot be done—not simply in the legal or legislative sense but in terms of what is publicly acceptable. The basis of public relations is that organizations can only succeed through a public consensus that allows them to pursue their legitimate aims.

Decisions in the public sector are being shaped, influenced or implemented by civil servants, politicians, government researchers, local authority members and officers, lobby groups, national assemblies—and international assemblies, such as the European Parliament, the European Commission, NATO, OPEC and the United Nations.

Oddly, much of what we describe as 'public relations' is actually closer to private relations—communications between defined groups of people, largely not involving the 'public'. Of course, public relations is only so defined in the sense that the communications audiences are the 'publics' upon whose consent the organization depends for its success ... though these publics could be a handful of financial analysts, a pubful of union leaders or a clubful of civil servants. Indeed, public affairs can be one of the most important elements in a broad public relations programme, for it is involved with the planned management of those political and public issues that decide the future of the nation and, therefore, affect the organization.

Business leaders need to be familiar with the programmes of the main parties, particularly those in power or likely to be in power. Not only can legislation be a factor but changes in employment rules, social services, investment, planning and regional policies can also have a direct impact. Increasingly, local and national governments are becoming involved in public issues such as the environment, safety, food, health and hygiene— which means the organization also needs close coordination between its issues management plans and its public affairs activities, as these are likely to overlap.

Public affairs requires an understanding of how public opinion is shaped, whether by pressure groups, by specific opinion leaders, through planned, focused campaigns, by special interest bodies or the media. Our legislators (and those who advise our legislators) are all influenced by the same process. The public relations adviser also needs to remember the importance of what is happening at local level in county and city halls, at international level ... and the interaction between all these and the statutory bodies that exist to manage sectors of our public life.

Knowing 'what is what' is the key

One of the most important and difficult tasks of the public affairs adviser is identifying what matters from the volumes of published and private information that may have some relevance. If he is to provide an effective service to the management of the organization, then he must be able to sift, sort and precis just that information that is important, at exactly the right time. To filter this material demands a full understanding of the organization's business and a clear brief on where the managers see it headed. Possible sources of information in the UK would include trade media reports, surveys and studies by specialist associations and pressure groups, parliamentary papers and government publications, speeches by political leaders, party publications and summaries of the proceedings of the European Assembly and Commission.

It is also essential to build a data base of those individuals who are the key players in the movement of opinion on your topic of interest—for example, those MPs on committees that will promote change, those public figures, academics and researchers whose views are respected. Commercial organizations run computer services that offer a rapid analysis of experts and interested individuals but that can be no more than the starting point for an understanding of the influences at work.

Understanding how this affects the organization

Of equal importance as knowing the information is knowing the relevance of it. The public affairs adviser needs to be able to interpret and analyse the basic information. For example, at what stage is the thinking, how likely is it to result in change, what factors may affect its progress, how would this impact on the organization, does it involve the whole business sector, are there others who may be affected who will be interested in having some input into an initiative to modify, redirect or reverse the proposition, which public figures, experts, opinion leaders (who have already or are likely to air views) will carry weight?

So, what do you do about the political snowballs?

Knowing what is what and the possible impact of it are only parts of an effective lobby. It is what you do about it that matters. The preparation of the programme of activity can be crucial. Direct approaches may be relevant where a key politician or official needs to know your view. This must be presented factually and positively. Remember to cover the possible arguments against your case. Third parties who will be influential may need briefing so that they will support your views.

On some major public issues, it is appropriate to 'go public' and involve the more respected and influential media. This needs careful consideration. A carefully presented case may be convincing if put privately. Public or media pressure can sometimes jeopardize this and create antipathy. However, once entrenched positions are established and it looks like confrontation, then it may be sensible to appeal to public opinion—accepting that any behind-the-scenes influence is usually abandoned by then.

The construction of the political lobby requires special skills and may well involve the employment of specialists, many of whom are not in general public relations at all. However, whether the public relations adviser is running the lobby himself, employing a specialist or the parliamentary division of a consultancy, it is useful to appreciate a few broad principles:

1. Particular attention to identifying the right individuals is central to success.
2. An effective and thought-through case, with evidence, must be developed.
3. The counter-arguments (and the strengths and weaknesses of these) need to be understood and may need to be discussed when seeking support from people who will be asked to back your case—they cannot afford to look ill-informed and get shot down in flames.
4. Timing of the presentations is critical—for some attempts to persuade are made too late, when views have been developed beyond the point of influence.
5. The identification of those who are likely to be supportive should be carried out early for they can become ambassadors for your case.
6. Those who need persuading from different views can be tackled later, when the tide is beginning to build up in your direction.
7. Do not overlook those who have an interest or responsibility in the

relevant sector, such as constituency MPs (and MEPs), as you should receive, at least, a friendly hearing for your perspective.

8. Check out those on the special interest all-party committees, for example, as they may already be informed on the subject matter and receptive.

9. Mount a parallel approach in Whitehall as well as Westminster, you will need Civil Service backing behind all political initiatives.

10. The parliamentary media can often put weight behind your case if it offers an interesting story for them, but use as much diplomacy and skill in briefing them as MPs, MEPs or civil servants.

11. As all legislation has to go through the Lords and many of them have special expertise, briefing the right peers can be invaluable; some have government posts and many of the more-active have the ear of ministers.

12. When generating support, take advantage of all offers of help and make specific suggestions of where help will be most valuable.

13. Brief everyone involved very thoroughly, particularly if changes are necessary in strategy or tactics, explaining the reasons why.

14. Keep all briefings friendly and businesslike with no more than appropriate hospitality.

....keep all briefings friendly and businesslike with no more than appropriate hospitality

15. Sometimes short office meetings with one or two people will be more valuable than long discussions over the dinner table.
16. Make sure that you always advance a positive argument rather than only being critical of alternative proposals, for everyone likes reasons for action.

COMMUNICATE WITH FRIEND AND FOE ALIKE

As well as the various parliamentary and legislative audiences relevant to a broad public relations programme, there are likely to be other influential groups that will require special attention. These may include trade and professional bodies, educationalists, pressure groups and local government. To communicate effectively with such groups it is very important to identify their own aims and appreciate how these might relate to the organization's aims.

The public relations programme aimed at opinion leaders will only be successful if it can create understanding between these special interest groups and the organization. Wherever possible, it should *also* be an aim to create goodwill and support. However, where the special interest group is directly opposed to the interests of the organization, this does *not* mean that no attempt should be made at communications ... or that it is impossible to achieve understanding.

As an example, a medical research centre that uses animals in its testing programmes should still be communicating with animal welfare groups opposed to such practices. It is unlikely (and possibly unnecessary) that the organization will succeed in changing the attitudes of the pressure group. But, it will ensure that the animal welfare group is arguing from a factual base. They will have less freedom to distort the argument and create public opinion which is directly opposed to the interests of the research group.

No such group would want to have its arguments defeated on factual grounds and will, therefore, tend to use any factual information which is made available. This will help to narrow the arguments into areas where the organization can justify its stance—away from emotive sectors.

PRESSURE GROUPS CAN CREATE HELPFUL CHANGE

Let us look in a little more detail at our hypothetical example. In the absence of any fact or information, it would be possible for an animal welfare group to mount an appealing campaign to get animal testing banned by law.

This emotional argument is less convincing when it is presented against a background of established fact. For example, suppose legislation on the introduction of new drugs or foods requires these to be tested on animals.

Are such manufacturers to gamble with the safety of their customers, defy the law ... or not introduce new products?

Suppose, all animal testing laboratories are subject to close official supervision and have to operate to strict standards relating to the discomfort that can be caused to the creatures. Emotive claims about uncontrolled or unscrupulous testing or wilful cruelty would then tend to be shifted into perspective. All such information will tend to ensure that the argument is conducted on a more factual basis.

It is even possible that the pressure brought by the animal welfare group could result in changes in legislation that could be to the advantage of the testing organizations. As an example, such pressure may change the law to allow imported products that have passed approved tests in other countries to bypass the UK testing procedure. Perhaps modifications of existing products may not need to go through the complete process. Or a public indemnity scheme might be proposed to help manufacturers marketing certain groups of products which might not be required to be tested on animals.

It is possible that public concern over animal testing may well influence the situation in the marketplace (as happened with the fur trade). The additional cost of replacing animal-tested products with new substitutes might become acceptable to the public. Certainly the producers of such products can only benefit from informed public debate of the topic. Secrecy leads to misunderstanding or misinterpretation by the public of the organization's motives. The public relations adviser must have the courage to recommend that his company or client stimulates a vigorous public debate.

THE INFORMATION DEMOCRACY WORKS

It is the responsibility of the public relations adviser to understand the position of all important external groups—particularly those trying to exert pressure for change, such as a campaigning consumer body, a group of dissident shareholders or the animal welfare organization, exampled above. What is their case? Is it factually based? Who are they trying to influence? How are they attempting this? Of course, if the public relations adviser feels there is validity in their claims then, equally, it becomes his responsibility to advise management and try to institute appropriate policy changes within the organization. (For this reason, a key target for pressure groups should be the public relations advisers to the organizations they are attempting to influence!)

Political democracy is intended to work in the best interests of *most* people. Similarly, the information democracy should ensure that all the arguments are presented and the opinion which emerges is in the best interests of most people.

Certainly, the organization should think very carefully before refusing to communicate in sensitive areas. Any communications should be through the same media used by the pressure group and every critical comment or negative news story should be dealt with promptly with a properly counter-balanced company statement. Des Wilson, the driving force behind Shelter and, later, the Campaign for Lead Free Air has often stated that his lobbies have been more successful because of the inability of the opposition to handle their case properly. The same has been true for Greenpeace and Friends of the Earth.

In some circumstances, the hostility of the pressure group can be turned to the advantage of the organization, if their arguments can be exposed as being unreasonable. This is the judo technique—where the organization rides with the argument rather than countering it. The opponent is pulled off balance and thrown over the corporate shoulder, rather than directly resisted.

Take a case to illustrate the point. One rural bus company found itself in the difficult position of having to cut a number of routes. It found itself under very considerable pressure from one or two well-organized groups which produced petitions against the closure of certain of these country routes. However, this pressure was completely defused. The public spokesman in a television interview agreed that the bus company was reluctant to close bus routes. However, he countered that if the people who had signed the petition had shown as much interest in using the buses, it would not be necessary to take such action!

KNOW WHEN TO ACT ... AND WHEN NOT

An important decision facing the public relations adviser is when to act, when to react and when to take no action. These decisions are a matter of balance and timing. Often, the decision whether to act or react can be decided on the amount of public attention that is likely to be focused on the issue in question.

An unfortunate accident at one of the company's plants has resulted in an injury or death. One of the company's products has been shown not to perform to standard. A packaging design has to be modified to avoid confusing consumers. If these are issues that are likely to come to public attention, may be discussed and could have an effect upon the reputation of the company—then the decision must be to act, rather than to react. Indeed if there is a question of ethics or responsibility involved, then the company must act first. These points are covered fully in Chapter 31 on contingency procedures.

PUBLIC AFFAIRS MATTER TO PRIVATE ENTERPRISE

In much of Europe, the role of the public affairs adviser is still not fully accepted. The function is far better understood in the US, where the concept of the political chief executive has been identified as one of the key features in the development of communications over the last decade, according to eminent public relations practitioner, James Fox. In contrast, many British (and many European) businesses do not seem to recognize the need for political monitoring and political action.

There are two principal reasons for this situation. First, many business-men believe that an occasional social contact with politicians, topped up by sporadic doses of information from the media, constitutes an adequate background against which to spring into action should the need arise. The second reason for the limited awareness of the need for political intelligence by some businesses is the number of trade associations that claim to have a competence in political monitoring; in many cases this barely exists. British public affairs adviser, Douglas Smith, quotes the chilling experience of hearing the head of a major trade association seeking to calm fears over an impending bill, saying, 'Relax, we are still squaring it with the civil servants.' This statement was made blandly in the Palace of Westminster itself, with MPs in the audience, on the day when the bill under discussion had its first reading and all concerned knew it would be guillotined into law within months. Too many companies may be leaving political monitoring and lobbying to trade associations that do not have the expertise to tackle this critical area.

Indeed, much of the lobbying undertaken by some trade associations, individual companies and organizations is extremely rudimentary: it may make them *feel* good, but will have very little influence on the shape of legislation. Too often, the case is being presented far too late and without enough authority or substantiating evidence.

An intelligent public affairs campaign should not be required only to deal with contingency situations. The public relations advisers to the organization should be maintaining continuous parliamentary contact and monitoring developments. They need to be aware of possible trends and political feelings at a very early stage. This will eliminate the need for emergency measures at a late stage in the legislative process.

DEVELOP RELATIONS AT ALL LEVELS

In the public affairs area in the UK, there are many levels of the decision-making process, from junior civil servants through the senior levels, from back-bench MPs through to cabinet ministers. The organization which wishes to influence the decision-making process will be working at all relevant levels. While the European level is of paramount importance, lobbying at national parliamentary level continues to be important.

In general, it is the ministers who can be most valuable. Often their active involvement will help establish their own reputation for action, upon which their political future is based. In planning any presentation to a minister or a ministerial department, it is helpful to have an idea of the style of the minister and his department. This can usually be established by watching the public performances of the minister concerned, reading all his policy statements, speeches and watching his performances on television. These are also likely to indicate his areas of special interest; also it may be sensible to ask the advice of your local MP.

Perhaps the most important factor in developing the presentation of a parliamentary case is to understand how the parliamentary processes work, the roles of the MPs, civil service and ministers and an appreciation of the importance of timing.

As with so many areas in the complex world of public relations, there can be no real substitute for employing the best professionals possible to handle specialized sectors. The less-experienced public relations adviser or the general manager with a responsibility for parliamentary affairs does not necessarily need to know how to handle all issues. However, he does need the skill to know when to call in expert advice. There remain basic aspects of good communications which have an influence in the parliamentary area. These need to be handled by the public relations specialist as part of a broader communications programme.

Start with your local MP

Every organization should ensure it has a satisfactory relationship with all relevant constituency MPs. This must be regardless of what their parliamentary allegiances may be. These MPs should know the company and have an understanding of the style of its senior management and what it is trying to achieve.

At the very least, this understanding will ensure that there is an informed view on the organization within the Houses of Parliament. Remember, too, that the constituency MP may not just be the one associated with the organization's head office—there will be a constituency MP for every depot, regional warehouse or distribution point. Each should be briefed and meet the senior manager at each location: a Friday may be most convenient as many MPs are then in their constituencies. Having established the initial contact and given the MPs the opportunity of meeting senior management and seeing the organization at work, it is perfectly proper to keep the members up-dated on company developments and management views on any proposed legislation. After all, the MP represents the managers of the *companies* who live in the constituency, as well as the individual employees.

However, as we said earlier, a working relationship with a constituency MP is *not* parliamentary relations. In an information democracy, it is reasonable that the best case will emerge through a process of argument and counter-argument. All sides in every case have the democratic right to present their case in the best way they can. Consequently, it is fair to say that an improvement in parliamentary liaison by companies would help create better understanding ... and, possibly, a more sympathetic climate of parliamentary opinion.

In the information democracy, the principle is ... 'let the best case win'. Although there is freedom for every side of any case to be presented, it is a rough sort of justice where only one perspective is adequately presented.

This does not negate the concept of information democracy; after all, if there were consistently only one candidate at political elections, democracy would not be abandoned. Probably, attempts would be made to make it easier or more attractive for candidates to present themselves. The same situation applies in some areas of the political lobby. Powerful, well-organized groups present their case (as is perfectly fair) but there is no real freedom of decision because the alternative points of view are not being equally well presented.

As an illustration, the success of the National Farmers' Union in the UK in representing farmers' interests is outstanding and a good demonstration of an effective political lobby. Key to its success is that it works on a local as well as a national level and mobilizes its membership to the full.

However, it is arguable that this is not necessarily in the best interests of either the food processing industry or the consumer. Certainly, some observers feel that the official bodies representing the food manufacturers and processors have not been nearly so effective in projecting the case relating to their part of the food chain, either in the UK or in Europe.

The opportunities to influence legislation exist not only for trade associations and commercial organizations but also for charities, professional groups, social bodies and societies. Perhaps the best starting point for parliamentary relations for these groups would be the party back-bench committees and the all-party committees relevant to their interest areas. Such committees welcome input from informed organizations on current issues; it is possible to find a committee in the British Houses of Parliament on virtually any area of professional and business interest.

The public relations adviser working for an organization may decide to undertake parliamentary relations directly if he or she has the necessary expertise. Alternatively, as we observed earlier, if the campaign is likely to involve a high degree of sophistication or know-how then it might be advisable to retain a parliamentary consultancy.

Consideration might be given to retaining an MP as an adviser. But, it must be recognized that while the MP can provide information and guidance, he will have very limited time available to help the organization. Equally important, as the MP has to retain independence, he is far less likely to want to put forward the client's point of view than might an ordinary constituency MP. Public relations practitioners are advised to ensure that any special relationship is properly published. MPs should always declare any special interests whenever this is necessary, and always in parliamentary affairs.

LEARN THE EUROPEAN SYSTEM

Of course, the public relations practitioner needs to understand the legislative processes in the country in which he operates. Clearly, this book cannot detail the many systems and concentrates on the UK perspective. But Britain, with its eleven partners (at the time of writing) in the European Community, shares a unique position in world legislative practice—the twelve EC members are subject to both national and binding transnational legislation. And, clearly, the transnational legislation of the EC will continue to be of increasing importance.

The system is somewhat different from the British Parliament in that the European Parliament is an advisory body. Draft legislation is initiated by the Commission. The European Parliament advises on this and the final decisions are taken by the Council of Ministers. However, since 1987, the Single European Act has given the European Parliament real powers of co-legislation, along with the Council. In practice, the European Parliament can now amend proposed legislation, and, where the Commission endorses parliament's amendments, the Council must be unanimous to throw them out. This has given the parliament a far stronger role than its earlier 'advisory' responsibility.

It is possible for organizations to make direct representations to the Commission in Brussels; however, it is also possible to direct an input through UK parliamentary channels. Examples where this has been achieved include the debate over the fishing limits, the retention of the mile and the pint as UK units of measure, the protection of door-step deliveries of milk and many others.

It must be recognized that the UK parliament does not have enough time to debate all impending European legislation. There are select committees on European legislation from both the House of Commons and the House of Lords and they are expected to identify all draft directives and regulations which should be discussed in the House. An organization wishing to present evidence to either of these committees should arrange to discuss this with the clerk to the committee.

It is also helpful to remember that every organization in the UK is within the constituency of one of the 81 British contingent of the 518 members of the European Parliament. Organizations should consider presenting their case to their constituency MEP. Although there is a limit to the power of these MEPs, they can discuss the thinking of the Commission. One advantage of the British decision not to opt for any form of proportional representation has been the relatively few changes in Euro-MP representation. The British contingent is among the most experienced in the parliament.

To date, British organizations have not been positive enough in presenting their case. Possibly this is a result of the limited understanding of the workings of the European parliamentary system. Useful sources of information for would-be campaigners include the House of Commons library (which will list all committees and all party groups), the *Civil Service Year Book*, the *House Magazine* (the unofficial guide to parliamentary activities), the commercial parliamentary monitoring services, the European Commission and European Parliament Offices in London, which provide guides and information. The PRCA has published a useful introduction to European lobbying, written by MEP Ben Patterson. The Department of Trade and Industry is also particularly helpful and will provide information and advice.

UNDERSTAND THE POLITICAL STRUCTURE OF EUROPE

To appreciate how to influence the legislative process in the European Community, it is important to understand the structure of the inter-linked elements. Let us look at a little background.

The United Kingdom became a member state in the EC on 1 January 1973. There are three 'European Communities' to which the 12 member states all belong, which make up the EC to which we informally refer: the European Coal and Steel Community (ECSC) set up by the ECSC Treaty signed in Paris on 18 April 1951; the European Economic Community (EEC), set up by the EEC Treaty signed in Rome on 25 March 1957; the European Atomic Energy Community (EURATOM), set up by the EURATOM Treaty also signed in Rome on 25 March 1957.

However, of more current relevance are the four main community institutions, all of which play a role in shaping legislation; the Commission, the Council, the European Parliament and the Court of Justice. It is a little complex but essential to understand if the public relations practitioner is to be able either to offer intelligent advice or brief specialist EC lobbyists.

The Commission This proposes community policy and legislation. It is then for the Council of Ministers to discuss and, if appropriate, adopt or amend the proposals; it also implements the decisions taken by the Council of Ministers and supervises the day-to-day running of community policies. The commission is the 'guardian of the treaties' and can initiate action against member states which do not comply with EC rules. It has its own considerable powers in some areas, notably competition policy and the control of government subsidies.

The Council This is the community's decision-making body. It adopts legislation on the basis of proposals from the Commission. The term 'Council' embraces not only ministerial meetings (the Council of Ministers) but also council working groups of officials from the member states and the committee of permanent representatives of the member states in Brussels (COREPER) which prepares discussions in the Council of Ministers.

Specialist councils have evolved dealing with particular areas of policy. The main ones are: foreign affairs (including trade policy and general issues), agriculture, budget, finance, industry, the internal market and research.

Councils are attended by the relevant ministers from member states and by the Commission, which is present as of right and participates in discussion as an equal partner. The relevant UK minister is usually obvious from the title of the Council. For example, the UK is represented on the internal market and on the industry and research councils, by a minister from the Department of Trade and Industry.

The European Parliament This is a directly elected body of 518 members, 81 of them from the UK. Under the EC treaties, its formal opinion is required on most proposals before they can be adopted by the council. Members are elected for a period of five years: 1994 and 1999 are election years. The secretariat of the parliament is in Luxembourg, although the parliament's plenary meetings are held in Strasbourg and its committee meetings in Brussels.

Most of the detailed work is done by its specialist committees, divided by subject area, who examine Commission proposals before they are put to the parliament. When the parliament is consulted on a proposal, it refers it to one of these committees. The committee appoints a 'rapporteur' for the proposal, that is, an MEP charged with preparing a report on it. The committee then discusses that report and may amend it. Each report includes a draft opinion on the Commission's proposal. This draft opinion is put to the parliament as a whole by the specialist committee, and is adopted (sometimes with further amendments) as the parliament's opinion.

The European Court of Justice This rules on the interpretation and application of community laws. It has 13 judges, including one from each community country. Judgements of the court are binding in each member state. (A *court of first instance* has been created to relieve it of some of its excessive workload.)

How does Brussels work? It is important to understand the realities behind the structure. The EC is not just a set of procedures and institutions but is run through a complex matrix of individuals, all with their special responsibilities and perspectives. Remember also that in all the community institutions there are 12 nationalities working together. This makes for cultural and linguistic diversity, and some quite marked differences of approach. However, all EC officials are committed to the same treaty objectives and there is therefore much common ground between them.

Virtually all EC officials speak several community languages. French and English in that order are the most widely spoken. Written texts for internal discussion are usually produced either in French or English. More formal documents, such as draft proposals from the commission to the council, are translated into all nine EC languages.

In addition to the formal channels of communication, there are also informal ones. Officials working in different community institutions on the same subject are likely to be in close touch with each other. There are also close contacts between EC officials and other Brussels-based personnel, such as the member states' permanent representatives and the Brussels press corps. It is worth being aware of these cross-currents. For example, one EC contact may well be able to introduce you to other useful contacts in other institutions.

HOW TO INFLUENCE EC DECISIONS

There are usually three stages in actually influencing decisions in Brussels:

- gathering information
- agreeing your action plan
- making the necessary contacts with whom you need to discuss your perspectives.

The DTI has prepared some helpful information and will always offer more topical advice than can be presented in this book. However the following suggestions should be useful.

The first step in any campaign to influence decisions in Brussels is to obtain clear and up-to-date information on what is happening. One thing the community legislative process produces in abundance is information. Additionally, many publishers and consultants offer newsletters and information services, drawing on the basic documents. So how do you set about establishing what you need and how to get it?

Trade associations and chambers of commerce often can help. The DTI publishes information covering the current EC legislative programme, while specialist industry publications, from trade associations or elsewhere, may help the public relations adviser to stay in touch with the community issues likely to affect his business. Consultants with expertise in EC matters can also help with gathering and interpreting data.

The public relations professional will also need to decide how much time and effort to devote to influencing decisions in Brussels. Clearly, direct involvement will take up more time than working indirectly through trade associations or chambers of commerce.

Whether the organization approaches the EC directly or indirectly, it is important to bear in mind that dialogue with Brussels is a two-way process. The public relations adviser will want information from the Commission and the other community institutions about their plans and will want to influence those plans. But they in turn will value the information the organization can offer about its particular sector. The Commission relies upon information from various outside sources in order to draw up its forward proposals.

Generally, for any piece of legislation, there will be a list of key contacts the executive responsible for the lobby will need to make and maintain. Make sure these contacts have a written note of the organization's concerns. But do consider face-to-face meetings too. Remember that the Brussels machinery is accessible and willing to listen to a well-prepared case.

Consider using specialists

The efficient trade organization with a parliamentary lobbying brief (or the specialized public affairs consultants) will concentrate on establishing effective contacts at all levels throughout both Houses of Parliament and in the European parliamentary system. This cannot be undertaken on a part-time basis by a general public relations practitioner operating across a broad spectrum of company communications activities—or, even, operating within the consultancy world. As a consequence, the importance of the specialist public affairs consultant is increasing steadily. Some large companies (and larger consultancies) employ public affairs advisers to concentrate on this area.

It is generally agreed that public affairs is an important challenge for the public relations industry. Indeed, as one of the UKs most experienced parliamentary affairs professionals, Douglas Smith, points out, the public affairs responsibilities in many of the United States corporations have now been taken on by the corporate lawyers. This consolidates their relationships with the political chief executive, who has an increasing presence in the United States. It is a realistic possibility that this could happen in the UK and other democratic European countries.

Certainly no public relations professional should allow such a critical area to be neglected or become the responsibility of an executive who may not have the appropriate communications skills and sensitivities.

POLITICIANS, LEGISLATORS AND OPINION LEADERS

Communicating with special interest groups

1. As always, have we defined the audiences, the messages, the attitudes, the objectives?

2. Can we establish the motives of any special interest sector that might be in conflict with our interests, for example, environmental groups or union leaders?
3. Have we discussed and agreed the priorities and established where we have a responsibility to establish good communications?
4. Are there audiences that might be better covered by our trade body or association?
5. If we are criticized, what procedures exist for handling this complaint and monitoring public interest?
6. How will we establish the factual basis behind any criticism and those aspects that may not have been appreciated?
7. Do we know when to treat criticisms privately and when we have to go public in our response?
8. How are we ensuring we behave to our agreed ethical standards to minimize legitimate complaints?
9. Are we communicating regularly the good news about our achievements, policies, ethical stance and so on?
10. Do we monitor the public perception of our organization to ensure that any problems will be weighed against our good track record?

Public affairs

11. What systems do we have for monitoring proposed legislation?
12. Do we have a separate early warning system or do we rely on our trade body?
13. What professional guidance can we call on to help us present our case to the legislators and influence proposed legislation?
14. Have we identified which MPs, lords, government and civil service departments have special interests in our sector of operations?
15. Do we have proper links at the right parliamentary and civil service levels?
16. Are we keeping these elected representatives and officials informed about our views and interests?
17. Are we in regular contact with those MPs where we have operations, sites or whose constituencies are directly affected by our actions?
18. Have we established the same communications links at local authority levels?
19. What systems exist to monitor the effectiveness of our work in these areas and any adjustments to the activity or budget that might be necessary?

The European dimensions

20. Is the same monitoring undertaken and attention given to the European parliament regarding proposed legislation?

21. Have we studied the operations of the European parliamentary system and identified the key pressure points?
22. Would it be advisable to retain a specialized parliamentary monitoring and/or lobbying organization to assist us?
23. Do we know how and to whom we should be presenting our case in Europe?
24. In influencing European legislation, have we:
    (a) processes for gathering information
    (b) an agreed action plan with responsibilities
    (c) a list of key contacts and how we propose to approach each?
25. Have we identified:
    (a) the responsible commissioner and his cabinet member handling our area of interest
    (b) the relevant officials in the UK government departments
    (c) the UK members of the appropriate European Parliament committee
    (d) any MEPs with special interests or a brief on the subject?
26. How can we cooperate with other bodies with similar interests, including UK and European trade associations?

The international scene

27. Have we established similar parliamentary procedures in every country where we are operating?
28. How do we coordinate all the local monitoring efforts at the international level?
29. Have we prepared an international public affairs policy to brief the individual advisers in each national operation?
30. What processes do we have for monitoring the effectiveness of our international public affairs and improving its cost-effectiveness?

TWELVE
THE FINANCIAL COMMUNITY

BRIDGE THE CITY/MANAGEMENT GAP

The financial operations of a commercial organization cannot be separated from its trading activities. It must make sense to project the financial credibility of the company and the skills of its management, just as strongly as promoting the products and services that it offers. The relevance and importance of financial public relations have grown in recent years. The specialist in this sector, today, has direct access to the chief executive and has become an important boardroom adviser. With the interlocking aspects of the financial, corporate, parliamentary and marketing relations, there is a strong case for that adviser being a public relations professional. But, if he is to be credible to his board colleagues, he needs very special expertise, courage and skill.

The focus of public attention on the *trading* performance of public companies and the growing understanding of the role of marketing are creating a much healthier business environment. The 'city' is no longer an introspective group of financial institutions. Visionary business management is focusing not only on its production lines, its retail outlets or the services it offers, but is also raising its horizons to look at the market, competition, international development—and seeking the backing of financial institutions to make rapid and successful growth possible. The public relations adviser who combines the responsibilities of marketing communications, corporate *and* financial relations is fortunate indeed, as these are the three most important areas of an integrated company communications programme. It is not enough for a public company to be efficient and profitable. It is essential that the policies it follows, the products and services that it offers, are known and understood by the publics with whom it works. It is equally important that all financial institutions on whom the company depends are fully informed about the organization, understand the policies and respect the management capabilities.

Finance is probably more international than most business

It is important that the commercial and trading activities of the company are closely related to its financial reporting to the city. As with everyone, financial advisers prefer to work with companies they know and respect; no matter how specialised the operating sector, it is important they understand the significance of the business, the quality of its management and the potential for commercial development.

It used to be a criticism of the city that it always seemed to be one crucial step removed from the business activities of the companies concerned. This is certainly less true today (if at all), for a number of factors have changed both the financial realities and public perceptions in recent years. These include the growth in public interest in financial matters (remember when the city pages were the city *column*?), the increasing internationalization of the financial world, the boom in private investors and the opening of new opportunities for smaller companies to raise finance through a public shareholding.

Now, the financial services sectors (including banking, merchant banking, broking and the major stock exchanges), are internationally competitive—not just as a result of European harmonization, but through the development of 24-hour global trading and the geographic position of London, New York and Tokyo, as the financial centres of the world. These are located in the three main international economic centres, Europe, the Americas and the Asia/Pacific region; by happy chance, they are also spaced across the global time zones, so that trading activities are spread almost throughout the 24 hours.

Major companies are able to decide where to float, where to raise capital and which multinational advisers to help them across, say, the dozen or more financial communities which may be of significance to them. (Of course, there are many smaller exchanges and allied financial communities wherever there is a significant business sector. In the British Isles, for example, there are exchange offices in Birmingham, Manchester, Glasgow and Dublin, while across Western Europe and most of the industrialized world there is a full-scale national exchange in most capitals—many of these are also significant internationally.)

The liberalization of the city in the UK (and similar developments around the world) and the later international share decline and subsequent recovery, were but elements in the steady progress towards more freedom, opportunity, scope, relevance and professionalism in the financial community. The financial public relations industry has also matured alongside this development. Most general practice public relations consultancies of any size now offer specialist financial relations advice—and those companies that concentrate solely on this area have grown in both number and size. At the same time, the public relations adviser in major corporations has found that financial relations for his company has become an increasingly important part of his work—as well as one of the services where his management colleagues expect the greatest expertise and judgement.

The central element in financial public relations is to create the environment within which the management of the company is best able to achieve commercial aims. Those making investment judgements about the organization are highly professional and working in one of the toughest business environments imaginable. Therefore, public relations people trying to establish effective communications with them will need to be equally as professional. This will usually involve building effective relations with four main groups:

1. The major institutional investors, such as insurance companies, international groups, pension funds and investment trusts.
2. The professionals who advise and represent the major shareholders, such as the stockbrokers, merchant banks, the corporate lawyers and accountants.
3. Private investors and shareholders (increasing in number, no longer always small players and, collectively, often of critical importance).
4. The financial media, trade publications and commercial research and investment services that inform and influence these groupings.

Public relations practitioners in the financial area need to be very close to the corporate policymakers they are representing. Their activities are regulated by the law and some rather strict regulations—tightened since the concerns over insider dealing in New York, London and Tokyo. In the UK, these include the various Companies Acts, the Stock Exchange regulations and the takeover codes.

Insist on quality information

The company will be judged by its performance ... and much of the appraisal of this performance will result from the accuracy, candour, timeliness, integrity and overall quality of the information being issued. If the public relations adviser is to serve his management or clients well he must insist on being on the inside, involved in policy and properly briefed, ahead of the game. This puts a substantial responsibility on his shoulders ... and explains why timid people do not survive in what can sometimes become a fierce world where much depends on the effectiveness of both the advice and the implementation. In a takeover battle, like a cup final, there are no prizes for coming second!

There are legal obligations upon companies which have their shares listed on the Stock Exchange covering the information about their performance that they must issue to shareholders. This includes the announcement of results—usually preliminary, interim and year-end. The publication of the annual report and the agm (at which shareholders and their advisers are briefed on and can ask questions about the performance of their company) can also be significant in the financial calendar.

Notice of the announcement of results is usually issued in advance. The timing and control of the information is particularly important and the public relations executive will normally be handling the advance notice to the Stock Exchange, preparation of news releases, briefing relevant journalists, planning meetings with analysts, any press conferences and individual interviews that might be judged appropriate.

There are also regulations relating to the issuing of information which could have an effect on the share price, such as new issues, board changes, disclosures, changes in holdings, acquisitions, significant investments or disinvestments, major product or corporate developments, mergers and other takeover activities.

Understand how stock exchanges work

A market in securities which works efficiently is necessary for both the confidence of the investor and the companies whose shares are being traded. The responsibility of a stock exchange is not just to regulate the buying and selling of shares but to ensure that the prices of transactions are based upon reliable information, made available at the same time to everyone involved. Clearly the information issued by the companies is an essential part of this communication process.

For some years now, dealings through the International Stock Exchange (which covers the UK and the Republic of Ireland) are no longer transacted on the traditional trading floors—a development mirrored by most of the major exchanges around the world. Members of the UK exchange use an electronic system, the Stock Exchange Automated Quotations (SEAQ) for their dealings. The growth in the volume of trading has meant that traditional paper announcements cannot meet the needs of the market makers, particularly as they are now widely spread.

To overcome this potential problem, the Stock Exchange also established an electronic financial news distribution system, the company news service, usually called CNS. This is a screen-based information service which carries the full text of companies announcements; it is complimentary to the Topic viewdata service run by the exchange—an edited news service carrying only the key points of price-sensitive items. It also allows those involved in the markets to obtain the full text of business statements released through the company announcements office of the exchange.

The essential elements of CNS, with which every public relations person operating in the UK financial sector needs to be familiar, are that it:

- receives announcements from companies and their agents
- prepares these into suitable form for release
- disseminates these equitably to all subscribers.

It is the responsibility of listed companies—including those on the Unlisted Securities Market (USM) and the third market—to notify the Stock Exchange of the type of information which may affect the share price, as noted earlier. Such information must be issued to the exchange first so that it can be released simultaneously to all subscribers via CNS.

Note: The International Stock Exchange in London publishes a very helpful booklet on these services, available from their company announcements office.

All messages to corporate audiences must be consistent

The public relations practitioner will also need to ensure that other communications relevant to the commercial performance of the organization present consistent and effective messages. Corporate, marketing and financial public relations must be closely related and consistent—even if they are projecting different facets of the same picture. For example, information and literature that might be particularly important would include the annual report, trading summaries, background briefing documents on markets and products, bid defence documents, major speeches by senior executives, parliamentary evidence and summaries for special audiences such as employees, customers, suppliers and so on.

Corporate advertising can be an effective public relations tool and a powerful method of putting controlled messages in front of broad audiences quickly and efficiently. However, it can be costly and does not involve the two-way communications element of, say, discussions and presentations— nor does it have the third party credibility of media comment. But, with the size of audience involved today in some financial communications situations (such as large privatizations), it can be effective to back-up other activities.

In recent years, television has joined the press as a medium and a broader range of advertisers are involved, including privatization candidates, banks, insurance companies, building societies and other financial service groups. Some of this advertising is not presenting financial information but is corporate in nature, projecting the strength of the organization; equally some of this advertising appears to be selling financial services but is really designed to do a corporate job on behalf of the advertiser—all financial advisers are also personal buyers of financial services.

However, advertising has often been used as a technique to inform shareholders about developments in, say, takeover battles, though its effectiveness needs to be carefully considered in these circumstances—any hint of 'panic communications' (interpreted by investors as a belated effort to cover a perceived previous lack of communications) could well be counter-productive.

Relate your financial public relations to corporate, parliamentary and marketing communications

Planning for financial crises—such as an unwanted takeover bid—should be considered alongside other crisis planning activity, even if different communications specialists would be involved. The whole of the company issues planning strategy should be coordinated—a manufacturing disaster, for example, could affect employees, investors and customers.

Similarly, financial affairs must be integrated into the broader corporate public relations programme. In some companies, financial public relations may be closely linked to parliamentary relations. As an illustration, there could be a parliamentary dimension to such eventualities as a bid which may need to be referred to the Monopolies Commission, significant redundancies, the exposure of international trading barriers, the opening of new international markets and developments in relationships with those government departments that may be customers of major corporations.

Professional investment specialists are still influenced by attitudes; effective communications will not counter any evidence that they judge professionally, but *can* add an extra element. This might enable a company's share to stand out from the thousands of others currently quoted on the UK's stock exchanges.

DO NOT TAKE SHAREHOLDER LOYALTY FOR GRANTED

Until the 1980s, some public companies only recognized the importance of the loyalty of their shareholders when they were threatened by a takeover. In the past, it was not unusual to find that the public company did not even have a complete record of its shareholders and so was unable to communicate with them directly and promptly. While no share register will ever be fully up to date, modern technology brings this possibility closer. The publicly-quoted company will also have a complete current list of all advisers who might influence investment. Occasions may arise during the year when the company will wish to issue information directly to them. This must be done with discrimination. Investment professionals tend to view with suspicion any apparent extravagance—such as glossy brochures and unnecessary reports on company progress.

The simplest guideline is to issue only information which is helpful to their professional decision-making. For example, if there were a significant change in the company's market, the organization might have undertaken research which indicates why they should be making a particular investment. This analysis may well be of some interest. A corporate brochure on a new expensive housestyle may not.

As noted earlier, it is important that the communications adviser understands the Stock Exchange restrictions on the release of price-sensitive information. A helpful guideline covering this and other city matters has been published jointly in the UK by the IPR and the PRCA.

Financial advisers have to be very concerned about the loyalty that needs to be shown to the shareholders—who are able to withdraw their money at a moment's notice. As a general rule, it is safer to assume that there is *no* automatic shareholder loyalty and that investors invest only for the return that they get. Therefore, if a company wants to be able to carry its shareholders through difficulties then it needs to be communicating consistently with them over a period of time. It is of limited value taking emergency whole-page advertisements to try to establish some rapport with the shareholders. Of course, if the speed of developments requires a very prompt response, then such a technique can be used to convey information, but it must be no substitute for regular communications: certainly such actions do not always generate goodwill. Some research even suggests they undermine existing confidence. Every public company needs planned and coordinated communications over a period of time to build confidence and support. City support is essential at all times but particularly, for example, when a rights issue is planned or a new acquisition or market development is being negotiated.

MAKE PERSONAL CONTACT CENTRAL TO COMMUNICATIONS

There can be no substitute for the value of the face-to-face type of meeting to help strengthen the credibility of the company. Many companies with strong relations in the city ensure that their chairman, managing director and finance director hold occasional but regular meetings with advisers in city circles. This reassures the city that the company is making efforts to maintain contact and be accessible. It must also be remembered that the projection of the capabilities of the management team is central to good financial relations.

The city columns of the national and provincial press and key trade publications provide an important source of information for people making investment decisions. In dealing with the media, it is essential that the public relations spokesman develops a reputation for accuracy, speed and honesty in all press statements. Any blurring of the truth, evasion, exaggeration or inaccuracy will damage the practitioner's reputation. News stories need to be sharp and short. It is essential that as well as the name of the public relations executive responsible for the story, the company director to whom the media can talk is also included.

USE EDITORS' TIME SPARINGLY

Individual meetings with city journalists (not necessarily editors) and the chief executive are not normally as necessary as some chairmen feel. These are really only productive when there is a major story that can be discussed at the meeting. This might provide an exclusive article relating to the growth of the company. Alternatively an informal press lunch might provide an equally valuable opportunity for an individual editor briefing on the background to an expansion into a new market.

Very few city journalists are likely to look in much depth at most listed companies, except at the times of the announcement of the interim and final results, acquisition activity and possibly the publishing of the annual report. The agm is usually of limited media interest unless the chairman is making an updated statement on performance or some extraordinary activity is expected from shareholders.

Briefings for investment advisers can include some background on the company, its development, its attitude towards the market, future potential, investment policies and expansion plans. It would be normal for these to be presented by the chairman or managing director. For convenience, many of these are held over lunch—but a good lunch should never be a substitute for a good presentation. These meetings can be particularly important for companies with provincial headquarters, who might not have quite such regular access to city advisers.

KEEP THE ANNUAL REPORT REALISTIC

Obviously, one of the most important influences on attitudes towards the company will be the annual report. Remember that the figures are always the most important part. The emphasis should be on the clarity in presentation of the information. If the company is operating in a specialized sector, then a section which looks at the overall operations of the company may be acceptable; this must be kept separate from the accounts pages. Similarly, the chairman's report should be kept crisp and factual and he should not be allowed to indulge in over-optimistic language or industry jargon. Pictures of the directors should be treated with considerable caution to avoid the suspicion that the annual report is being used as an ego vehicle!

More and more companies who are considered leaders in this field are improving the quality of presentation of the annual report and accounts. However, it is no coincidence that these companies also concentrate as much attention on the depth and clarity of the factual information. They do not make the mistake of substituting an attractive overview of the company for a concise analysis of the company's performance; such an analysis can be helpful as it will generally go beyond the statutory information requirements.

FINANCIAL RELATIONS AND COMMUNICATIONS

Establishing good financial relations

1. Can we identify what groups of people and/or institutions own our shares and the proportions in each sector?
2. Which have proved to be the best direct and indirect methods of reaching these groupings?
3. Do we have a programme of financial media relations and how is this run?
4. Have we the staff or consultancy resource to develop communications with shareholders and other financial sectors?
5. Are there opportunities in the course of the year for us to mail information direct to our shareholders and potential shareholders?
6. Do we provide opportunities for shareholders to advise us of their opinions, for example, by reply-paid cards or questionnaires in annual reports?
7. Are there occasions, other than the general meeting, where we might invite our shareholders to meet the directors?
8. Do we ensure that we send news, copies of the company newspaper, technical literature and other interesting items to these people?
9. Have we got products and services for which we could offer special arrangements to our shareholders, for example, discounts or introductory offers?
10. What financial groups outside shareholders are of significance to us such as investment advisers, bankers, accountants and so on?
11. Are we only providing information about our trading performance or do we keep these groups advised of developments, trends and other activities?
12. Do we tackle the presentation of the company to financial sectors as if it were a professional marketing exercise?
13. Are we prompt, candid and accurate in the information that we issue, particularly during times when there may be some debate about our activities?

14. Are we using media advertising to reach the financial community?
15. What budget have we allocated for the total communications activity?

Developing financial communications

16. Can we see alternative communications techniques deployed by our competitors or other respected companies in similar industry sectors?
17. How do we monitor the effectiveness of the various existing elements within the campaign and any new techniques we might consider?
18. Would we be expecting to rely on shareholder loyalty should the company be going through a difficult situation?
19. Do we have contingency measures to mount a high speed communications exercise in such emergency situations?
20. Are we constantly monitoring financial trends, competitive performance, our training success and other activities to see how we compare?
21. Have we organized a programme of regular briefings for financial advisers?
22. Do we ensure there are opportunities for the chairman, managing director and finance director to meet key professional advisers on regular occasions?
23. Do we have an executive responsible for maintaining good relations with city editors?
24. Would city editors feel that our company was accessible if they needed to get an urgent comment from the chairman or chief executive?
25. Do we look very carefully at those occasions when a conference or press lunch might be appropriate?
26. Do we watch that our material is tailored to the requirements of city editors and is not woolly, extravagant or written in unacceptable language?
27. Are we constantly updating our mailing list of shareholders and professional investment advisers?
28. Have we looked at the possibility of putting this information on to computer or word processor?
29. Do we always ensure, with editors or advisers, that we never substitute a good lunch for a good presentation?
30. Have we considered moving our agm around our regional facilities for the benefit of the shareholders and media in those areas?
31. Do we maintain relations with financial and industrial correspondents, particularly in those provincial papers where we have operating facilities?
32. Do they get the opportunity to meet the chairman or chief executive once a year or so, for example, by an invitation to the agm?
33. Do we always make sure that we concentrate on quality of information and do not substitute quality of presentation?

34. Are we consciously working to make sure that all our financial relations activities are consistent and continuous?
35. What steps do we take to ensure that the financial projection on the company is consistent with communications in other sectors, for example, marketing–and vice versa?
36. Should we consider regular planning meetings between the professionals in corporate, marketing and financial public relations?
37. Have we evaluated all those financial contingencies that could possibly affect the company and integrated them into our broader issues planning?
38. What coordination procedures do we need to handle communications at the international level to ensure simultaneous and consistent information to both internal and external audiences?
39. How often do we survey the key investment decision-makers to ensure that we are communicating at least as effectively as our peers in our business sector?
40. Should we consider a full audit of external and internal financial communications to ensure that all our efforts are both effective and cost-effective?

THIRTEEN
MARKETING, ADVERTISING AND PUBLIC RELATIONS

EFFECTIVE MARKETING DEPENDS ON PUBLIC RELATIONS

Public relations as a marketing-support technique is well understood. Marketing is defined by the Chartered Institute of Marketing as the management process responsible for identifying, anticipating and satisfying customer requirements profitably. Implicit in this definition is the need to create goodwill between the organization offering the products and services and the purchasers of these.

The best-laid marketing plans can sometimes be devastated by factors that are outside the control of marketing management. Confidence in products has been shaken by health, safety or pollution scares which often attract wide news coverage. A handful of angry shareholders at an agm has been known to attract more attention than the announcement of a massive new production facility. A few neighbours have been influential in stopping planning permission for extensions to factories.

In many companies, marketing management does not have the responsibility for communications with many important audiences that can significantly affect the success of the organizations; as well as neighbours these can include employees, shareholders, suppliers, national government, local authorities and pressure groups. In recent years, some companies with a strong marketing orientation have put all their public relations muscle behind their brands. These companies risk some dangers from adopting the low profile approach—such problems can arise in the areas of public goodwill, consumer pressure, industrial and parliamentary relations. Consistently, organizations with a recognized public personality are subjected to less criticism and tend to operate with greater public support.

Though public relations has a prime corporate role it can be used to support marketing in many areas—by improving awareness, projecting credibility, combating competition, evaluating new markets, creating direct sales leads, reinforcing the effectiveness of sales promotion and advertising, motivating the sales force, distributors/wholesalers/retailers, introducing new products or services, building brand loyalty, dealing with consumer issues and in many other ways.

Of course, some of these aims will be important for the advertising effort. Therefore, liaison between the advertising and public relations must be close and effective.

GET PUBLIC RELATIONS AND ADVERTISING TOGETHER

Coordination will only be possible if marketing management brings the advertising and public relations people together and establishes mutual understanding and trust.

Both sides may resist the restrictions which the need to work together inevitably imposes. It is as important to establish areas of independence as it is to agree on the common ground between them. For example, it might be necessary to coordinate the timing of the advertising and public relations events around the launch of a new product—but it may *not* be necessary for both to work to the same creative approach.

Planning

Little coordination will be achieved unless the advertising and public relations people sit down as equal partners at planning meetings. This applies to company staff in advertising and public relations, as well as the outside agency or consultancy.

Timing is critical

Briefing Both advertising and public relations will have a contribution to make to the development of the marketing plan. Each should be invited to submit separate recommendations on proposed action to meet the agreed marketing objectives. This may mean that the outline promotional plan will include elements from both the public relations and the advertising pro- posals. For example, the campaign may combine a strong advertising approach to the prime customers while public relations covers media relations aimed at the broader market and secondary audiences.

The quality of the brief is important though this tends to be an area where advertising has traditionally been more disciplined. As Edward Lincoln, UK consultant and one-time public affairs director of Wilkinson Sword, has said 'Too many public relations consultants give the impression they know what is required. They accept with dangerous alacrity a half-brief and go away only to produce a half answer.'

Timing The schedule of public relations and advertising activity is critical. For example, the public relations launch of a new product needs to be timed so that editors can report on it *before* the advertising appears. This could obviously affect the advertising schedule. No editor will write about a new product if his readers already know all about it from display ads in the same or previous issues. (Remember too that advertising copy delivered to publishing houses may well be drawn to the attention of journalists by their advertisement colleagues.)

Many editors are also sensitive to any implication that advertising may have influenced the editorial coverage, and so it is wise to seek editorial coverage in issues in which the product is not the subject of any major advertising.

Roles

It is difficult to effectively coordinate advertising and public relations without having a clear view on the special strengths of each craft:

Audience Advertising can be directed very accurately at a specific target audience. Media relations activity may well be directed towards the same audience, but there can be no guarantee of the exposure, as this is dependent upon the news value and readership appeal. (Public relations techniques that do not depend on the media for reaching the audience, such as competitions or sponsorship, can also be difficult to focus onto a narrowly defined audience.)

Impact Because the advertiser buys the space or the time, he is entitled to say whatever he likes, law and decency permitting. The media relations part of the public relations campaign depends upon the intermediary of the journalist and so has to be more circumspect in both style and language. In compensation, the impartiality of editorial or airtime can often give the message far greater weight.

Function When to choose advertising and when public relations? Often advertising can be used to sell a deal, but public relations may be more effective where the market needs educating. With new products or services, it will be usual for the public relations to lead the advertising, to take maximum advantage of any news opportunities. Public relations is most effective, perhaps, in changing opinion and winning goodwill. Advertising is best for impact and awareness.

In simple terms, public relations tends to be highly credible but cannot always be totally controlled or always guaranteed to deliver precisely the agreed messages to precisely the defined audiences at precisely the agreed times. Advertising can be controlled and can be most effective when the same message needs to be presented consistently to a defined public ... possibly a number of times. It works less well in controversy, debate or sophisticated argument, for the obvious reason that people know where it is coming from and, therefore, view it with some 'they-would-say-that-wouldn't-they' caution.

.... people know where advertising is coming from

Paperwork

However the liaison is organized, it is essential that all parties exchange those reports that are necessary for the proper planning of the campaigns. This will eliminate many of the conflicts or duplication that can result from poor coordination. Such progress reports can be used as the agenda at public relations/advertising coordination meetings.

Budgets

The advertising and public relations elements of a campaign should each have their own distinct budget. Once the budgets have been agreed, there should be no competition for expenditure between advertising and public relations.

The effective coordination of advertising and public relations could be assisted by following these 10 simple suggestions:

1. Involve both disciplines in the marketing planning.
2. Define complementary public relations and advertising objectives.
3. Allocate separate and firm budgets to each.
4. Agree responsibilities and planned activities.
5. Establish practical routines for coordination.
6. Have regular joint liaison sessions.
7. Get public relations/advertising to present their campaigns to each other.
8. Arrange for them to make a joint presentation to the organization's management.
9. Ensure regular exchange of all documents/information.
10. Insist that all parties work together this year—or they might not get the chance next!

ADVERTISING DELIVERS THE MESSAGE

While it is important to appreciate what public relations can achieve, it is equally sensible to understand what it can *not* do. Public relations cannot correct valid criticisms or counter a justifiably-earned poor reputation. Media relations cannot generally create continuous publicity, time and again, with products or services where there may be no news interest. Nor can it easily reach the same people, again and again, or be targeted on demand to a narrow market sector. And it is not always possible to ensure that the message is transmitted exactly as the sponsoring organization would wish.

However, as noted earlier, media advertising can deliver the company message, exactly as required, to a very clearly defined market sector, as and when required, and as often as the budget will allow. A comparison between media relations and media advertising identifies more clearly the role each should play in a campaign. While the message can be completely controlled in advertising, the editorial message has been shown in tests to have more credibility with the reader, to a factor of perhaps three or more. This is because the editorial has the authority of the publication, while the advertising is clearly seen to be a paid-for message.

There is one area where close cooperation between the advertising and public relations can pay very substantial dividends. This is where a campaign theme is developed which can be projected through both communications techniques. The 'we try harder' Avis message was a good example of this. For a major UK mushroom organization, the advertising agency created a campaign based on the theme 'make room for the mushrooms'. This had obvious appeal to the shopper and housewife when developed as a TV commercial. It was also projected through the public relations consultancy to the trade where the message had a different meaning—give the product shelf space. The theme was used on all presentations, information leaflets and press packs as part of a complete coordinated campaign.

Where the news aspects around the company and products have limited potential for development, then a public relations campaign broader than one solely based on media relations will be necessary.

PUBLIC RELATIONS CAN DEFY THE LAW OF DIMINISHING RETURNS

Advertising can often provide effective promotional support for mass-selling products. At some point, the law of diminishing returns can begin to apply; with large advertising budgets this may mean that an additional 10 per cent could be spent on public relations far more effectively than the same sum expended on increasing the advertising volume.

As an illustration, £1 million might be spent on media advertising to support the introduction of a new consumer product—say, a new range of leisure and sportswear. A 10 per cent increase on this sum would only increase the advertising effectiveness by a maximum of 10 per cent—and possibly less. However, this additional expenditure of £100 000 would allow a significant level of public relations support activity that could increase overall campaign effectiveness by much more than just 10 per cent.

Such a campaign might include a number of activities such as: the launch of the range to national press, radio and television, provincial papers, trade and sports writers; the introduction of the range through a series of presentation evenings across the country; a 12-month continuous media relations campaign; a sponsorship in sports relevant to the new kit; the retention of a group of leading sports and showbusiness personalities to endorse and project the range through personal appearances; national newspaper and magazine competitions aligned with the product design; a series of sponsored books on sports training tips; wall charts and posters for sports clubs, retailers and schools; a national young sports stars of the year competition; a national trade sales conference held in a European sports centre; a training scheme for young sports performers of potential and many, many, others.

All such ideas could be developed to favourably project the client name and the product qualities. Which should marketing management buy—a significant campaign of broad public relations support, or a small percentage increase in the advertising impact?

RUN THE CRAFTS IN PARALLEL

Public relations should not be seen as being competitive with advertising, sales promotion or other publicity efforts. An effective marketing campaign will ensure that all techniques run in parallel and are complementary to each other. As David Ogilvy has said, advertising can help define the brand personality. Today's public relations techniques can help project this personality and the credibility of the organization behind the product.

In the planning of the budget, it is often useful to assess the overall promotional figure (see the calculations in the budget section, Chapter 7) and allow the public relations, advertising and sales promotion specialists to present their own cases for their allocation from this budget. The marketing director needs to decide what opportunity he wishes to give for his professional agencies and consultants to present their campaign ideas. At the beginning of a new campaign it may be a useful exercise to make this a competitive presentation, open to two or three nominated advertising agencies, consultancies and sales promotional houses.

Once the organization has made its decision on which professional partners it wishes to work with, it is not fair to look at competitive presentations. This can be counter-productive and seriously reduce commitment.

WATCH THE BUDGET CARVE-UP

At the planning stage, there may be no need to finalize the details of the proposed budget; from their knowledge of the company, the agencies should have an understanding of the likely level of budget involved. They will recommend a level of expenditure necessary to achieve the objectives, the techniques which have proved effective and those areas where a further investment of budget might be advantageous to the company.

This friendly competition between the crafts can only work where the company employs separate advertising agencies, consultancies and sales promotional houses. The use of such different specialists ensures a competitive element in their recommendations. It also gives the company access to wider perspectives and ideas: separate advisers can make the campaign less vulnerable to personnel changes at the suppliers, personality clashes or other factors beyond the company's control.

In contrast, the use of a publicity organization that has an in-house advertising, public relations and promotional operation can bring economies both in overheads and in manpower. In some cases, liaison between the promotional organization and the client may be improved.

HOW TO SELECT AN AGENCY

The manager responsible for business communications may sometimes be required to identify the need for an advertising agency and establish the selection procedures. Some of the principles are the same as for selecting any key supplier. Indeed, the steps outlined in the section on planned action (Chapter 6, covering the selection of a public relations consultancy) do provide a general guideline that can be adapted.

The role of the manager responsible for the selection must be clearly explained to all the candidate agencies. For example, is he solely responsible for the selection process or will he be responsible for monitoring and controlling the work? Who will be responsible for policy, budget clearance, final copy approval and so on. Who will sign the agreement and approve the financial arrangements, conditions, termination and notice clauses?

It is essential in any selection to treat all trading partners fairly; you must protect and enhance your organization's reputation. Let us assume that you identified a dozen potential agencies on your initial list before producing your shortlist of two or three and making your final choice. If you handle this project sensitively you will have one good agency appointed. You will also have eleven others who will respect your decision and acknowledge the professional way in which you handled the negotiations. This fair negotiating ability is one the professional business communications manager must develop. In summary, always treat others as you would like to be treated and you will not go far wrong.

CREATING PUBLIC RELATIONS TO SUPPORT ADVERTISING AND MARKETING

1. Have we identified the immediate marketing audiences with whom we are trying to develop good relations?
2. How will the public relations efforts relate to the organization's long-term marketing plan?
3. What business changes might be anticipated that will need particular public relations support to achieve?
4. Will the nature of tomorrow's business affect our public relations approach to creating the environment for the development of the organization?

5. Does this mean that public relations will be used to help move the organization into new product, service or geographical market sectors?
6. How might competitive activity be expected to develop, particularly in the communications sector?
7. What steps need to be taken to monitor competitive communications so that the programme can be adjusted, as necessary?
8. To what extent will our efforts need to be educational, in terms of introducing new technology, new product concepts or company diversification?
9. Will there be a requirement for a parallel communications activity within the organization to match changes in the market place or among external audiences?
10. Has a policy decision been taken on prices so that the stance in public relations and advertising relating to value and quality can be established?
11. What specific support will be required for the salesforce from communications, for example, regional promotion or sales leads?
12. What additional promotional techniques might be deployed which need to be coordinated with the public relations effort?
13. For example, have decisions been made on media advertising to indicate those areas where public relations might need to be complementary or reinforce the advertising effort?
14. What is likely to be the timing of the campaign in relation to other sales promotional support efforts?
15. How will the budget be controlled and related to each element within the broader campaign?
16. Should specific public relations activities be developed to support specific sales or marketing objectives, such as dealer conferences or trade competitions?
17. Has consideration been given to methods of separating the achievements of public relations, advertising and sales promotion, so that the cost-effectiveness of each can be evaluated?
18. Have all members of sales, marketing and advertising management had the opportunity to submit their ideas and suggestions in the public relations area and vice versa?
19. Has the final promotional plan been circulated to all these managers for their agreement and approval?
20. Has particular attention been paid to those areas where public relations and advertising might overlap or need to be very closely coordinated, such as, exhibitions, audio-visual, research, conferences and seminars?
21. Have we studied all the creative aspects of the advertising or sales promotional recommendations to see whether these have public relations exploitation potential, for example, the use of slogans or show-business personalities?

22. What procedures have been established for the efficient coordination of the work of the marketing, public relations, advertising and other promotional executives?
23. Have we allocated an intelligent budget for measuring the effectiveness of the campaign?
24. Does the calendar of promotional activity make allowance for the different time scales needed for public relations, advertising and sales promotion activities?
25. Have the calendars for all promotional activities been compared to ensure that they are coordinated and make best use of available management time?
26. How will the executives responsible for sales, marketing, advertising and public relations exchange information on the development of the campaign?
27. What systems have been set up to provide the necessary feedback from the market place on the impact of this activity?
28. Can the objectives relating to sales and marketing be related to the long-term communications attitude objectives?
29. Have we looked through the other checklists relating to this area, such as those on objectives and budgets?
30. What procedures have been agreed for monitoring the results achieved by all aspects of the promotional activity?

FOURTEEN

PUBLIC RELATIONS IN SALES SUPPORT

CREATE THE SALES ENVIRONMENT

The role of public relations in sales support is perhaps the best understood; it is also probably true that this *still* remains the greatest potential development area for public relations.

Many organizations using public relations understand the publicity aspects and the support this can give to the sales effort. However, publicity is perhaps not the most valuable contribution that public relations can make to supporting the sales effort (or any other area, such as charity or political appeals), where a particular message needs to produce direct response on the part of the recipient.

By far the best contribution that can be achieved by public relations is to create the right environment within which such sales efforts will take place. To misquote a famous McGraw-Hill advertisement, the customer leans across the desk to the keen young salesman and says: 'I don't know you or your company. I have never heard of your products. In my eyes you have no track record. Your reputation is non-existent, while your competitors are reputable, well established, familiar and know how to work with my company. I don't like working with unknown suppliers. Now, what are you trying to sell to me?'

Newspapers, trade and technical publications, radio and television programmes all need constant news material. New companies with new products, new services and new sales approaches can organize themselves to create a lot of news coverage. This public relations activity can be continued over many years, so that the personality of the organization emerges clearly through these many individual news stories; its reputation, its standards, its contribution to the particular industry sector, its responsibility, its social commitment, its part in the local, regional and national economy and many other factors.

It is a realistic aim for the public relations to create the situation where the salesman is greeted by the prospective customer: 'I've heard of you, I know your company and like its style. Your products are well known and your service and reputation are quoted as examples in the industry. Your company's reputation and trading policies are admirable. You must be an excellent man to work for such an excellent company. Now tell me how you can help my organization.'

USE PUBLIC RELATIONS TO HELP THE SALE

In drafting the objectives, the public relations practitioner will have discussed these areas with the sales personnel and ensured that the programme is projecting the particular points that are necessary to make the salesman's job more productive.

The salesman will get in to see fewer customers if his company has no reputation; he will spend a lot of time in trying to build up a relationship and credibility. An hour of efficient sales talk may not achieve as much as a good story on his company in the *Sunday Times*, *Newsweek*, in the business columns of his own local paper or in a leading trade publication.

Engineers read and believe *The Engineer*. Companies trying to sell to the engineering industries will begin negotiations with a lot more credibility if the hard-headed journalists on *The Engineer* have decided that they have a story worth telling. (The same argument applies to grocers and *The Grocer*, architects and *The Architects' Journal* and so on.)

MATCH THE THEME TO THE COMPANY AURA

It may be a prime function of the public relations activity to actually promote products. Therefore this publicity effort should be planned to be consistent with the goodwill objectives. Today's sales must not be achieved at the expense of the corporate reputation.

As an example, a major electronics company decided to introduce a new item of business equipment in to the UK market: this would supersede the existing model. They decided to put a special promotional effort behind clearing these products. The scheme was built around a clever mail-shot, based on taking the gambling out of buying such equipment. As an incentive give-away, all respondents to the mail-shot would receive a set of poker dice.

However, the combined intervention of the public relations manager and his consultancy succeeded in getting the scheme rethought. The reasons behind this were that, while it might achieve the objective of clearing these products, it was not consistent with the reputation that had been developed by the company. Indeed, it seemed likely that this promotion would actually be in conflict with the agreed business objectives. The tone of the 'hurry, hurry, while stocks last' mail-shot was in complete contrast with the standards established for this leading professional systems supplier. Equally important, the public relations consultant advised against any mail-shot which was built around a gambling theme. While most people would accept this was a light-hearted approach, there are some people to whom gambling is unacceptable. Undoubtedly, Murphy's law would apply and those who objected would turn out to be the largest and most important customers.

USE PUBLIC RELATIONS TO GENERATE SALES LEADS

Many organizations set an objective for their public relations activity to create direct enquiries for the salesforce. This can be invaluable in helping produce a direct commercial return on the budget investment. Campaigns to create sales enquiries need to be carefully planned. The level of enquiry needs to be agreed: with some trade publications it is possible to get coverage of routine product changes or new literature details. Many enquiries will be from information departments, students and business libraries wishing to update their files. How valuable this is to the organization needs to be assessed; the mere numbers of enquiries involved may be no measure of value. In other cases, one or two enquiries can be enough to justify the campaign.

As an illustration, early in my career, Dunlop were considering phasing out a type of industrial belting which had not achieved anticipated sales levels. The press office was invited to look at this product, to see whether it could undertake any activity which would focus more attention on the benefits offered. As the press officer responsible for this product sector, I came across one of the few applications of unusual interest. The belting had proved to be the only practical solution for a company undertaking gravel excavation in a well-known beauty spot. The use of the belting made this possible with the minimum visual disturbance. A particularly interesting series of photographs was commissioned. These produced some favourable trade press reaction, including a good picture story in the *Financial Times*. As a direct result of this piece, the salesmen for the division received a number of useful enquiries. One was from a major construction company who saw the belting as offering exactly the solution they needed for a number of installations. This enquiry came from a senior director of the construction company; ironically, it was a company where the salesmen had been trying to present the product to the buyers for months.

Ultimately, some very substantial orders were placed and the product was not only rescued but thrived and is still being manufactured and sold in significant quantities today.

Sodastream obtained distribution through Asda, some two years after the first approaches to the retail group. This followed an in-depth Sodastream company review in the *Financial Times*—quite an achievement itself, considering the company, at that time, was not public and had no intention of floating. A copy of the story was passed by a director of the store (interested to know their policy on this product sector) to the relevant purchasing executive; he, in turn, called in the company sales manager and shortly the product won its place on the shelves.

RESPECT THE SALES PROFESSIONAL

One of the first targets for the public relations must be the organization's own salesforce. The public relations manager should demonstrate to the salesforce the value of public relations. This needs to identify the contribution that it will make to their success. It is important that the personnel involved in running the public relations programme should establish good relations with both the sales management and field salesmen. Naturally, there is considerable suspicion among many salesmen about public relations personnel. In some cases, this arises from lack of experience but, too often, it is fuelled by an ineffectual public relations executive unable to respond to the sales needs.

To win the credibility of the salesforce, it is essential that the public relations adviser understands the work of the salesforce and what motivates them. He must appreciate that the customer pays for absolutely everything and it is the sales people who are the link between the company and the customer. Most salesmen have to work on their own initiative; it can be the most lonely of jobs. Good sales personnel must have confidence, balanced personalities and the highest levels of drive. Successful salesmen must be respected for their achievements.

SPEND TIME AT THE SHARP END

There are many ways that the public relations practitioner can get closer to the sales team. The efforts expended will pay dividends. The first requirement is to insist upon spending time on the road with the salesforce.

Such visits will give a real indication of the situation at the 'sharp end'. You must make it clear that you are not reviewing the performance of the salesman. You are interested in the reactions in the market place: you will lose goodwill if you appear to be snooping. There is no grapevine like the salesforce grapevine!

One of the central groups of people with whom the effective public relations adviser will regularly be in discussion must be the sales management team. These meetings might need to be on a regular quarterly or monthly basis. At the same time, it is very helpful to talk to as many individual members of the sales team as possible. Sometimes this can be done face-to-face, particularly if they have regular sessions at head office. Alternatively, these discussions can be held on the telephone. Try to talk to several different salesmen every week or month. Another helpful technique is to circulate a questionnaire to all members of the salesforce to get their views on problems where public relations could assist them. This can produce some indication of the type of activities they feel might contribute to improving the sales environment.

Be certain that you and your public relations colleagues attend sales meetings. Sometimes, you may ask for public relations to be an item on the agenda for discussion. If you do participate, get the agreement of the manager on your role. Your views on the public relations implications of sales policy may be welcome: your comments on sales effectiveness may not.

GET INTO THE SALES SYSTEM

Once or twice a year, it can be very helpful to write a paper on the public relations role in supporting the sales effort. Circulate this to all members of the sales team via the sales director or send copies to each of the regional sales meetings so it can be an agenda item for discussion.

With many public relations programmes, members of the salesforce will be providing the leads for the stories; a presentation at the national sales conference can be a good opportunity to demonstrate the effectiveness of this part of their contribution to the effort. At a sales conference organized by a leading construction group, the public relations consultant mounted all the press coverage that had resulted from the salesforce suggestions on to a giant roll of paper. This was then unrolled right round the sales conference room. Some companies make an award to the salesman who nominates the most stories used in the year. All are simple but effective ways to acknowledge the contribution of the people at the sharp end.

Try to set up some method of monitoring the possible news stories that will be suggested by members of the sales team. This can take the form of a simple form which sales personnel complete when they come across a story of interest. Or it might simply mean the addition of a section in the call report which they tick when they feel a story may have potential.

TELL THE SALES TEAM WHAT MAKES NEWS

You need to give them some indication of the type of stories that might be of interest. By judging each order against some agreed criteria each salesman can identify the potentially newsworthy orders. These guidelines have been simplified to make them self explanatory. They were originally developed for the manufacturers of instant accommodation, Portakabin, but the concept can be modified for any product category:

Prestige orders These can be a prestige contract from a well-known company, such as Rolls-Royce, sales relating to special projects which are themselves in the news, such as a new airliner, an unusually large contract, sales linked with famous names and places (for example a contract with royal involvement or for a famous establishment like Lords) participation in a major project (say laboratories for a world research centre). Remember, incidentally, the strict rules on the use of Royal connections.

Problem-solving orders These include situations where the product has provided a solution to a particularly demanding need. For example, the purchasing decision could have been influenced by the speed of supply, tight budgetary restraints, flexibility in use or making optimum use of space. Repeat orders can also provide interesting stories as they reflect the belief of the customer in the quality of service offered by the company. Contracts won which have assisted in the rapid expansion of a company, contributing to commercial success, present an excellent public relations platform.

'Added value' contracts Where the product has added to the quality of the working life of the customers' employees or added a new value to their business can make suitable topics for case history features. Examples might include computer or control rooms, hospital facilities or VIP entertainment suites.

Unusual orders An unusual order may well present an opportunity to undertake photography which could interest the national, regional or trade press. Such an order could be unusual either in its application or its location:

1. Applications could cover pubs, shops, churches, animal houses, research projects, mountain rescue centres, penthouse suites, training establishments or film/TV locations.
2. Locations could include inside a building where you would least expect to find such a construction (e.g. St Paul's Cathedral, Stonehenge), oil rigs or isolated sites such as a hillside, beach or moor.

Sympathetic associations There can be good stories where the products are used with clients or projects that have human interest or strong popular appeal, even though the applications may not be unusual. For example, these might cover goodwill causes (such as the Lord Mayor's show), fundraising activities, public projects (the restoration of Durham cathedral), charity events (London Marathon), social events (Wimbledon or Henley) or community projects (welfare centres, 'Shelter') and so on.

Do be certain that the press coverage generated is promptly distributed to the salesforce. This could be in the form of a regular 'what the papers say' bulletin. Some salesforces use material from publications as third party evidence in support of their sales presentation.

Dexion, the storage and materials handling specialists, make maximum use of good news stories. The company also developed a system for using shortened case histories (written at the same time as the news stories) in their sales presentations, together with appropriate public relations pictures. This gave them a complete catalogue of application, cross-referenced by type of materials handling situation, as well as by industry category.

ACKNOWLEDGE THE STORIES

As well as issuing the cuttings and broadcast transcripts to the sales team, some companies like to circulate the news releases. Certainly, the public relations adviser needs some method of advising salesmen on the progress of stories they have submitted as story suggestions. It is better to acknowledge a story and turn it down, rather than to simply leave it in the air; this can be very demoralizing to the salesman who has put the effort in to giving the subject some consideration. If a story has to be rejected, do be certain to explain why.

Sometimes it is possible to train the sales personnel to become their own public relations specialists; they will often be the only representatives of the company within some regional areas. With assistance, they can become spokesmen for the company and can often achieve valuable local editorial coverage. With word processing, it is possible for the public relations department to 'tailor' stories to suit the local situation. This means that the sales executive or the regional sales manager can become the spokesman quoted in the story for that region.

Many salesforces do not sell directly to the product user but through trade, wholesaler and retailer outlets. Public relations can be a very conspicuous promotional technique: it can also be used to develop relationships with the intermediaries in the sales chain.

For a relatively modest investment, the right public relations campaign can create a lot of activity. Such efforts can be a practical demonstration to the trade of the support the company is giving to the product or service.

PUBLIC RELATIONS SHOULD LEAD INTERNATIONAL DEVELOPMENT

As the organization expands outside its national boundaries, public relations must be one of the disciplines guiding the management, making sure they not only say the right things at the right time ... but that they also listen to local points of view. The greater the distance between the transmitter and the receiver, the greater the break-up and distortion of the message, the more static on the line and, overall, the fuzzier the communications—if they do not break down completely! In Chapter 5 on communication guidelines, we looked at some principles of international communications; it might be helpful to look at some of these as they might operate in practice.

These examples are for a manufacturing company, strong in a domestic market, expanding through various stages into new international markets. Initially, most companies need to go through an export phase before they become truly international, with operations in each region, run and staffed by nationals. Is IBM an American company operating overseas, an international company or a multinational with its head office in the USA? This company successfully ran a campaign identifying its contribution to the British economy—such as £120 million investment in one year alone and 11 000 British suppliers.

Campaigns to contribute to international sales objectives need to be planned and run within each sales territory, ideally by using local professionals, either recruited to the staff or through consultancies. Economies and market size may not make it possible to start with a substantial local public relations campaign in each overseas market. It is possible to develop towards this from campaigns run from the home territory.

Perhaps the earliest stage at which public relations can be deployed is in the opening up of new markets. For example, it is possible to issue news stories about new products, export intentions, successes in selected markets and international company developments that will help create an interest in chosen overseas markets. Obviously, any company venturing into exports needs professional export advice, but it can help to deploy the limited company resources in those markets where the earliest maximum return might appear likely. The more difficult markets can be tackled later.

News stories can also be written to interest prospective agents and distributors in selected markets. The response to these gives a company a measure of the interest that there might be in their products or services.

When an executive of the company is considering visiting a particular market, it is often helpful to issue a story in advance to local media. This will help attract attention to the visit and can sometimes produce direct enquiries from prospective trading partners. When the organization has reached the stage of appointing distributors and agents, public relations should be discussed as part of the promotional support activity within the market.

FOUR STEPS LEAD TO EXPORT PUBLIC RELATIONS SUCCESS

News stories can be issued from the home base to achieve world coverage—although there are obviously considerable limitations on the effectiveness of any media relations campaign handled from a distance. The organization can issue stories itself. The level of attention that these will receive from news editors increases very significantly if they are translated competently into the appropriate language by nationals of the country or by one of the professional translation agencies.

Beware the fluent linguist who does not understand the technology of the industry concerned. The world-ranging sales director of a giant electrical machinery manufacturers recounts ruefully an experience on a sales mission to China. Some of the technical information on the machinery being displayed at an exhibition he attended had been enthusiastically translated by a local colleague into perfect, idiomatic Chinese. He was therefore stumped when asked by a stand visitor to point out a special feature of his machinery, the 'wet sheep'. After some confusing discussion, he identified the component as 'hydraulic rams'!

Stories for the UK can be given world-wide cover through a number of channels: through the government-sponsored Central Office of Information, through the BBC external services and through a number of commercial news distribution agencies. These will also undertake the translation and distribution. Some of these business news services are outstanding in their quality, particularly in handling technical and specialized news stories. British companies can participate in joint promotions through a number of government-sponsored agencies. Similar agencies exist in most industrialized nations.

LOOK FOR LOCAL PUBLIC RELATIONS SUPPORT

At some stage, it will become necessary to have a presence on the ground, ideally a national of the country. It is essential to use local skills, particularly in communications. The arguments for and against using an enthusiastic amateur or a dedicated professional are exactly the same as those for the home market. It may be more difficult to justify a seasoned public relations professional in some overseas markets.

Quite often, it is within the realms of practicality for the home-based public relations consultancy or public relations staff to set up a training programme for overseas agents. This can cover the basic principles of public relations and operations. To these, each regional manager will add his expertise, knowledge of the market and the local flavour that is likely to make the campaign a success in his own country.

This type of training can be augmented with a public relations guidance manual; visits by the public relations representatives to the head office; visits by the public relations professionals in the home market to the overseas companies to give them assistance on-the-spot.

AIM TO EMPLOY PROFESSIONALS OVERSEAS

At some stage, the advantages of recruiting a staff public relations specialist in overseas markets will become overwhelming. This person will have the advantage of knowing the details of the public relations practicalities within that market, will have his contacts, will know the media and, obviously, will be a fluent writer in the language concerned.

It can still be realistic for an overseas public relations manager to work to an overall coordinating brief from the parent public relations specialists; he will need to report back on a regular and agreed basis. The head office public relations adviser must ensure that each overseas public relations adviser regularly receives news and material that might be suitable for adapting for use in his own country. An international exchange of media coverage, press comment, visits, new product activity, case histories and so on is extremely helpful. Many of the more sophisticated companies produce an international public relations bulletin. This monthly or quarterly publication collects all this material on a regular basis producing an invaluable source of ideas and information for each public relations specialist within each country.

The alternative to a staff public relations specialist within each country is the use of an established local consultancy. This may be a practicality in Western Europe, the English-speaking nations, the Middle East, certain parts of the Far East, Africa and South America. It is certainly worth evaluating. In Third World countries, this type of organization does not yet exist. In these cases, the use of a staff man may be essential.

The use of one of the established international consultancy organizations should certainly be considered. (These options are discussed in Chapter 6 on planning the resource, Chapter 7 on the budget and Chapter 8 on programme planning.)

It is essential that head-office public relations executives responsible for making recommendations listen very carefully to local advice; this does not mean automatically *following* local advice. The principles of selecting and working with a public relations consultancy apply in broad principle to the choice and use of an overseas operation.

MARKETING ACTIVITY						
Research	Product development	Branding and packaging	Trade support	Product support	Advertising and sales promotion	Feedback and results

PUBLIC RELATIONS ACTIVITY

PR Activity	Research	Product development	Branding and packaging	Trade support	Product support	Advertising and sales promotion	Feedback and results
Discussion	Public relations will need to be represented at policy planning meetings in all areas						
Advisory	Can we include questions in research that will help create public relations news material?	What innovations might create news? Are there trends in public attitudes we need to reflect?	Can the brand reflect our corporate communications policy? What about pricing?	Will the new range give us an opportunity to strengthen our trade reputation?	Can we present in consumer promotions our financial strengths?	All activity needs to be consistent with policy to stress our stability not our pace	Can our monitoring of media and key audiences help measure effectiveness?
Presentations				Plan and organize sales conference	Speakers trained for presentations to selected groups	Campaign could make a presentation at marketing conferences	Visitors book to record all attendance at every presentation
Media briefing		Lunch with business editor of local paper to work towards a feature on the innovation behind the product	Exclusive for one of the design magazines	Interview with sales director. Regional trade stories	National press conference. Regional home writers briefings	Exclusive interview with marketing director and selected journalists	Report on all reaction by journalists, particularly trade comments they have noted
News stories		Picture story on testing for technical page of the *Financial Times*		Contracts, orders, trade reaction	Material for press pack plus background article	Release campaign details to marketing press	Follow up story on sales results at 6 and 12 months
Press office	Press officer to spend several days with the development team to research background articles			System for public relations stories from sales team. Feed out reader enquiries	Consumer writer service. Articles/features photography prepared		Monitor coverage and record enquiries and advise marketing

Public relations print	Reprinted articles for their recruitment campaign	Consumer club leaflet to go into product boxes	Weekly sales bulletin. Monthly trade newspaper	Guide to domestic security for editorial enquiries	Presentation brochure to be prepared to help overseas distribution	Reply cards from security guide recorded and actioned
Audio-visual	Extracts from public relations items onto slide for induction of new staff		Tape/slide for regional events and consumer video	Video presentation for consumer media and special groups	Campaign on slide for showing to agency/consultancy personnel	
Competitions	Technical students to be invited to participate in design competition		Salesman of the year. Trade buyer holiday scheme	Regional press offers. Observer special competition		Christmas weekend for best story lead from salesmen
Events	Factory tour to include research facility by the star of the TV commercial	Giant product model to be donated to local technical college	Regional trade evenings with the TV personality	An at-home with the star for competition winners	Safety survey to be sponsored and run jointly by public relations/advertising	

Chart 14.1 Planning the public relations campaign to support the sales and marketing activity creates many opportunities. It can be helpful to look at the main sales and marketing responsibilities and see how public relations might relate to these. A simple headline chart can be invaluable. Of course, each activity would be subject to separate recommendations but it is useful to have a broad picture of the activity on one sheet. From this the schedule of timing and budget can be prepared.

In this case, adapted from a recent example, the event is the introduction of a new home security system that will be sold through electrical wholesalers and distributors and aimed at the house owner who will buy from do-it-yourself and high street electrical outlets. Both trade and consumer public relations are important.

But one factor the professional public relations practitioner must ensure that his colleagues in sales management appreciate is that public relations is central to creating the best business environment in which the sales personnel can work. An investment in public relations pays handsomely in sales returns. This is as true in international marketing as in home markets.

USING PUBLIC RELATIONS TO SUPPORT SALES

The opportunity

1. Have we looked at the sales objectives and identified those areas where public relations can assist the salesforce to do their job more effectively?
2. From this, can we write sales support public relations objectives with some quantifiable, measurable element, such as sales leads, reader enquiries or trade awareness?
3. Does sales management understand and support the contribution public relations should make to create the optimum sales environment?
4. Should we hold a planning session between public relations and sales management to assess opportunities, experiences, strengths and weaknesses?
5. Has the function credibility with the sales executives or will the first stage need to be public relations for public relations?
6. Can this be undertaken by a closer involvement of the two crafts?
7. Would it be helpful for public relations to be a topic for a presentation and discussion at national and/or regional sales conferences?
8. Have members of the public relations teams spent time on the road with members of the salesforce?
9. Could a representative of the salesforce be assigned to work in the public relations department for a period to present his observations at a sales meeting?
10. Does the public relations programme include regular news stories on new products, services, price changes, appointments, new contracts, interesting orders, new literature, sales aids and so on?
11. Is this activity regularly reviewed with sales management and reported, say, on a monthly basis?
12. Could the media relations campaign be extended to developing long-term good relations with those publications identified by sales management as those reaching their target audiences?
13. Have we considered articles by or on the sales management, interviews, facility visits, invitations to briefing sessions, sales meetings and conferences?
14. Can we extend similar activity to appropriate radio and television programmes, local stations and regional business editors?

15. Have we established a system for gathering news opportunities through members of the sales team?
16. Is this on their call reports, a separate form or perhaps a telephone call basis?
17. Have we identified what might make a possible news story such as:

    (a) associations with a prestige project,
    (b) an application solving a tricky problem,
    (c) involvements with a celebrity,
    (d) an unusual product in an unusual setting,
    (e) participation in a worthwhile cause?

18. Does the system ensure that all suggestions are processed and acknowledged even where they cannot be used?
19. Are there opportunities to train members of the sales team to act as spokesmen for the organization, for example, with regional media?
20. Can we tailor stories to suit the local or regional situations and support the sales personnel on the spot?
21. Should we take the public relations effort out to support the sales teams where they are relating to customers, with regional events such as:

new product launches	campaign announcements
top executive lunches	technology roadshow
trade presentations	entertainment evenings
annual business dinner	sponsored events?

22. Are we sending copies of news material, features and articles to members of the salesforce for use in their customer presentations?
23. Have we got a fast and efficient system for handling reader enquiries and advising the relevant sales person, where appropriate?
24. Can we present to the sales team an annual review of the public relations effort, the coverage, stories suggested by sales personnel, those covered and so on—either at the conference or in a special edition of the sales bulletin?
25. Have we established methods to assess the effectiveness of public relations in helping to meet the sales objectives, including, if possible, attitude surveys of main target sectors?

International support

26. Are we using public relations fully to support our sales efforts in overseas markets?
27. Do we look at the special requirements of each market separately and define for the public relations personnel the sales structure, distribution, awareness, market, penetration, competition, and other essential factors?

28. At the simplest level, have we a public relations campaign originated from head office to support sales efforts in those markets that are not yet sufficiently developed to have their own public relations resource?
29. For example, have we analysed the media available and media relations opportunities that we could develop with news articles, pictures about our organization and its plans?
30. Do we need to complement this with our own company-produced media, such as local editions of the external house journal in the appropriate language?
31. Should we support with public relations all export visits by our executives to each territory to help create interest among potential agents, distributors and customers?
32. Have we a product or story of such potential interest that we should consider inviting editors to see our facilities at head office, hear our plans and ask for their views?
33. Is all our activity in the appropriate language and checked by a local to ensure we are respecting national conventions, sensitivities and attitudes?
34. If our organization has developed to the point where we have agents or distributors on territory, how can we help them in their public relations efforts to support our sales?
35. Can we offer to train a senior member of their team to take on the public relations responsibility under our guidance?
36. Should we offer to assign a member of our team to work alongside their management until they can pick up the public relations responsibility?
37. Can we hold an international public relations conference as a training and familiarization activity for the representatives of a number of territories?
38. Could we prepare a suitable manual produced in cooperation with a local public relations adviser to help them plan and develop this resource?
39. Are we monitoring the growth and development of our overseas companies so that we can advise them at what stage they should consider recruiting a public relations executive onto their staff?
40. Would it be wiser for them to retain a local consultancy that we could help brief, advise and supply with basic public relations material for conversion to local use?
41. Should we consider an independent local operation in each region or one of the international networks to support us across several or all markets?
42. What budget and executive resource should be deployed to support this local sales effort (see budget, Chapter 7)?
43. Have we discussed with our international sales colleagues the possibility of additional sales discounts that might be offered to distributors on

condition these are spent on promotional activity approved at head office?

44. What systems will be established to ensure that public relations is considered a priority by local top management and that all company actions are consistent with corporate communications policy?

45. How will the activity be monitored and measured to assess effectiveness relating to the programme resource and/or budget?

FIFTEEN

NON-COMMERCIAL ORGANIZATIONS

KEEP IT BUSINESSLIKE

Public relations practitioners sometimes argue that there are very special requirements for the non-profit or non-commercial sector. Perhaps, the similarities are greater than the differences. The public relations specialist working with a non-profit organization needs to be very sure that any emphasis management places on the special nature of the organization is not simply an excuse for being unbusinesslike. For example, a children's charity can create great warmth and may attract many well-meaning people as willing helpers. Yet, the organization and running of a successful charity demands the strictest business disciplines.

Some of the world's most successful charities—Save the Children or the Worldwide Fund for Nature are very good examples—have been successful because of the efficiency with which they have been run. The public relations for a charity (or any other non-commercial activity) must be structured on strictly professional grounds. This means that there must be clear objectives, responsibilities, reporting procedures, resources, commitment by the organization to the function—and proper delegated authority for the public relations team to undertake the necessary activity.

Perhaps the peak of 'non-commercial' public relations is that undertaken on behalf of democratic governments. The British government was one of the first to undertake proper communications programmes. This initiative has been matched by many other countries, notably France and the Netherlands. Former director general of the Central Office of Information and a previous press secretary to several British prime ministers, Henry James, has commented on the role of public information in his evidence to a parliamentary select committee investigating government relations with the media. 'There is a conflict between countries operating under different systems of government. A democracy may be at a disadvantage as it cannot control the free flow of information. It nonetheless is strengthened by genuine consent and the greater credibility of its information at home and abroad.'

This basic factor of credibility relates to all aspects of public relations but nowhere more critically than in the non-profit sector.

FOLLOW A LOGICAL PLANNING SEQUENCE

In general, the primary objectives for any organization are likely to fall into three broad areas. These apply equally to a non-commercial organization:

Sales Every organization is 'selling' something. Many non-profit bodies do not identify very clearly what they are selling and to whom. For example, quite clearly a local authority is selling bus services, healthcare or education. A technical college will be selling places to prospective students. A sports club will be selling the benefits of membership. An environmental group might be selling peace of mind, donations or, as we shall see later, votes.

Support It is helpful if the organization can identify those activities which it sells in exchange for the resources it requires. The organization requires support and this will be an important objective for the public relations activity. For example, the sports group may need the endorsement of the sports authorities for its role in the community; the technical college needs the approval of the regional educational department; the environmental group needs political votes. Identify exactly what support is required, as a quantified objective, if possible.

Finance All non-profit organizations will be working to budgets; public relations will have a role in the communications aspects of meeting these targets. These can cover sales budgets for commercial services (for example, those supplied by a training centre, research institute or public utility), fund-raising targets, the endowment of a chair in education or buying buses for the handicapped. The public relations professional will be identifying how the public relations programme will work to help achieve these.

THE MESSAGE CREATES THE PROGRAMME

With the objectives defined, it is necessary to look at the audiences that matter. These groups might include customers, shareholders, investors, potential contributors, volunteer helpers, staff, business leaders, politicians, key journalists and so on. The aim of the public relations activity will be to help develop goodwill and create favourable attitudes towards the organization. But what should these attitudes be? What are the existing attitudes?

A larger organization may be able to afford research to investigate this in a quantified way. Smaller organizations may do this on a more informal basis. For example, if the aim is to create goodwill towards the local scout group, a simple neighbourhood discussion group will help identify what attitudes exist and, quite likely, what needs to be done to develop these. If, on the other hand, you have the responsibility for organizing the next Olympic Games, then the size of the project might suggest that, say, one per cent of the budget should be spent on research to establish existing attitudes.

The Order of St John runs many public services, the best-known of which is its voluntary first-aid and ambulance operations. Along with Barnado's and Save the Children, it is one of the charitable organizations that operates its public relations activity on a truly professional basis, though often with tight resources.

'You tell me once more you expect I was at their opening ceremony and you'll be needing them.'

Figure 15.1 The St John Appeal caught the public imagination and not only appeared in the editorial columns but became the subject of popular comment, such as this cartoon reproduced courtesy of Giles and the *Sunday Express*.

The effort put behind its centenary generated some 50 thick files of press coverage, plus countless national radio and television news items, interviews and feature programmes. The reason was creative thinking, including such initiatives as the formation of a junior division with special uniforms, called the St John Badgers, a series of centenary postage stamps, the largest ever children's party held in London's most famous park, the naming of a railway locomotive and many other ideas.

How do you wish your non-profit organization to be seen? Good intentions are not enough. A strong body of enthusiastic volunteers around the central core make it even more important that everybody clearly understands the organization. This means that the messages to be projected must be properly defined. Is your charity a friendly low-key operation with its main objective to involve people in some small area of childcare ... or is it a hard-nosed operation that is going to raise millions to tackle national and international injustices? (Some major groups in the latter category behave as if they were in the former category.)

Similarly, is your sports group established to provide a friendly meeting forum for sports enthusiasts and others in the local community ... or is it a lobby group to persuade local authorities and businesses to fund better sports facilities? These policies may appear clear to the people at the top: but they are often very distorted by the time they reach the willing helpers at the bottom.

PLAN THE PROGRAMME, THEN COST IT

The techniques to be deployed in the public relations programme will be selected for their relevance and cost. Indeed, it is often preferable to construct the public relations programme to meet the defined aims and then to cost this to calculate the necessary budget. An adequate budget is essential. Voluntary enthusiasm is rarely as good as paid professional effort.

If we take a charity or fund-raising activity as an example, administration and promotional costs should not exceed 10 or 15 per cent of the sum to be raised. The proportion could well be down to one or two per cent of the total with the larger organizations: this is obviously a more acceptable level.

Professional public relations assistance can actually *reduce* the overhead percentage deducted from funds raised. As an illustration, a small charity wishes to raise £100 000 to finance a holiday home for handicapped children. A professional fund raiser, public relations consultancy or freelance professional is found who is prepared to tackle this as a project; he calculates that the cost necessary to put this over to the right people to produce that level of sum will be £15 000. This is a significant proportion of the amount to be raised.

However, there may be very little *real* difference between the effort needed to raise £100 000 and £150 000. With professional assistance, it is easy to raise the target to £150 000 which means that the costs have been reduced to only 10 per cent. And the organization has succeeded in raising £35 000 more than it might have done *without* proper help.

One method some non-profit bodies have used to enlarge the budget available for professional assistance is to undertake cooperative campaigns with business sponsors. Indeed some generic programmes, such as fund-raising for Olympic teams, are good examples of this synergy at work—although strictly most of these are so closely involved in commercial objectives that the approach is closer to that outlined in the marketing section.

TAILOR THE MESSAGE TO THE RECIPIENT

As with most missions, the essential element is a commitment to success. The public relations advisers within the organization must keep on reminding themselves of the value of their objectivity: their perspective is *not* the same as those with whom they are trying to establish two-way communications.

Let us consider the fund to provide a holiday home for handicapped children. This is likely to be a passionate commitment for those directly involved. To the local businessman asked to provide support it can be something else. It could either be an interruption to a busy day, an embarrassing appeal, moral blackmail, or a meaningless request, (particularly if he has no children and is not local to the community). One thing is certain . . . he is unlikely to be as enthusiastic as the sponsors.

For the organization to achieve success in getting his support they have to be very specific in their request. The promotional adviser has to identify very clearly what the product is, the benefits it will offer, the back-up and service, the credibility of the organization, the ability to deliver the goods as promised . . . and what this proposition will cost.

FOLLOW PROPER SALES PRINCIPLES

Consider your charity deal in exactly the same way you would a commercial proposal:

What is our product? Show the businessman the home that will be built, identify for him the number of children that need this type of assistance, show how this will contribute to their welfare. Above all, do this rapidly, efficiently and professionally.

What are the benefits? Make sure that in presenting your product you stress not just the features, but the benefits. In other words, not the number of rooms in the holiday home, but the number of holidays it will provide for the children: not just the range of educational courses that will be offered, but the broadening of the youngsters' horizons.

Indeed, many charities find that it is very helpful to have their literature produced by professional promotion houses who appreciate the need to present the message clearly and powerfully.

What back-up do we offer? If you sell products, then you have to have a guarantee and service. The prospective donor will want to know what back-up resources will be supporting the home.

Look at the structure of your charity, its strengths, its continuity, its links with the community, its supporters, its foundation, its presidents and trustees, its track record. All of these will provide essential conviction. They demonstrate the back-up to the new children's home.

What is the price? You need to identify clearly the price you are putting on the appeal that you are offering. Obviously, the capital and the running costs will have been calculated: but what are you expecting the businessman to contribute?

TELL THE DONOR EXACTLY WHAT YOU WANT

Some years ago, one of the most successful appeals ever run in the UK was organized by the Salvation Army: they recognized the need to tell the public exactly what they should contribute. From this simple concept, they developed the slogan ... 'For god's sake, give us a quid!' The importance of this message was that it saved the donor the problem of deciding what was a fair contribution. Many people will refuse to give, rather than risk the embarrassment of giving either too much or too little. This simple campaign concept still has not been bettered.

Some fund-raising activities quote different appeal sums for different benefits. The Institute of Marketing launched a multi-million appeal for their College of Education and spelled out what each level of contribution would achieve—the dedication of a room, a reception area, a particular building, an item of equipment and so on.

In contrast, some charities are very disappointed when they write to famous personalities and get a refusal. They should examine their appeal very carefully. Who would buy double glazing without a price tag? Why should a business manager commit himself to something, unless he has some idea of what is involved?

In some cases, getting support is as important as getting money. This enables the appeal to publish a list of early contributors which has a snowball effect in encouraging other people to help. It is perfectly fair to write to early supporters, such as local businessmen, national leaders or show business personalities with a specific request.

'Please send us your favourite recipe for a book we are publishing for our appeal' ... 'Please send us one of your old ties which we can auction' ... 'Please send us £50 and a letter of support' ... 'Please send us a tape with a two minute anecdote that we can compile into a radio broadcast to celebrate our appeal' ... 'Please give us 10 minutes of your time for a photograph to go into our appeal document' ... 'Please allow us to quote your name on our literature as a supporter of our cause' ...

CONSIDER ORGANIZING A PARLIAMENTARY LOBBY

When your non-commercial body is looking for political support or seeking to amend legislation, this is likely to require a political lobby. Of course, MPs, MEPs, congressmen, senators and all elected representatives are sensitive to public opinion, as is demonstrated most dramatically at election times! Therefore, the well-organized lobbying group will undertake activities to ensure that there is the maximum possible public support for the cause.

In the UK, parliamentary lobbies have been undertaken successfully by organizations as diverse as Shelter, the charity for the homeless, the British Franchise Association, the Campaign for Independence in Medicine, the Royal Society for the Prevention of Cruelty to Animals, the British Field Sports Society and many others.

Of them all, perhaps the National Farmers' Union is the most influential pressure group in parliament. Hard work and some very good organization have achieved a high degree of influence. This is remarkable when it is considered that less than 3 per cent of the population can be classified as farmers. The NFU has achieved its effectiveness through a very good ground-roots organization and effective direction from the top. (See also the section on planning a European lobby.)

LOOK AT LINKS WITH COMMERCIAL BODIES

As with the example of the Chartered Institute of Marketing and its association with some very well-known companies in the commercial sector, it is possible for voluntary organizations to link themselves with commercial companies.

An example of one of the better known cooperative techniques is the on-pack offer, sometimes used as a sales promotion activity. The participating company undertakes to make a contribution to the worthy cause, with the use of some form of coupon, label or on-pack offer which demonstrates proof of purchase. Schemes like this have been used to raise money for such causes as sending teams of athletes to the Olympics, buying life-boats for the Royal National Lifeboat Institution and minibuses for use by Barnardo's and other children's charities.

The potential for promotional projects which can be structured involving a charity or appeal is very considerable. Roadline UK cooperated with the children's television show, 'Blue Peter', in collecting charity parcels for their annual appeal. The British Heart Foundation ran an annual sponsored slim, usually supported by a well-known manufacturer of a low calorie food. The Save the Children Fund mounted enormous public jumble sales in cooperation with women's publications.

Many non-profit bodies use outside consultancies working on normal commercial terms. Some, such as Christian Aid and Barnardo's have built up staff departments of a dozen or more people. In most cases, the public relations function is identified as being part of the responsibility of the chief executive.

Yet insufficient resource is applied by some bodies to public relations. In view of the quite outstanding results that it can achieve this may be short-sighted. The importance of public relations to a voluntary organization, charity or other non-profit body can be very substantial. These bodies are increasingly working in a competitive market-place, where more and more appeals are being made.

IS CHARITABLE STATUS A HELP?

In the UK, an organization which has charitable status is registered. It is interesting to note that the charity commissioners deem that education and information are charitable activities, but some pressuring and propaganda are not. As a result of this, the charity commissioners have refused charity status to some pressure groups who have been seeking social reforms. Equally ironically, they have allowed charity status to some bodies, who have been demonstrated to have a very limited 'charitable' nature, including some religious groups.

It is likely that the charity laws will be tightened. At present, a registered charity can be in serious problems if it strays into the political area: it is legally possible for the trustees to be held responsible for funds which have been spent on activities which do not fall into the charitable sector. If the organization is to be an identified pressure group involved in parliamentary lobbying, then it may well find it neither possible nor advisable to achieve charity status.

Whether your body is a charity, a trust, a foundation, a research or educational establishment, or any of the other non-profit organizations discussed, the public relations adviser must remember basic disciplines. What are we trying to achieve, whom are we trying to influence, what attitudes exist, how would we like attitudes shaped, which messages do we wish to convey and how will we measure success?

PLANNING COMMUNICATIONS FOR NON-PROFIT ORGANIZATIONS

1. As with every organization, have we clearly identified those people upon whose goodwill we depend for success?
2. For practical communications purposes, can these be arranged into convenient groups, e.g. volunteer helpers, regional officers and so on?
3. Have we decided how we wish to be seen by these groups, in other words, have we drafted our mission or purpose?
4. Has this been circulated, agreed and approved by all relevant managers?
5. Would this help us to write down the messages about the organization which we wish to project?
6. What steps can we take to evaluate the attitudes that exist towards us among key audiences?
7. In what areas will improved communications help us to improve such attitudes?
8. Do any gaps indicate where we might need to change our policies?
9. What communications channels already exist to keep these audiences informed?
10. Which of these provide feedback to enable us to monitor reactions to information, development of attitudes and so on?
11. Can we make some assessment of the relative effectiveness and, therefore, the cost effectiveness of these existing communications methods?
12. Do we have colleagues who would contribute to a brainstormer to develop alternative methods of communication?
13. Can we make an estimate of the likely cost and effectiveness of these other options, so we can make a comparison with existing techniques?
14. Does this give us an alternative programme of communications which we could consider?
15. Are we deploying all voluntary resources that might be available to assist us in our public relations efforts?
16. Have we provided proper training and briefing for any such voluntary assistance for our public relations objectives?
17. Is there any requirement for a parliamentary or public affairs campaign to support the aims of the organization?
18. Are we allocating a realistic resource in manpower and budget to achieve the public relations objectives that have been agreed?
19. Have we established clear procedures for measuring our effectiveness in achieving communications objectives?
20. How will these influence the activity for coming years and the appropriate budget?

FOUR

Figure 16.1 The public relations professionals are often behind great state events as well as at the centre of commercial activity. The meetings of Mrs Thatcher and Mr Gorbachov (this one at a formal state function in London) were both political and public relations trials.

SIXTEEN
DECIDING WHICH TECHNIQUE

CREATIVITY CAN BE DEVELOPED

The programme of activity to achieve the agreed public relations objectives will be constructed using a number of techniques. Some of these will be well established, others more innovative. Creative public relations professionals are introducing new ideas all the time.

The fact that a particular method is well-proven does not mean it should be rejected for something more novel. Equally, just because an idea is new, does not mean that it is better. However, there should be no embarrassment about borrowing and adapting existing ideas. The public relations adviser needs to be able to demonstrate a degree of imagination in proposing solutions to problems. Such creativity can be developed: it might be helpful to make a few suggestions on developing a repertoire of creative ideas.

At an early stage in his career, the public relations executive should develop the habit of thinking laterally, monitoring what other professionals are doing on the public relations scene and constantly trying to develop alternative solutions to communications problems. The results of this effort may well become an invaluable personal file. Certainly in a consultancy or public relations department, someone enthusiastic should be nominated to build and run an ideas and public relations services file; do not delegate this to the most methodical clerical assistant *unless* they have the vision and imagination to make this central to your public relations thinking.

Whether it is you personally, or a colleague, certain things must be done. Read every publication and book available on the subjects of public relations, advertising and publicity. There is a constant flow of new ideas being published. Make a note of every imaginative promotional technique.

Open a public relations ideas file and a cross-referenced index on these. For example, the ideas could be indexed under the promotional technique such as mailing, exhibitions, seminars ... or to the audiences they reach, such as shareholders, local community, suppliers, and so on.

Visit every marketing services exhibition or send someone round to every stand with your business card. If that is not possible, get a copy of the exhibition catalogue. The promotional suppliers will ensure you are on their mailing lists for all their services. This will create a useful library of promotional techniques.

Telephone every classified advertiser in the trade publications who provide marketing promotional services. In the UK these include *PR Week*, *Marketing, Campaign, Marketing Week, UK Press Gazette*, and so on. File all the literature and suggestions—cross-referenced as above.

Not only will it be invaluable when you suddenly find you want to hire a hot-air balloon or an open-topped bus or a stage coach with six white horses or the only boxing kangaroo in Europe or the man who can dive 50 metres onto a mattress ... in fact, the actual index itself will provide an invigorating way of stimulating new ideas.

Today, with the word processor it is simple to index and cross-reference such a file. It should be used every time you are planning a campaign. Remember that disciplined logic should be applied first to define the audiences, the attitudes, the messages, the measurement of success and the objectives. Creative solutions can only be effective if they answer real problems.

There can be many dull ways to influence the audience and many exciting ways. Every public relations planning session should have a creative ideas discussion. Some form of brainstorming meeting, involving other colleagues can help. Read the books of Dr Edward de Bono to stimulate thinking abilities. When you have decided on the techniques, be certain that you incorporate a facility for the two-way flow of information. Otherwise you are not achieving 'communication' but merely dissemination. Feedback is essential to tune the campaign as it progresses.

The following are sections covering some of the main proven public relations techniques and operating areas. Though only an outline of some important aspects of public relations they should provide a foundation from which effective and creative programmes can be structured.

SEVENTEEN

MEDIA RELATIONS

COVERAGE RELATES TO NEWS INTEREST

Commercial media exist to provide news that is of interest to their readers, viewers or listeners. This simple statement of fact should be obvious. But it means that the public relations adviser must be ruthless in the application of critical standards to the preparation and issue of news material.

Is it logical for the chief executive of a company to expect his own morning newspaper to concentrate only on issues that are of major public interest ... yet expect that same paper to report some change in one of his products that, realistically, might only be of interest to engineers?

Some journalists seem to believe that a news sense is a very rare quality. In truth it is largely common sense. Bad news is *not* the only news. But it is the exceptional which is the definition of news. If one taxi driver sets fire to his vehicle then it is news. The fact that several thousand others do not, is of no consequence. One naked football fan running on the pitch may be news, but the 500th will not be. There are two main reasons why bad news gets better coverage. First, it is more exceptional: murder, hijack and fraud are not yet the norm. Second, people experience morbid curiosity in disaster and tragedy, perhaps because of the relief that they are not the victims.

Companies can use this 'new is news' factor to their own advantage. The first chairwoman of a public company may be news. The first major contract for the sale of an unlikely consumer product (such as electric kettles) to Tibet is news. A survey that shows the average man has three (or thirty!) pairs of underpants is news. A 63-year-old char lady being invited to open a new high-technology laboratory is news. The winner of a travel scholarship who has never been abroad is news. The invention of a safety device by an apprentice is news. The invitation of all company pensioners to the launch of a new product is news.

It only takes observation of how the media work to recognize that central to any effective media relations campaign must be a hard core of news. And it is perfectly legitimate to *create* news. If it is new, has never been done before, is interesting and relevant ... it could be news.

Obviously, what is news in an engineering publication may not be news in the parish magazine. What is news for a local radio station may not be right for national television news.

This book cannot cover the detail of how to prepare, write and issue news: there are many excellent publications on this subject. But, the efficient public relations practitioner must have this skill. Clever news headings, impeccable typing, personal messenger delivery may all be helpful, but there can be no substitute for a strong news story.

Sheila Tate, White House press secretary at one time, ran an informal survey among Washington correspondents. It revealed some interesting facts that probably apply to journalists in any situation, in any place in the world.

For example, some 92 per cent rated candour as a key quality in an executive responsible for public relations. The same percentage also said that they would be more likely to deal with public relations people that they knew personally. When asked to evaluate the helpfulness of various press materials, fact sheets and speech texts were top, with expensive printed items such as brochures and annual reports coming bottom.

There was virtually unanimous support for the fact that a news conference should only be held to handle a major news announcement where questions were essential. Some two-thirds of the respondents felt that news conferences were abused as a communications technique, yet virtually all claimed to read press releases. Hand delivery improved the chances of stories being read by two in every three journalists. Again, nearly all were happy to be telephoned as a reminder for a press event.

Let us look at some of the elements of a media relations campaign.

News releases Only issue news to those journals which will have a direct interest unless you want to damage your media reputation. Do not scatter stories to all. Always provide a contact name and telephone number. Be certain that the telephone is properly manned, if necessary, 24 hours a day, 365 days a year.

It takes many years of training and experience to be able to present information in the concise and direct style necessary for news releases to be used by editors. A basic writing ability is essential. But, with care and practice, an average writer can be developed into a good news writer.

There are some guidelines that may be helpful:

1. Develop your writing skill. Draft, redraft, edit, polish and perfect the

copy. Read publications and understand what makes news and how it is put together. Analyse the writing skills of good journalists. Understand the good, criticize the bad.

2. Always ask who, what, why, where and when and be sure that these questions are answered in every news story. Train yourself to eliminate as ruthlessly as you add. If material does not answer one of these questions, what is it doing in your story?

3. Write stories to suit the style of the publication. If, for practical reasons, your story has to go to a wider range of media, always draft it in the style to suit the most popular of these. Better still, produce different stories for different types of news outlet.

4. Always keep the copy tight, concise and factual. Never fudge an issue or create a misleading impression. Substantiate any claims. Separate fact from belief by putting the latter into quotes. (Research chief John Brown confirmed the vehicle exceeded 200 m.p.h. 'We believe it's the fastest in the world', said . . ., etc.)

5. Write the story from the point of view of the journalist. Although it is a statement from your organization, it should be presented so that it can be used directly in the publication with the minimum of editing. Comment, observation or speculation can only be included in a story, in quotes or footnotes.

6. Get the main newspoint into the first paragraph and preferably the first sentence. Organize the paragraphs so that the most newsworthy are at the top. This will allow the journalist to edit from the bottom. The paragraphs you can most easily afford to lose, therefore, should be the ones towards the end of the story.

7. Keep sentences short, use positive and not negative statements, use active verbs, avoid subordinate and inverted clauses, and cut out any subjective material or superlatives. Keep separate points in separate sentences. Break each collection of points into separate paragraphs.

8. Put the copy into modern journalistic style. Eliminate any old-fashioned phrases, formal or pompous language, jargon peculiar to the industry, cliches or colloquialisms that are not accepted as standard current English (or appropriate language).

9. When you have written your story, check through and make sure that it meets *all* these criteria. In particular, be certain that the news is at the *beginning*. Often draft news releases can afford to have paragraph one taken out!

10. Go through your copy, tighten, edit, improve, check all spellings and punctuation. Get someone else to read it before it goes for release. Ask them to criticize and query. Avoid becoming sensitive about your own copy. Learn to be self-critical. Push yourself to the highest standard possible.

Letters Publications like to receive authoritative letters on topics of interest to their readership. Be sure your company writes where relevant. Agree a corporate policy. Encourage regional personnel to write letters to appropriate media. Help them in their initial drafts. Be certain that any response to a published item is very fast; some letters can actually be sent by fax, telex, telephone or hand delivered. Look for opportunities to open a debate, as well as contributing to an existing discussion.

Interviews Within your organization will be some fascinating and authoritative people. Present them to selected media for interview. Prepare briefing notes, arrange a convenient time and place for the interview, provide travel arrangements, lunch or other facilities that would be hospitable, but no more. Brief the person interviewed and, separately, the journalist. Before the meeting takes place, both should know the areas to be covered.

Train your interview subjects in media techniques. Help your interviewee with any tricky questions that may be asked. By all means attend the interview to effect the introductions, pour the coffee or whatever. Do not take part unless the interview is going off the rails. In the worst case remember that you *can* stop an interview: you cannot ask a journalist to forget what has been said. Trust journalists and get them to trust you. Say as little off the record as possible. However, never lie or hide the truth. If the timing of a question or discussion is not convenient, then explain to them why you cannot help: offer to give them an early story as soon as it is possible.

Editor meetings Make sure that you regularly meet the key editors for your industry. They should know you well enough to be able to talk to you at any time they wish. Make sure that your meetings with them cover some items of substance and are not merely social occasions. Therefore, pick up a strong news story for each editor meeting; then follow it up every 6 or 12 months, as may be necessary. Arrange for key editors to meet relevant senior personnel within your organization if necessary (see 'Interviews' above).

Articles Many publications carry authoritative articles. Make sure you are monitoring all publications relevant to your industry. Recognize opportunities for articles. If you see a news story which is contrary to your company's views, suggest an article as a follow-up. If you see a trend in the industry that others may not be aware of, suggest an article. If one of your management colleagues introduces a new technique in his area, consider an article.

Always agree with the editor the deadline, length and style. And always meet the deadline. Clarify with the editor whether this article is to be published as a by-line piece from the company or as if it had been prepared by an independent journalist.

Edit drafts or background notes into acceptable journalistic style. Never allow yourself to be overruled by any manager who has less public relations experience. Take responsibility for final approval of all copy issued by your organization. Explain early to all managers preparing drafts that you will be editing this copy. If any executive is unreliable in delivering on time, then suggest that the main thoughts are put onto tape. Alternatively, ask to interview the executive.

Features Many publications carry regular features that look at particular subjects that will be of interest to readers. For example, home journals may regularly look at bathrooms. Industry journals may regularly look at marketing or exports. These often provide opportunities for contributions—again, perhaps by-lined by an executive of your company. Suggest a facility visit to your organization for the survey's editor. Alternatively, arrange an interview with a senior executive or provide company background notes.

To identify opportunities, ask relevant publications for their editorial features lists. Calendar those features that come up regularly at the same time each year. Write regularly to the features editor with new ideas.

Press office You have to have a press or information office to deal with media enquiries. There must be enough telephone lines to deal with the expected level of calls, including emergency situations. Be sure that there is a proper procedure for dealing with telephone press enquiries. Press officers must know to whom to turn for information. Every call must be answered immediately. If the information is not available, then the call must be returned within the time promised. Journalists respect public relations people who meet deadlines. Do not offer to call back if you know the information will not be available. Say so. Explain why. Do not be tempted to present information that you cannot give. Do not allow your colleagues to hold back information which is already openly available. Avoid unnecessary secrecy.

Be sure the press office holds up-to-date photographs of all the senior management, together with short current biographical details. Only use effective pictures and hold a range of situations—formal, in action and so on. Build a complete library of news photography in black and white, in colour negative and colour transparency. Cover, for example, all manufacturing processes, products, export activities, factory locations, the field work of your society/charity or other relevant items.

Make sure that all current statistical and financial information relating to the organization is readily available. Build a library of company information and standard articles which can be sent in the post, immediately on request. It is helpful if the press office is equipped with telex and facsimile transmission. (In the UK, subscription to one of the commercial news distribution services and a London messenger service is also invaluable.)

Read every newspaper and trade publication relevant to the industry. Senior executives must be advised of any relevant references. Follow up any news opportunities that result from this media monitoring. Make sure that there is a telephone number available 24 hours a day, 365 days a year. Make sure all public relations personnel have the telephone number of every key publication and the home numbers of senior executives.

At all stages the executive responsible for planning the public relations activity needs to relate the communications objectives to the sources of information available to these audiences. Across the world, the news scene changes rapidly—new publications, radio, television, and other media opportunities are constantly arising. The result has been a major increase in outlets for broad distribution of news. At the same time many audiences are bombarded with information and are becoming more selective.

The effective media relations executive should be able to balance the need for broad news distribution and targeting communications at narrower identified audiences and opinion leaders.

PLANNING MEDIA RELATIONS

The earlier checklists looked at broader questions to give some indication of the areas where decisions need to be made by management. The checklists that follow each chapter on techniques are more specific and try to look at each communications method in a practical way.

News releases

1. Do we have a programme of issuing regular news information?
2. Are we sending these to the journals we have identified that cover our agreed target audiences?
3. Do we consider carefully the timing of the release to get maximum news impact?
4. Have we up-to-date mailing lists of media, including named journals, as appropriate?
5. Do we select publications relevant to each story rather than using a standard general list?
6. Where possible, are we adapting the story to suit different publications?
7. Do we have a process for regularly updating this media and editor contact list?
8. Are we self-critical in ensuring that we only issue stories that have real news value?
9. Have we a procedure for controlling the number and frequency of stories released to each publication, radio or TV programme to avoid overkill?

10. Are we ensuring that each story is written to the shortest length reasonable?
11. Do we identify the news element right at the beginning of each story?
12. Does every news story offer a source for further information or comment, in addition to the public relations adviser?
13. Is every story complete with all names, facts, details and the answers to who, what, why, when and how?
14. Are we watching the writing style (see notes on drafting news stories) to ensure that it is appropriate to the target news editors?
15. Have we a system to compare actual coverage with the stories issued to enable us to develop news interest and style?
16. Do we put subjective observations or company comments into quotations?
17. Are we checking and approving these with the executive who is quoted?
18. Does he know how to deal with any media follow-up as a result of being quoted?
19. Are we ensuring that every story is impeccably presented?
20. Do we have a style guide to ensure that we are consistent and up-to-date in presentation, regardless of who may actually type or prepare the news story?

Articles and features

21. Are we taking every opportunity to write articles as part of our media relations campaign?
22. Do we monitor media to be aware of features or surveys where we might negotiate placing an article?
23. Have we asked publishing houses to put us on the mailing list for their editorial feature advance notices?
24. Are we developing a team of our management executives able and happy to draft articles?
25. Have we given them the training and guidance necessary to prepare these drafts?
26. Do they appreciate the need for their copy to be professionally edited by us to journalistic standards?
27. Have we suggested to our busier or less articulate potential authors the possibility of preparing draft copy through interview or on tape?
28. Are we negotiating each article with the appropriate editor well in advance of publication date?
29. Do we look at opportunities to provide background material which will make a feature for a publication staff-writer?
30. Do we also offer fully-prepared articles by-lined by one of our colleagues?
31. Do we ensure that all articles are appraised for consistency in copy style and editorial objectivity?

32. Have we considered certain articles with broader appeal for possible syndicated release?
33. Do we look at each article to see whether it could be adapted for different, non-competing publications?
34. Are we checking secondary audiences to whom we could mail reprints of favourable pieces?
35. Can we organize regular management discussions to review policy on articles and create ideas for new opportunities?

Picture stories

36. Are we considering captioned picture stories as an alternative to news releases?
37. Are we constantly looking at the opportunities for illustrating our news activity?
38. Do we have reliable photographers to meet head office and regional or overseas requirements?
39. Have we prepared a general brief on the organization for all photographers, so they understand what we are trying to achieve?
40. Do we individually brief every photographer on the requirements of each picture assignment?
41. Have we got an up-to-date and well-maintained photographic file to enable us to issue pictures for immediate press release?
42. Do we look at every photograph to see whether there are additional uses, for example, the annual report, notice boards and so on?
43. Do we regularly check our media photographic coverage with competitors and other similar organizations?
44. Are we issuing pictures to maintain our presence in those regular features where an article may not be practical or appropriate?
45. Have we checked the section in this book (Chapter 19) on achieving good photography?

Interviews and meetings

46. Are we regularly checking with our management colleagues on the opportunities for editor meetings or interviews?
47. Do we know all members of the executive team who might be suitable for media interviews?
48. Can we offer training, where necessary, to those who have the personality and potential but not the experience?
49. Do we prepare briefing notes in discussion with every management colleague who will be taking part in an interview?
50. Are we discussing the potential angles and direction of each interview with the editor concerned?

51. Do we send the company background, biography and briefing notes to the journalist well before the interview?
52. Have we identified potential tricky questions and agreed the policy on answers?
53. Is our interviewee fully briefed on these areas and the need to avoid off-the-record and off-the-cuff comments?
54. Are all the physical resources arranged, such as travel, interview room, telephone, hospitality and so on?
55. Have we clarified to both the interviewee and the journalist, the role of the public relations adviser in the interview?

General

56. Do we have proper systems for dealing with media enquiries—including the necessary procedures for dealing with crises?
57. Are there trained, experienced media executives able to provide information and other facilities?
58. Has our press office got all the necessary secretarial, administrative, library, filing, and other resources to provide an effective service?
59. Are we combining in our media relations the correct balance between broad distribution of information and efforts targeted to identified audiences?
60. What suggestions do we have for monitoring the effectiveness of our media relations and using this information to fine tune our programme.

EIGHTEEN

MEDIA CONFERENCES

PRESENTATION AND DISCUSSION IS THE KEY

An ill-planned or unnecessary media conference can spoil the potential for successful future events. If you waste journalists' time, do not present the right information, are not well organized—then you may well receive poor coverage of your event. Even worse, you will find it difficult to get them to report future activities, or attend other events.

Different rules apply to press receptions and to the media conferences we are discussing in this section. To clarify this point, a press reception is usually arranged to provide an opportunity for executives and media to meet, perhaps to provide background, often as a social or semi-social gathering at an event that the media are already attending—say, a tyre manufacturer's reception at a motor show. However, a media conference is a news event where new information is to be presented and *discussed* by the media.

Be very objective when considering a possible media or news conference. The first question to be asked is whether the conference is really necessary. If the information could be better handled by issuing a news story, arranging an interview or placing an article then it is probably not necessary to hold a news conference. It must be remembered that a weak conference may attract the media—but only once.

Some companies feel that they should hold an event because it is about time they met the press or they want to introduce a senior executive or, even, that there is sufficient budget to allow such an event. Unless there is hard news, resist this temptation: perhaps you could hold a suitable reception when the opportunity arises—say, at your next national exhibition.

There are a number of factors which would make a media conference advisable:

The news angle It is essential that there is a strong, urgent news angle. A review of company progress or update on the market is unlikely to be strong enough. Ask yourself if the journalists you propose inviting will be as enthusiastic about attending when they know the story.

Discussion opportunity If the implications of the news require discussion, then a media conference might provide the ideal opportunity. If the news needs to be interpreted in different ways, by different publications or by the broadcast media, it can be sensible to call the journalists together to give them the opportunity to ask questions.

The personality aspect Some new developments have a human relations aspect and this can be difficult to put over in a printed news story. If you have a good news story *and* a magnificent boffin or a powerful new marketing director, then this might be welcomed by your industry journalists wishing to establish contact with these executives.

Technical complexity On occasions, the sheer complexity of the story makes this difficult in the printed form; this may mean that journalists will appreciate the question and answer nature of a conference. This might apply in high technology sectors, or with a new campaign launched by an environmental group, or a major change in a company's overseas investment programme.

Direct relevance Some announcements are of such importance to specific industry sectors that the relevant specialized journalists expect to hear these first hand. (If there are only a few publications concerned, this might be better done as a personal briefing with the editors concerned, possibly over a working lunch.)

Location Your capital city is probably most convenient for trade press but may be inconvenient for regional press, radio and television. Try to judge whether the interest on location, say, is stronger than the convenience and possibly better attendance of an event in the capital or regional capital. If it is a completely new process, test facility or production development, or an historic building renovation, or conservation project, then a site visit may be appropriate. If it is a product launch, a production expansion, or an appeal announcement, then it may be better held in the city.

Air Products successfully opened a new plant located in an inaccessible part of Cheshire, England, with a press conference at their head office. This utilized up-to-the-minute photo displays and a television link to site for the switch-on. Today, in the UK, Europe, the US, and some other countries, television satellite links are possible.

Journalists on national newspapers or consumer publications are most unlikely to spend a day visiting a remote facility unless it is of the utmost significance. One persuasive argument to get heavyweight journalists from behind their desks is to give them the opportunity to meet the top people they cannot normally reach.

The pressures on the limited time of trade journalists equally must be considered. An excursion may be justified if the story is strong enough, or if they will see processes or meet people important in their industry. Some companies have special facilities and a reputation that ensures good attendance. JCB created an imaginative demonstration centre at their main plant near Uttoxeter in England. At this, 'ballets' of their excavation and other vehicles are performed complete with lights, music, commentary and film. (These vehicles also go 'on tour' to events around the country.)

Venue In-plant or hotel? Again, the decision depends on what is to be seen. Often a media conference will be timed to run over lunch. Therefore, catering facilities will be important—this will probably give a conference venue or hotel the edge.

Often a convenient hotel room is all that is required. But sometimes an imaginative and relevant alternative can be located. Effective media conferences have been held in universities, hospitals, training ships, historic castles, even aircraft. One US manufacturer launched a heating system at a restaurant overlooking the tropical house at the zoo! An essential point is to check carefully any possible venue personally. Make sure that the standards are acceptable. Novelty will not excuse poor facilities, inconvenient location or bad catering.

Timing Do not run an event longer than necessary. Complete the business briskly. Journalists under pressure will be able to get their story quickly and leave. Those who want to probe further will be able to stay on. Most successful press conferences are held late morning or late afternoon. It enables them to run on to refreshments, buffet, or even lunch or dinner, as appropriate.

Try to allow a few minutes for latecomers at the start of your conference; this can be done by arranging the start to run over coffee or drinks.

Hospitality Your guests should be treated as important business guests—in other words, as appropriate to the occasion. If the event is to run over lunchtime, a buffet is normally preferable to a formal sit-down lunch, that way people can circulate. Hospitality should be good—though not lavish. There's an old editor's saying that still holds good—'What counts is news, not booze.'

A formal lunch might be best for a handful of senior financial journalists meeting the chairman. A buffet would be more suitable for several dozen journalists.

Programme Try to plan to complete the business *before* the less formal hospitality part. Lunch before the business should be avoided even when travel times may mean a delayed lunch.

A typical programme for a city centre event might be:

11.30 Arrival, sign in, presspacks and coffee,
11.45 Introduction by a senior director,
11.55 Product demonstration (or, as appropriate),
12.15 Questions and answers,
12.30 Drinks and lunch.

Any travel, assembly and meeting times would be additional for, say, a media conference on site.

Reception One of the public relations team should receive your guests, check them in (against the list of acceptances), hand out any press information and introduce them to the senior director hosting the event. The public relations reception official needs to have the necessary cloakroom facilities, a telephone, typewriter, train times and other information journalists might require.

Badges are more acceptable these days, though some journalists still object. Certainly your own staff should carry their names and positions in large clear lettering on their badges. Avoid guest badges that can tear delicate materials or adhesive ones that will mark suede and leather.

Invitation Draw up a press list and send your invitations between three and six weeks in advance. The date must be checked to ensure it does not clash with any competing or major public event: in the UK this can be done with the *UK Press Gazette*, the Press Association, the IPR, the PRCA and your own trade association diaries.

Printed invitations are sometimes useful to set a theme but are not essential. A personal letter with a reply-paid card is probably best. Be sure you give enough detail to enable the journalist to judge whether he wishes to attend. Draw up the acceptance list and ring round nearer the date to check any non-respondents. Confirm any substitutes or replacements.

Content Try to put life, style, activity and pace into the event. Avoid unnecessary gimmicks. Always demonstrate a product or system where you can. Keep it smooth flowing and professional. Use film, video, tape, slides, charts, models as relevant and necessary. Ensure you only use articulate and well-informed speakers. Keep the number presenting to a minimum. Make the presentation positive and direct but not a sales pitch. Avoid panels of 'worthies'. Train and rehearse your speakers. Brief all other participants, particularly on handling the media and dealing with questions. Agree answers on all difficult areas.

Presspack Printed information supporting the story should be collated into a suitable media pack. A specially printed folder may be relevant if your organization will be holding many such events. A standard folder is acceptable provided it is attractive: it is the contents that count.

The folder will contain the news story and main news picture. Other items might include copies of speeches, background industry statistics, personality pictures and biographies, organization profile. Do not overload with unnecessary material. Include no standard items: all copy should be prepared particularly for this event. Certainly think carefully before including publicity items such as sales leaflets.

Follow-up On the day of the event, mail the information pack to those journalists who are interested but did not attend. Note any special requests from attendees and process these—such as requests for pictures or facility visits. Issue appropriate thanks. Collate all costs and check against original budget. Hold a debriefing session with the responsible executives to analyse good and bad points. Record these to influence future projects.

Media conferences can achieve very dramatic results. From recent experience, a media conference has enabled one office equipment manufacturer to sell the whole of his first year's production; a small provincial company to significantly cut staff turnover; a manufacturer to improve relations with factory neighbours and a construction company to secure better financial backing from the city.

To make a media conference work, however, you must help your organization define exactly what you intend it to achieve and ensure that these are realistic aims. Your immediate market at the conference is the journalists who attend. Their primary responsibility is to their readers, listeners or viewers.

If what your organization has is of relevance and news interest to the public served by the media you will have an effective conference. If not ... you should not have called one!

ORGANIZING MEDIA CONFERENCES

1. Do we consider running a media conference only when this is the best method of conveying the information to the media?
2. Have we clearly differentiated between those occasions when a news conference, a reception or a facility visit might be most suitable?

3. Do we always check that the date is convenient and does not clash with any other competitive event?

4. Is there a critical path outlined and agreed which will take us through from start to finish?

5. Have we clearly identified the objectives that have to be achieved in calling the media together?

6. Are we providing adequate opportunity for questions and media feedback?

7. Have we detailed and agreed the programme for the event?

8. Do we have a proposed timetable that allows adequate time for each element and flexibility to cope with minor changes on the day?

9. Have we looked at the necessary travel arrangements to and from the event and considered poor weather alternatives?

10. Does our programme require special facilities at the venue and have we checked that these can be provided?

11. How will we ensure that all of these facilities have been tested and are up to standard, for example, sound and audio-visual systems?

12. Will our proposed programme for the day require presentations by any of our colleagues?

13. Have we advised our speakers that they will be required to prepare their papers in advance for approval and attend rehearsals?

14. What arrangements have we made to support them with appropriate visual aids?

15. When will we decide which media representatives will be invited to attend this event?

16. Have we ensured that all arrangements will be confirmed so that these invitations can go out between six and three weeks in advance?

17. How will we record who accepts the invitation and contact any proposed substitutes?

18. Are we going to be following up nearer the date and, if so, by further letter or telephone?

19. What arrangements will we be making to cover the possible news interests of those who are unable to attend the event?

20. Have we looked at the material that will be necessary for the presspack, including news stories, biographies, photography, speeches?

21. When will we have a final run through all the necessary catering, travel, security and other on-site arrangements?

22. Will everyone attending the press event be fully briefed on his or her role and responsibility?

23. In particular, will they all be briefed on how to deal with press enquiries and questions which will arise during the informal discussions?

24. Have we prepared a list of difficult questions and agreed the policy on any sensitive issues, including those topics which can only be handled by nominated executives?

25. Do we have a plan to follow up this event with personal letters, reminders, additional information and so on?
26. Have we costed all the special requirements so that we can agree the overall budget?
27. Have the objectives, checklist, timetable, programme, critical path and budget been approved by relevant colleagues, where necessary?
28. How does this news event relate to other activity within the broad media relations campaign?
29. Can we check the effectiveness of this media event in comparison with other alternative communications techniques?
30. Have we established the criteria by which we will be assessing the success of the event when it is completed?

NINETEEN

PHOTOGRAPHY

GOOD PICTURES INCREASE MESSAGE IMPACT

Senior public relations professionals place considerable emphasis on the ability of recruits to be able to handle the language—both spoken and written. This is sensible but it might be helpful if equal emphasis were to be put on visual skills. Few public relations people have a really strong feeling for design and consequently prefer to think their ideas through verbally. To take just one obvious example, an effective way of adding a pictorial element to ideas is to use photography. Most public relations programmes can be increased in effectiveness many times by combining verbal and pictorial elements. Studies have shown that the retention rate for information can be doubled if verbal presentations are supported pictorially. It is still true that a picture is worth a lot of words (if not, the proverbial thousand!)

The usage of stories by editors, for example, often increases very substantially when they are accompanied by good pictures. Many readers skim through publications and pictures can stop the eye at least as well as a punchy headline. My own consultancy has handled campaigns where it was agreed *as a policy* that no story would ever be put out unless it could be accompanied with a good picture. If there were no good pictures ... then there would be no story.

The way to get good photographs that are used is *not* for the public relations person to be his own photographer. Photography is a highly skilled and professional job and requires a substantial investment in equipment and training alone. The emphasis on the role of the professional communicator is inevitably changed when client, press and other colleagues see him acting as an amateur photographer. If you need good pictures, use a good photographer. The responsibility of the communications adviser is better met by deploying resources rather than *personally* undertaking as much communications activity as possible.

Be certain to brief your photographer properly. Exactly what are the pictures intended to communicate? Where will they be used? How? Will you be wanting these in black and white, colour negative or colour transparency? Are these for records only? Do the verticals need to be vertical? Are these personality pictures or intended to create an impression? Has the photographer scope for the use of his own ideas? Will he be able to stop the activity? Has he got to capture the event as it takes place? Who will be there to assist him on the day? Will he be able to make a recce in advance? What will he be able to change if it does not match up to your instructions? . . . These are the type of questions that you should attempt to answer in the brief.

Build a list of trusted photographers with whom you can work on a regular basis. Sometimes you may need more than one photographer in each location—because of their special skills and abilities. A studio pack-shot may require completely different disciplines to an animated portrait of the chief executive . . . or a dramatic shot of the new process in operation . . . or the presentation of a charity cheque.

TREAT YOUR PHOTOGRAPHERS AS COLLEAGUES

Get to know your photographers. Get them to respect the importance you attach to the quality of good pictures. Treat them as professionals. Demand that they produce the best results. Attend as many sessions as you can yourself until they have an understanding of what you are trying to achieve.

Care about pictures. Look at pictures. See how they are constructed and edited on the page. Look at the photographic work of your colleagues and competitors. Flip through the presspacks at an exhibition. See how other people are managing photography. Watch the trade press and see what pictures get used.

A *little* technical understanding will help. Ask your photographers questions. Get them to come in to talk to your colleagues at briefing sessions. Get to know when telephoto or a wide angle lens may be better. Understand when you need 35 mm and when 5 × 4, when colour negative is better than transparency.

If your photographer is good, let him get on with it. But if you feel that the picture he is getting is not the best, let him take that one . . . but *then* suggest your own alternative. Direct this the way *you* would like it to be. Never rely on luck, particularly when you will not have the opportunity to take the picture again. If you *think* that the chairman had his eyes closed, or the 100-year-old pensioner had his back to the camera, help the photographer by stepping in and asking him politely to do it again. If you have the confidence and poise, you can do this acceptably with practically anyone (except, of course, the royals!).

Analyse the quality of pictures you produce. Constantly look at ways of improving them. Discuss these points with the photographer so that he can put his views. Hold regular briefing sessions with your staff to review photography standards.

Use the pictures properly. Good photographs can enliven many communications media including print, displays, exhibitions and conferences. When working with the media, the public relations specialist has to prove he is a picture professional. Identify those publications that use pictures. Decide when an exclusive photo might get you better coverage. Get to know the picture editors. Look at different shots for two or three different publications. Find out the deadlines.

Know those publications where colour can be used—even on the cover. Negotiate exclusive colour shots with the editor. Take your first pictures speculatively. Once you have proved you can deliver the goods, the picture editor will come back for more. Work hard on your reputation for producing good, useable photographs.

Learn to work with photographers assigned by journals to cover your stories. They are not on your payroll or commissioned by your organization but they will appreciate your help. Provide all the necessary facilities for the magazine or newspaper photographer. Suggest any angles or special shots your inside knowledge suggests.

Learn when to call in a news agency photographer. Although there will be no charge for news event coverage, their time is valuable. You want to get a reputation for providing good news picture situations, efficiently organized. General interest pictures can sometimes be arranged as an exclusive with one agency—in the UK, say, the Press Association. Good pictures may appear in dozens of magazines and provincial papers.

TARGET YOUR PICTURES FOR TOP PRESS COVERAGE

Really strong news pictures can be negotiated with the popular dailies. They will normally cover national news stories. More unusual situations can often be negotiated as exclusives.

To take some examples. The opening of a new dam by a member of the royal family might be attended by most national newspapers but may not get much coverage unless something unexpected happens. Such events are not always welcome! The coverage that results from the marquee blowing down or the minister falling asleep in the seat next to the Queen might not be the news angle expected. Therefore, see if you can create your own picture situation. Would it be possible that the switch-on could release a torrent of water to give the photographers a dramatic backdrop to the VIPs? Might the ceremony be better at the *bottom* of the dam, with its massive dominating height behind, rather than at the top where the shots may simply suggest a modest strip of concrete across a lake? Think about it in picture terms.

The launching of a charity appeal by an international zoologist, say, will require invitations to be organized. If the event is not news it will get no coverage—even if every newspaper is represented. All picture editors reject dozens of photos for each one used. Photographers are often covering assignments in case something unexpected happens. Their attendance does *not* mean the event has automatic news value.

Rather than taking a chance on misfortune creating your news coverage, plan the unexpected. If your famous zoologist is concerned about penguin welfare, ask him to launch the appeal at the zoo. Better still persuade him to go into the penguin pool. Better still put him into a penguin suit in the penguin pool. If he objects, discuss whether the publicity or his dignity is most important. If the latter, perhaps you need a more extrovert show business celebrity to launch your appeal—and leave the zoologist to do the serious bit.

Sometimes these picture situations are better arranged as exclusives. For example, perhaps the zoologist has produced an esoteric study of penguins. It might make a good picture for one of the popular newspapers to arrange an exclusive of him sharing breakfast at his laboratory bench with one of his penguins.

The serious national dailies appreciate high/quality industrial pictures for their business pages. Consider an exclusive on that new process or major export order. In the UK this might be for the *Financial Times*, the *Guardian* or the business pages of the *Sunday Times* and so on. Some papers will accept prints. Others prefer to use their own photographers.

Remember that the television companies like to use transparencies behind news items. In the UK, transport executives have commented on how many road transport stories feature most attractive pictures of Roadline vehicles. This is because the company had the intelligence to send a selection of excellent transparencies to all television stations. This gave the TV news staff access to a good transport picture when a good transport story comes up.

Make the pictures work for you: they may be the best investment from your budget that you will make. An investment in developing skills in using pictures will repay itself many times over. Photography is integral to so many aspects of communication.

Photographic briefing sheet
Copy to photographer: copy to project file

Any Company Limited
Address
Telephone

Commissioning executive:
Telephone:

Available to discuss:

Brief for photography
Company—   Instructions to—   Operator—

Job description
Location: Special factors:
Reconnaisance: Lighting requirements:
Site contact: Assistance on site:
Telephone: Models/props required:

Pictures required for use:

	Format	35 mm	6 cm × 6 cm	5 in × 4 in	Other
Film stock suggested:	B/w neg.				
	Colour neg.				
	Transparency				

Agency: Deliver to:

Please discuss and confirm costing. An official order will be issued. No invoice can be accepted without quoting an order number.

Signed: Date:

Chart 19.1 The public relations adviser must treat the photographer fairly. As well as a proper brief, he needs to know any possible complications—these might not only affect the quality of the finished pictures but the price of the job. A simple briefing sheet issued by the public relations executive can be an invaluable aid to both parties.

ACHIEVING GOOD PHOTOGRAPHY

See also the section on media relations (Chapter 17).

1. In our communications campaign, which media provide opportunities for photography, for example:

media relations   annual reports
house journals   promotional literature
exhibitions   television
seminars/conferences   slide presentations
receptions   others?

2. Can we collate a list of all organization activities, products, services, locations, personnel, where we will require good photography?
3. Do we have established photo files for this material or are there areas where good pictures are required?
4. With the exception of unexpected news coverage, can we prepare a schedule over, say, 12 months, to photograph all the organization's aspects as listed?
5. What existing photographic resource do we have, for example, a staff photographer or a regular supplier?
6. Can we identify any of the photographic requirements that might need a specialist to handle, for example, high speed or high fashion photography?
7. Are we sure that our existing photographer is capable of providing the quality of work necessary?
8. If so, can we discuss the balance of these picture requirements with our staff photographer or preferred supplier to produce a shooting schedule over the agreed period?
9. If not, can we train our photographer, recruit a new one or use him as picture manager to control a suitable outside photographer?
10. Can we identify the potential uses for this photographic material so we can brief the photographer:

    (a) black and white print—for most press use,
    (b) colour print—for display or presentation use,
    (c) colour transparency—for publication and slide use?

11. Do we appreciate the basic camera formats:

    (a) 35 mm—fast, lightweight cameras; very flexible and produce slides suitable for standard slide presentation; interchangeable lens; limited enlargement from negatives,
    (b) 6 cm × 6 cm—single lens; often has interchangeable backs for different film stock; better quality larger format, but heavier camera; less shots per roll which increases costs where many shots required; good reproduction; (twin lens format, now outdated),
    (c) 5 × 4 (or larger)—flat sheet film cameras, best quality, often with rising front which means photographer can correct perspective; bulky, heavy and slow; not suitable for press work but good for top quality reproduction?

12. Do we have a procedure for briefing photographers to cover use of pictures, format, subject, who will be directing, when prints or slides will be needed and so on?
13. Can we motivate our photographers to produce imaginative, creative work by giving them the assistance and encouragement they require?
14. Do we ensure the maximum cooperation of, say, our production colleagues during photographic location assignments?

15. Are we allowing adequate time and budget for good photography, particularly being prepared to arrange for reconnaissance visits for major projects?
16. Do we supervise every photographic shoot possible?
17. Where an expert with a good photographic eye cannot attend to help the photographer, do we ensure that there is a proper discussion to supplement the written brief or order?
18. Have we taken warm, believable photographs of all our senior executives?
19. Do we insist on proper lighting for every photographic subject, rejecting dull pictures, straight flash and hard shadows?
20. When shooting on location do we check the background, ensure all areas are clear and clean, move unnecessary items and so on?
21. Are we careful in the use of our product or company name to ensure it is not too blatant or offensive?
22. When we use personnel in shots, do we check they are wearing the proper clothing and safety equipment, look natural and they give written clearance (on an appropriate form) for us to use the pictures?
23. Do we examine publications that use pictures to check those that work and those that could be improved?
24. Do we discuss the results of each photographic assignment with the photographer to see what was successful and how this might be improved on future occasions?
25. Could we invite our main photographers to talk to our colleagues about their resources, skills and views on photography?
26. Are we monitoring the photographic work of our competitors to be sure we are constantly improving standards?
27. Have we agreed an adequate budget to allow us to take advantage of all photographic opportunities?
28. Can we check that we have equally effective photographic procedures and resources for all our regional and/or overseas operations?
29. Is there a system for exchanging photographic material and recording actually what is available?
30. Can we monitor all photographic activity and use of budget to identify cost effectiveness and ways of improving this aspect of communications?

TWENTY

RADIO AND TELEVISION

The ability of radio and television to reach an audience can be appreciated from the cost of the advertising! Advertisers spend this sort of money because of the audience it delivers, the attention it achieves and, most important, the results it produces. Yet both radio and television are available media for good editorial ideas: too few of these come through public relations channels.

Programme opportunities Local stations are desperate for local news. In the UK, national radio programmes like 'You and Yours', 'Science Now', 'The Food Programme', regularly use commercial news items. Television programmes such as 'Panorama', 'That's Life', 'Tomorrow's World' also use commercial news items, presented in the right way.

Local and national radio and TV can reach millions. Programme makers are all in the ideas business. The sheer volume of radio and television currently being broadcast in the UK, means that there is a massive demand for good material. The same is true across much of Europe, in the US, Canada and in most industrialized countries of the world. In the US, there are nearly three times as many radios in use as the total population! Over 15 million are bought every year and it is estimated that 95 per cent of the population listen to radio every week with over 80 per cent listening every day. It is probably the major source of information for most US citizens. (Current trends in the UK would seem to reflect this development.) Yet a study carried out in the US by Audio Features showed that around half of the radio news editors surveyed were rarely contacted by public relations executives. Broadcasting standards are generally high but programme makers are as approachable and receptive to good ideas as newspaper journalists.

In the UK, the annual, *Who's Who in Broadcasting*, will help identify the people who put together programmes. A news release may be acceptable to put a factual news story in front of the news editor, though the personal approach is nearly always best.

Radio and television are immediate media. Stories will not last. Timing is critical. News stories need to be presented quickly to editors. Facilities for interview, location recording, studio guests and so on must be provided *immediately* they are required. Deadlines are tight and, with electronic news gathering, getting tighter. Live material from remote locations can now be directly slotted into news bulletins.

Some US associations and unions have established their own studios so they can offer TV stations an instant spokesman on key news topics. Some of these links are by satellite so they can transmit across the nation and, eventually, across the world.

But timing is important in another sense. The presentation has to be crisp, immaculate and professional. The radio and television audience have the ability to switch off or change channels almost immediately. As a result of this, broadcasters are constantly working to keep a high level of immediate interest in their output.

The effective public relations adviser will be creating broadcast news opportunities. But he needs to know how to handle a radio or television journalist when approached to provide information or facilities. Check what programme it is for. Will it be live or taped? Will the contribution be edited? Who else will be appearing? Who will conduct the interview or discussion? What topics or questions will be covered? Will there be an opportunity to see/hear the final programme before transmission? Will there be a live debate to counter any misunderstandings or damaging assertions from other participants?

Training There are many excellent training courses available to help you or your colleagues present your organization's case in the best possible way. Make sure that all senior executives who may be required to broadcast are trained in the techniques. Decide whether you, as public relations adviser, are going to act as a spokesman or the behind-the-scenes negotiator.

Radio interviews These tend to be less aggressive than television. This does not necessarily make them easier. The listener will be tending to have other things to concentrate on—driving the car or digging the garden. The power of the spokesman's personality has to come over positively. Gestures (or a fine face) will not help. The speaker has to get the interest into the words and voice. This is a skill that *can* be developed.

Ironically, although the speaker cannot be seen on radio, the studio situation can be surprisingly confusing. Often there is only a short informal build-up to radio interviews. The interview subject can be sitting down and, in seconds, going out live over the airwaves.

Always take advantage of any rehearsal opportunity. Run through the points, checking tricky questions. But, remember the interviewer reserves the right to ask *anything* he likes. This might include subjects that have not been discussed in the briefing session. If the interview is taped, the interviewee can refuse to answer; the silence will have to be edited out.

Television studio interviews On television, the concentration of the attention is onto the small studio area where the guest and the interviewer will be sitting. Therefore, it is easier to concentrate on the subject in hand. However, the surge of adrenalin can help some people sharpen their performance but stuns others into mumbling incoherence.

There is no substitute for experience. Watch television and see how it works. See how people deal with questions. Tape as many interviews as possible and rehearse your own answers to the questions. Learn to identify the effective techniques, the irritating habits.

News and feature programmes Learn the differences between the type of programme presented. News items are highly condensed, feature items might be slightly longer, while full-length investigative-type of programmes can often be hostile.

For example, many members of a waterways holiday industry group in England participated willingly with a television company to help make a film about the industry. When it appeared, it turned out to be a critical view of the damage being caused to the waterways, much of it, the programme claimed, by leisure boats. Several sequences featured what the broadcasters considered to be good television. The participants were very critical of these, such as shots with dead fish in the foreground, the use of telephoto lens to foreshorten perspective and make the waterways appear busier, unidentified waste being ejected into the water.

In another case, a developer working on a new shopping centre in a provincial university town provided facilities for a television company. The developer was horrified to find that the finished film used footage of attractive existing shops (implying they would have to close) that were not even in the development area: it avoided any shots of the derelict, characterless properties that were due to close.

Public relations practitioners need to be very clear and, if necessary, firm with the programme makers to avoid such unhappy situations. Every seasoned public relations professional will recount his own horror stories. Most arise from a simple misunderstanding over the objectives of the programme makers; they want to make interesting, relevant programmes, not promote your vested interests. Most will play this straight but some may be devious; all will put their viewers' interests ahead of yours—wouldn't you, in their place?

Special interest programmes Both radio and television present special interest programmes. These tend to be less aggressive because the broadcasters are working in the same industry week after week. ... These feature programmes are dependent on the degree of cooperation that they are going to get from people who work in these special interest sectors such as gardening, antiques, motoring or leisure. This does not stop the broadcasters being hard hitting, but it does ensure that they are reasonably accurate and fair in any criticism.

Be sure you know what the broadcaster is aiming at before you or one of your executives agrees to cooperate. Ask who else is appearing. Sometimes the name of the programme will tell you clearly the angle. The researcher may tell you the evidence to be used in other interviews.

Location interviews There are a number of ways that interviews can be organized. With major news events, a participant may be stopped and a camera or microphone thrust at him.

Be sure your spokesman is not caught out by such situations. If he has been in negotiation over a proposed plant closure, consider the possibility of an interviewer standing on the steps of the offices when your personnel director comes out. Think beforehand about what he is to say. If this is limited by the negotiations, construct something which will still give the broadcasters a piece of useful television or tape. However, remember that *you* are in charge. It is quite acceptable for your spokesman to politely excuse himself and break away when he has said all he wishes.

Telephone interviews On occasions, your organization will be asked to give a telphone interview: this should be resisted if possible. The quality will be bad; you have no control over the editing and the usage of the material—the viewer or listener even may get the impression that it was not important enough for your company representative to go to the studio.

If your executive is in a studio interview, he may well have a down-the-line interview—in fact, talking to a studio monitor. Your spokesman has to look as though he is having a real-life conversation with the interviewer. The best advice is to ignore the electronics and talk to just one real person.

The same principle applies on down-the-line radio interviews, where that 'real' person may be a microphone in front of the studio guest.

Panel discussions Advanced preparation, as always, is helpful. Consider the points you would like your executive to get over. It is not always a good idea to be the first person into a discussion. Equally, he should not let the discussions go too far before he starts to make points.

Make sure your spokesman puts over your organization's views effectively. Be sure he finishes when he has finished. Remind your spokesman that he should be quite prepared to put normal politeness quietly to one side. Warn him against being brow-beaten by the chairman: the interviewee must answer the question in the way he would like. Do not encourage him to be too clever by turning the question into the one that he would have liked to have been asked. This can only be done by *very* professional interviewees.

Syndicated radio interviews In the UK, there are now several organizations which will produce an interview on tape, syndicated to local stations.

The basic principles still apply. However, as your organization is paying for the service, you receive more help in the preparation. Remember that the final radio tape has to stand up to broadcast standards or it will not get used. The syndicating companies will not allow the interview to become soft. They want—and *you* want—good usable material.

Studio interviews Face-to-face interviews are invaluable because your speaker is not competing for attention, though he is competing for the time. If the interview is live, then he will know how much time he has. Because of this, there is likely to have been more discussion beforehand about the areas to be covered.

If the interview is to be filmed and edited, its length might depend on the amount of interest that the speaker is able to generate. Never allow a 5-minute interview that will be cut down to 30 seconds on-screen.

Consider carefully the points you want your spokesman to put over. He may need to identify the questions that are to be asked in order to weave these into his answers. Always treat the interviewer as a professional trying to do a professional job. His only major advantage is that he will have more experience. Do not try to challenge him on his own area of professionalism. But remember that he is extremely unlikely to know as much about the sector your spokesman is discussing.

Never bluff. Handle naïve questions politely. If the interviewer is asking a simple question it is because the viewers or listeners would like to ask the same simple question. There are many ways of presenting the truth but avoid misrepresentations. Listen carefully to the stance that the interviewer is taking. Quite often he will be representing the public at large. This is perfectly fair: you need to judge whether he has got a better measure of public feeling than yourself. You *should* have, for you are working in your sector everyday. If you need to challenge an assumption ('Many people believe...'), do it firmly but politely, using evidence where possible: 'I can understand you believing that, but our research shows that 80 per cent of the public...'

Broadcast guidelines You must put adequate preparation into what you or your spokesman is to say. Do not rely on being a spontaneous speaker. Concentrate on the good news and avoid temptations to justify yourself. Do not allow the interviewer to get on top of the situation. Keep your cool, concentrate on the essentials. Do not be diverted. Learn to convert technicalities into simple lay language. Do not say anything on-air or off-air that you might regret later. Prepare for yourself or your executive a brief of the main points you wish to cover.

Do not drink (under any circumstances) before the interview. Wear clothes appropriate to the situation. Avoid annoying mannerisms. Concentrate on what *you* want to say, not on what *they* want to say. Think of interesting ways of illustrating your points. Keep it enthusiastic. Avoid jargon. Talk through the interviewer to the audience. Do not allow yourself to be interrupted. Correct any inaccuracies in the questions.

Look honest, sound honest and be honest—then you and your organization might be believed.

More and more businesses are organizing themselves to handle media investigations in a thorough and professional way. For many years journalists had free rein and could inflict considerable damage. The fault lay in the lack of awareness by many organizations of a need to prepare for such situations.

Investigative television reporting will continue to get better and fairer, as organizations become better equipped to cope with the special requirements of the medium. The public relations adviser must know how to work with the broadcast media in his or her work in improving communications. These media will continue to increase in importance in projecting the organization's messages.

CREATING BROADCAST OPPORTUNITIES

Policy

1. Do we have a policy to take advantage of broadcast opportunities to communicate our messages?
2. Have we identified which of our audiences can be reached through radio and television?
3. Have we looked at our list of agreed audiences and tried to identify particular radio and television programmes which will reach these people?
4. Can we compare such broadcast opportunities with other communications such as press and house journals to ensure we are fully covering all audiences?
5. Are we organized to handle the special requirements of news and feature opportunities on radio and television?
6. Do we issue our news stories to relevant special interest programmes or appropriate radio and television stations?
7. Are we preparing special news stories for the broadcast media, when these seem appropriate?

8. Have we identified the key journalists and editors likely to be interested in our news activities?
9. Do we maintain personal contacts with those journalists who are directly relevant?
10. Are we inviting broadcast journalists to attend company events that may be of news or feature interest to them?
11. Do we have a system of monitoring such opportunities, updating our journalist records, recording and reporting on the coverage, and so on?
12. Can we provide the special facilities that might be required for radio and television such as interview rooms and trained spokesmen, particularly should these arise as a result of an emergency?
13. Do we have an efficient system for handling all broadcast enquiries and ensuring these are advised to the public relations department?
14. Have we established who may deal with any special enquiries, for example, at local level or regional level?
15. Is there a policy that all enquiries should be dealt with by the public relations manager or does he act as an adviser to local management?

Radio

16. Have we considered issuing syndicated taped interviews with executives to provide local radio feature material?
17. When discussing a particular radio item do we clarify for which programme this might be intended?
18. Can we find out what audience we will be reaching?
19. Does this affect the type of presentation, which spokesman we might nominate, the factual background and briefing necessary?
20. How long will the broadcast interview be, so that we can appreciate the depth that might be possible in the discussion?
21. Will the interview be broadcast live or will it be recorded?
22. Can we hear the tape played back before broadcasting or editing?
23. Have we nominated a trained spokesman able to handle the proposed discussion areas?
24. Can we hold a run-through of potential problem areas before meeting the interviewer?
25. Does he have the agreed policy answer on sensitive points?
26. Has our interviewee all the facts necessary to answer all likely questions intelligently?
27. Can we agree the key three or four organization points that we wish to put over in the interview?
28. Have we checked that our interviewee has these noted on a card to act as a reminder?
29. Can we avoid the telephone or doorstep interview and persuade the interviewer to use our special radio room or invite our spokesman to the studio?

30. Have we checked through with our spokesman the base points:

(a) speak in simple short sentences,
(b) leave the microphone and voice levels to the experts,
(c) do not use any jargon or shop-talk,
(d) keep your voice enthusiastic,
(e) answer the questions asked,
(f) but use these to lead into other interesting areas,
(g) do not be deferential to the interviewer,
(h) be firm in correcting any mistakes in their questions,
(i) but keep responses polite and calm,
(j) avoid spontaneous analogies or metaphors,
(k) back up claims with facts or evidence,
(l) always use positive examples and avoid negatives,
(m) discuss only your organization,
(n) avoid speculating on competitors or other third parties,
(o) keep away from any alcohol before the interview,
(p) do not use jokes or ad libs in any serious interview,
(q) remember that you are the official representative of the organization,
(r) plus any other factors specific to our case?

Television general

31. Have we established whether any participation is for news or feature use and in which programme?
32. Do we know what audience this will be reaching and how this relates to our defined audiences?
33. Will this affect the type of presentation or our choice of spokesman, back-up information and so on?
34. Can we find out the likely length of the transmitted item so that we can run the interview as close to this as is practical?
35. Will we be able to see the filmed/taped item particularly if any editing is proposed?

TV features

36. Can we arrange to see the completed programme before transmission to check how our contribution relates to other material?
37. Is the subject so sensitive or liable to distortion that we will insist on this as part of our agreement to provide speakers and/or facilities?
38. If so, have we carefully drafted this agreement to give us the power to back our position?
39. Have we asked the programme makers to tell us in writing what they wish to film and/or discuss before we agree to provide facilities?

40. Should we ask to have a live studio discussion immediately following the filmed documentary at which we will be represented?

TV news

41. If we are handling an urgent news situation on site have we established which programme, when and how long?
42. Are we coping with a crew that can transmit live material (through ENG—electronic news-gathering systems), can tape or is shooting on film, with or without location sound?
43. Do we understand the implications of each method of observing our organization:

    (a) 'live' means limited control and immediate impact,
    (b) taped means some control but allows editing by the programme makers,
    (c) film slows down the time to transmission and almost certainly means editing?

44. Are our procedures properly organized so that we are prepared and able to deal with urgent news demands at very short notice?
45. If we are handling an emergency and access to some locations is difficult, can we offer visuals, charts or graphics?
46. Is it better to provide controlled shooting of our site/facility rather than trying to enforce a pointless ban that will be broken by telephoto lens, snorkel cameras or helicopters?
47. Can we be as cooperative as is practical in providing information, background details, the latest developments, and trained, articulate spokespeople to present these?
48. Have we ensured that all our colleagues and all visiting media representatives know who is the single public relations executive responsible for all media coordination?
49. Can we be sure to provide all the physical resources necessary such as parking, weather protection, interview and/or rest rooms, telephones, coffee, toilets, and transport as appropriate?
50. Have we made arrangements to monitor the coverage, record or transcribe it, as necessary, particularly if we wish to follow-up a developing story?

TV interview (general)

51. Can we try to avoid the street, doorstep or airport interview, unless this is absolutely essential?
52. If this is the situation, is our interviewee prepared and able to cope with quick-fire, possibly unpredictable questions?
53. Have we helped him to decide the key points to get over and how to close an interview politely but firmly?

54. Is it possible to suggest that such news interviews take place in the organization's prepared interview room or suitable office?
55. Have we considered whether behind-the-desk, in an easy chair, or standing shirt-sleeved and so on, best suit the message to be communicated?
56. Before transmission/recording can we check through with the interviewer the areas to be discussed?
57. Does our interviewee have all the necessary information, background and authority to handle these?
58. Can we discuss and agree (privately) the key points we wish to get over during the interview?
59. Do we know the likely length of the on-air transmission so we can limit the interview and avoid studio editing?
60. Have we checked when the item is scheduled to be broadcast so we can monitor and/or record this?
61. Can we use only trained, experienced and prepared people to speak on behalf of the organization?

TV studio interview

62. If we have arranged a studio interview, have we checked the basic TV interview guidelines, above, with our spokesman?
63. Are they suitably dressed to reflect their role in the organization and the topic under discussion?
64. Can we check whether this is a live transmission or a recorded interview?
65. Do we know how long it will run 'on air' to guide our interviewee in the depth of answers necessary?
66. Can we check with the interviewer the subject areas to be covered in the discussion?
67. Does our spokesman have all the facts, information and policy clearance to cope with all these areas?
68. Have we identified the key points we wish to get over as well as a few back-up factors if time allows?
69. Would it be helpful to provide any visual aids in advance, such as films, charts, maps, graphs, products, models and so on?
70. Have we confirmed the studio location and time for the interview so that our spokesman will not be hurried?
71. Can we remind him not to drink to relax before the interview as this can be disastrous?
72. Does he appreciate that nothing should be said 'off-the-record' either in the entertainment room, prior to the interview, or after?
73. Have we established who will be conducting the interview so that we are prepared for his type of approach and style?
74. Can we check through some practical reminder points relating to the studio:

(a) check hair, tie or other dress items before going on,

(b) concentrate on the interview area and ignore distractions,

(c) look at the interviewer during the discussion,

(d) ignore the camera and any monitors,

(e) adopt an upright, composed posture, legs closed,

(f) keep your voice bright and interested,

(g) use modest hand movements only,

(h) avoid 'ums', 'ahs', 'you knows', jargon or cliches,

(i) talk 'through' the interviewer to the viewer,

(j) avoid familiarity with the interviewer,

(k) treat every question seriously,

(l) watch the use of humour in a serious interview,

(m) do not agree to unfair comments out of politeness,

(n) correct any inaccuracies or misunderstandings,

(o) keep your comments short, lively, cool and polite?

75. Will we organize a review or discussion after transmission to acknowledge the successful elements, identify weaker areas and take action to improve future performance?

CHAPTER
TWENTY-ONE
DESIGN AND IDENTITY

DESIGN IS PART OF COMMUNICATIONS

We all know that those who talk most, often do not communicate best. As David Bernstein said in his excellent book, *Company Image and Reality*, 'Communication is an over-used word and an under-used skill, particularly in business.' He identified some 24 major British companies that announced important (and sometimes threatening) changes all within the same one or two year period with variations on the words; 'We are confident...' the very phrase suggests the exact opposite and, as some of the companies noted have since been taken over, those expressions had a truly hollow ring.

As we discussed earlier, the company does not communicate just through its words but through its products, its services and all the visual aspects of the organization. What the French describe as 'media permanent' (such as sign-boards, vehicles and uniforms) can be extremely powerful in putting over messages about the organization. Therefore, design policy should be seen as part of the broader communications policy, for, indeed, design *is* communications.

Design services can be offered by a wide variety of organizations, from freelance graphic artists through advertising agencies, public relations consultancies to specialist design houses. Wherever the design skills are bought, it is essential that the design brief springs from the corporate communications policy. It is possible for powerful design to create a perception that does not match the reality. When design starts dictating corporate and communications policy, then trouble will be coming over the horizon.

The corporate identity is part of the physical presentation of the corporate personality. It therefore follows that the organization's corporate identity is more likely to be coherent, consistent and relevant if the organization has an agreed mission statement—or some written perspective on its corporate personality.

Make decisions based on objective study

While it is important that the company has an appropriate corporate identity, this does not always mean that the existing identity needs to be changed. In some cases, the identity might merely need tidying, updating or applying more consistently. Some company identities, such as those of ICI or Shell, have evolved very gradually over many years. Similarly, some

Figure 21.1 Companies often update their identities, sometimes dramatically but, more often, through making subtle changes that keep the design up to date and in keeping with current management philosophies. Examples here are BP, Eagle Star, ICI and Shell.

products have maintained their currency through steady but subtle changes, often over generations; examples include Coca-Cola, Persil, Swan Vesta and Oxo.

All decisions about the corporate identity should be based upon careful study and research. This alone may not provide the answers but it will certainly identify the key questions and give a clear indication of the existing perceptions among important audiences. (See Chapter 28 on research for further suggestions.)

A realistic brief for any change to the identity must be prepared (and sometimes the wisest decision may be 'no change'). A realistic budget proportional to the size of the organization and to the size of the task should be earmarked—but only spent if strictly necessary. Astronomical sums can be spent on creating a new identity, but these may not always be justified where the job has been allowed to inflate, mainly to match the ambitions of the managers of the enterprise.

Some managements find it easier to make decisions relating to such physical factors as corporate identity ... rather than those in the organic, dynamic and dangerous areas of human communications. Even where the design policy may involve the commitment of major budgets, such decisions (taken behind closed doors with friendly, polite and well-paid advisers) can be easier than those that relate to face-to-face communications with important publics. Budgets for design and advertising in some organizations may still well exceed those for public relations. It is the responsibility of the public relations professional to convince management of the power of this sector of communications—using research, as necessary to prove the case.

Changing the name—two case studies

Staying with the existing When the pharmaceutical giants Beecham of Britain and SmithKline Beckman of the USA merged, they chose the name SmithKline Beecham and gave a design consultant six weeks to create a corporate identity for their £3.7 billion company—at that time, the second-largest pharmaceutical group in Britain. The designers had to fuse the identities of the two companies to create a new corporate image, one that would suggest the new group was dynamic, innovative and international.

Vince Carra, creative director at Landor, the corporate designers, said the name SmithKline Beecham was chosen to capitalize on the fact that both had strong reputations in the healthcare industry, as well as giving equal billing to each company. To create a new visual identity for SmithKline Beecham, Landor staff talked to senior executives from both merger partners to establish the new company's core values.

The difficult task of putting across the new corporate values to the companies' staff involved some 300 personnel responsible for communications programmes designed to make employees feel part of the new company. Beecham had a reputation as a market-driven company that started out in consumer products before diversifying into pharmaceuticals. Its brands include Lucozade, Ribena, Bovril and Brylcreem. SmithKline did not have as strong a portfolio of consumer brands. As a result of this, it was more focused on its core pharmaceutical business. The challenge was to create a corporate culture that enabled the group to remain a leader in pharmaceuticals and health products—particularly in the fast-growing market for over-the-counter medicines. The new identity provided the broader public relations opportunity to fuse Beecham's consumer marketing skills with SmithKline's pharmaceutical expertise.

The image of the merged group also had to be sold to investors. They saw Beecham as 'lean and hungry' but SmithKline as under pressure, because sales of its Tagamet anti-ulcer drug, which had underpinned its strong performance since the mid-1970s, were stagnating. The new name was just the beginning for broad communications and marketing campaigns to position the merged company ahead of intense competition.

Opting for the new When Geoffrey Mulcahy, chief executive of Woolworth Holdings, the huge British retailing group, announced a proposed name change, not all the media coverage was favourable. One report called for a shareholder revolt against the board. Another accused them of misspending 'barmy sums of money'.

The reason for choosing a new name seemed simple. The composition of the company had changed dramatically in the previous five years. Then, the original Woolworth chain was responsible for less than half its turnover and was the least profitable of its retail activities. The board wanted the investment community to associate the parent company with its more dynamic divisions—such as the B & Q do-it-yourself stores and Comet electrical shops—rather than the 'pile 'em high 'n' sell 'em cheap' image that Woolworth had never really succeeded in shrugging off.

The company had drafted in a corporate identity consultancy, Wolff Olins, to come up with a new name. The result was the motif of a Kingfisher bird which, the board said, symbolized 'leadership, expansion and growth'. Unfortunately for Mr Mulcahy and his team, the press disagreed. One newspaper accused the company of paying 'daft money for a trivial service'. Another cruelly reminded its readers that kingfishers are prone to lining their nests with excrement.

Despite these hostile reactions, the company persevered and the designers implemented the new identity; the company developed from there and succeeded in the primary objective of separating the name of one of the operating subsidiaries from the group name—clearly a move which gave more flexibility for their planned expansion and acquisitions programme. One consolation for Kingfisher was that the reception to other corporate name changes has been no less hostile. The Wall Street Journal greeted the announcement that Burroughs and Sperry had chosen Unisys from the 31 000 names suggested by its employees with 'If Unisys was the winner, imagine how the losers sound'.

Name changes need courage and persistence

Kingfisher was one in a long line of companies to choose new names, following in the footsteps of Massey-Ferguson, now the Varity Corporation; International Harvester, which became Navistar International; and US Steel, now the USX Corporation.

The concept of a corporate name change is not a new phenomenon. For centuries, companies have changed their names after mergers and reorganizations. Persistence pays, for who nowadays thinks of Exxon, the US oil group, as Standard Oil Company (New Jersey); or BTR, the British industrial conglomerate, as British Tyre & Rubber? Yet the number of name changes has risen rapidly in recent years. The chief catalyst is the wave of corporate activity which has swept across the world's stock markets.

Some companies have changed their names to mark mergers or amalgamations. Other companies chose new names to escape from unhappy histories; for example, US Steel became USX while British Leyland resurfaced as Austin Rover.

Corporate identity as a major separate industry probably emerged in the US in the early 1960s, when the first wave of conglomerates was created. Initially, it was confined to creating names and logos. But in the late 1960s, when big business became a popular target of the peace movement, consultancies become involved with broader aspects of a company's image management. The international expansion of the North American, European and Japanese industrial groups means that the biggest projects now stretch beyond national boundaries, all over the world.

The public relations professional faces a major challenge. Has he the skill and seniority to control the design and identity functions as part of the broadest communications policy of the organization? Design groups have become very professional in recent years and are extending their services; the authority and vision of the public relations executive will decide whether the designer is viewed as part of his resource and a contributing colleague—or the person setting the pace in corporate positioning.

HANDLING DESIGN AND CORPORATE IDENTITY

Working with designers

1. Have we agreed a corporate design policy and issued this to all who commission design?

2. What authority do they have for commissioning such work and ensuring conformity to policy?
3. Do we have a design manual spelling out typefaces, corporate colours and other mechanical data?
4. Should we invite our regular designers to a seminar to discuss design and standards?
5. What procedures do we have for monitoring the design standards and procedures of the organization?
6. Do we keep a central file of copies of all company print and other design material?

Revising the corporate identity

7. Have we an agreed mission statement or comparable policy document?
8. Can we draft and agree a design brief from this?
9. Have we circulated this to all our key colleagues for their views and input?
10. Are there basic restraints we need to put on any possible revisions?
11. Which elements, if any, will we insist on retaining?
12. What research on key public attitudes to the organization exists, or should be commissioned, to give us a base for any revisions?
13. Have we collated actual examples of all current print, uniforms, emblems and other design items?
14. Do we have a short list of possible designers to give an initial response to the brief?
15. From these, could we select two or three to prepare a proposal?
16. Have we confirmed a possible budget and agreed the selection process for the design house?
17. To whom will they be reporting and what control procedures will be operated?
18. How will interim recommendations be presented, to whom and what are the processes for amendments to be made?
19. What plans are proposed for announcing and introducing the revised identity?
20. Can we allocate a budget to research reactions to this after, says, six or twelve months and, from this, appraise the effectiveness of the operation?

TWENTY-TWO

PUBLICATIONS

Print can still be an extremely effective medium of communication. In some respects, it has become a little overshadowed by developments in the broadcast and electronic media.

But print does have definite advantages. You can prepare the case exactly as you would like it to be. Often, you can take as long as you need in editing, in shaping the words, in illustrating them, in making sure that the whole layout projects your story in the best possible way. You can also spread out the story so that readers can go into as much depth as they may wish on different aspects. The printed item can be put in front of people to suit your organization's timing. It can also be passed from hand to hand. *You* control the medium.

A radio or television broadcast may reach millions of people—but only those that happen to be at their sets at that moment. An audio-visual presentation can be controlled—but will only be seen by those attending at a certain place at a certain time. In contrast, a piece of print can be mailed, can be given out at an exhibition, put into a pay packet or be enclosed with every product.

As public relations adviser, you will need to know how to prepare print. You do *not* need to be a designer, typographer, printer, print-buyer or production specialist. However, to get the best from these professionals, remember the basic rules; what are you saying, to whom, when and why are you saying it? And, of course: what is the budget? In few areas can the costs vary so enormously. To be sure you are buying intelligently, prepare a detailed specification for the print job and your required production schedule. Get competitive quotes. If the prices are within a few per cent go for the printer with the reputation. If there are wide discrepancies then there may be something wrong with your specification ... or your list of tendering printers.

Whenever possible, use the printers you know and can trust. If their prices are competitive and they have worked for you before, they will not let you down. The majority of your work may be placed with the same printers. The balance should be placed with printers you have not worked with before to ensure you are in touch with the market.

Do listen to the professional advice of your designer at design stage and printer at printing stage. Last minute changes can add considerably to the cost. Often the professional can suggest a satisfactory way of achieving what you wish at a fraction of the cost of an expensive alternative.

Wherever there is communication, there is likely to be a role for some form of print. This can come in every conceivable shape, size format ... but to examine the role of print in good business communications, it is helpful to identify four main categories, even if these are somewhat arbitrary—leaflets and brochures, house journals, corporate publications, and sponsored books.

Leaflets and brochures The products, services and policies of the organization need presenting and this may require a leaflet or brochure. While it may not be the public relations adviser's job to produce product literature, he should appreciate its function. There are important differences between advertising and public relations literature. In particular, the skills required for writing compelling sales support material are not the same as those for producing public relations copy.

If the public relations manager has the responsibility for producing publicity literature, it is usually advisable to appoint a specialist writer or agency. Remember, when checking copy, that the emphasis must be on the benefits and not the features: people buy benefits, not features. For example, it is not wise to assume that motorists will appreciate why yours is a better car because it has a fifth gear. This is a feature. The benefit is lower engine speed when cruising which means quieter, smoother travel with reduced petrol costs.

In some cases, the preparation of the literature copy may be organized in parallel with the public relations editorial activity. The public relations adviser may sometimes be able to produce the basic research—particularly if it involves case histories, for example. This material should then provide the framework for the professional advertising writer or agency to produce finished copy.

It does not follow that every piece of literature produced needs to be in an expensive format. With the arrival of high street instant printing and desk-top publishing, it is quite possible to produce certain types of literature at relatively modest cost. In some cases, it may be advisable to spend more on the cover, perhaps in colour, and accept low cost printing for the contents.

Do not spend more than is necessary to achieve the right impact. Equally, do not scrimp on costs if this is going to result in a sub-standard appearance. Many of these decisions are dictated by the environment in the market place. Check what your competitors are doing: look at what other similar companies are producing.

As well as the publicity material, you may be required to produce technical literature. Although this may be drafted by your technical colleagues, it is important that a professional communicator has the opportunity to check this copy for conformity to corporate communications policy. This is particularly important if the literature is to be used in other communications activities, for example, in presspacks for exhibitions or at the agm.

Of course, the organization will be producing many types of leaflets and brochures and not all of these will be in the area of sales and marketing support—for example, reprints of executive speeches, recruitment handouts, induction folders, information booklets, and so on. In all cases the quality of the print, the style and tone must reflect the objectives—what are you saying, to whom and why?

House journals The second main category of printed material is the company-owned medium—the house journal, which may be a newspaper, magazine or newsletter.

This may be produced for an internal or external audience. Be cautious about publications which are designed to try to reach both groups. The occasional copy of the internal journal that is passed to the well-known outside customer, the local MP or MEP, may be acceptable. However, if the internal journal is covering the company properly, it will be full of company gossip and trivia, debate, criticisms, personality news—most of which will be of no interest to the external audience. Indeed, some of this news may actually create the wrong impression of the company.

Check the simple questions—what are we saying, to whom and why? These will indicate that separate publications may be needed for internal and external audiences. Remember, though, that the external publications will be of considerable interest to your own employees by showing how the organization projects itself to vital external audiences.

Explain to employees any anomalies that will be apparent between the projection of the company outside and internally. A well-known food group once created confusion among a group of employees. The company had produced a publication for an external audience promoting a service where sales were well below target. Unfortunately, the management had forgotten the impact this publication would have upon the employees: they were in discussions about the possible closure of this operation. The optimism of the publication did not appear to be consistent with their knowledge that it was working very much under-capacity.

This problem illustrates the need to explain to internal audiences how the organization is projecting itself externally. (Of course, this principle applies to all promotional activity—employees should see the TV commercials before they appear on their screens and have the marketing logic presented to them and so on.)

Some house journals are published in newspaper format and some in magazine format: fashions on this point swing one way and then the other. The best guidance is to ignore fashion and make a decision on which is the best form of communication for the type of material to be issued. If you would like to use colour pictures and a feature-type approach, then a magazine might be more appropriate. If you wish to create a glossy up-market feel, then the magazine will almost certainly be the best.

In contrast, if you want a pacey, lively style with a strong sense of immediacy, big bold pictures and headlines, then the newspaper format may be better. Even within this, to use British examples, it is possible to have a format that might range from the *Guardian* style to the *Daily Mirror*. The frequency of publication is not the important factor in deciding whether to opt for a newspaper layout: with modern web lithoprinting processes, it is perfectly possible to produce a full-colour quarterly newspaper format journal using late copy right up to the day of publication.

To achieve such immediacy, the newspaper production timing needs to be arranged to relate to known activities within the company—the agm, the 'Driver of the Year' competition, the Christmas celebrations and so on. This establishes the news credibility of the publication. Other managers will more readily accept the argument that they should use the newspaper for the dissemination of company news before it is put out through any other source. This will obviously improve the readership interest if the journal carries information employees can only get from its pages. David Bernstein of the Creative Business quotes the example of the tabloid newsletter they created for a local authority. After the first issue, the client complained; it had produced a flood of queries and complaints. The reason was simple—converting what had previously been dull leaflet information into a lively newspaper had meant that residents were reading it and reacting. Good communications!

A regular area of discussion among professionals looking at house journals is their frequency and size. Is it better to have larger issues less often, or the opposite? Of course, it is *cheaper* to produce 8 pages every 2 months rather than 4 pages every month. On the other hand, the greater the frequency the more the publication becomes accepted as an essential channel of communication.

Therefore, aim to produce the publication as often as the editorial resource will allow, even if this means reducing the number of pages in each issue or cutting out other costly aspects (such as the use of colour). Some editors achieve a compromise: they publish a black and white or two-colour newspaper on a regular basis, but produce a special magazine once or twice a year using a larger number of pages or full-colour.

Perhaps the most lively area of debate relating to house journals is the responsibility of the editor. The best publications have a strong personality at the top and the editor is given a lot of independence. It is almost impossible to produce anything creative and imaginative by committee. It is difficult for the editor to satisfy the wide demands of an editorial committee. The publication either becomes bland and cautious or, if the editor is tough, then there will be constant disagreements. Everyone else in the organization has one boss. So why should the editor have a committee? Scrap it.

The best rule for the public relations adviser who may be appointing a house journal editor is ... pick the best man that you possibly can for the job. Give him a proper brief and clear objectives. Then let the editor get on with it. If the editor fails to produce the journal that meets the objectives and that the readers want to read, get rid of him!

Corporate publications The third main print category is the substantial organization publication. This might include the financial report, the corporate handbook and annual organization review.

The annual report is designed to convey financial information to financial people and must fulfill certain statutory requirements that vary from country to country. Copies of the annual report should be available for employees, say, on notice boards and in the personnel office so that anyone who wishes can inspect one. Copies should also be available on request. Under no circumstances should the company miss the opportunity to issue copies. Discrimination in information can be a most dangerous practice.

While the annual report should be made available to employees, a separate employee version can be helpful. This would cover the trading position and the overall state of the company, often in a more descriptive form. Such a presentation is not suitable for financial audiences who do not need a pictorial analysis of performance. Equally, the standard statutory financial presentation is not always the most comprehensible. This in-house edition must be produced to the same production standards.

Financial reports issued to employees are generally well-read. A survey carried out in Britain by Touche Ross showed that three-quarters of the sample of employees who received reports had all read these. Only two per cent claimed not to have looked at them at all. Some two-thirds found them interesting and around half of those surveyed would have liked more information. The overall requirement is to treat the annual report and any associated employee report as communications vehicles. Therefore, get the maximum return from the amount of money that probably has to be spent on it for statutory reasons.

Some companies use their annual reports as a marketing tool. Shareholders and financial advisers are not only customers, they are important opinion leaders. Ideas that UK leaders have used include pages of products, special offers to shareholders, cutout and pullout pages with indices. Kalamazoo cleverly featured its own business paperwork systems on the logic that many of the company's shareholders are likely to be customers. The food group, Reckitt & Colman, incorporated an unusual colour page with a dinner recipe utilizing many of the products from their range.

Of course, we have been looking at the annual report of quoted companies: the same principles apply to charities and most public utilities. Even privately owned companies can produce annual reports that can become valuable communications vehicles for external and internal audiences. Even if the organization decides not to publish full financial information, there can be cases where an annual report on progress and development can be a valuable promotional item of print. Also, there will be occasions when development activities suggest that a special project report may be advisable.

Some special reports will need to be produced in advance—this can be the case with a prospectus, a proposal for a new development, an investment opportunity, a charity appeal, an overseas expansion plan. The public relations adviser may also be responsible for preparing progress updates. These may not need to be to a similar expensive, quality format. For example, a series of regular project updates may be produced on light paper, in a newsletter format printed single colour. These will be designed to fit into the pocket in the project colour brochure or a specially prepared ring binder. Such low-cost items can also be used to meet general information needs and to help keep down the print budget.

Sponsored books The fourth main print category is publications in a book or booklet format but sponsored or endorsed by the organization. The cost of such publications has to be acceptable in commercial terms, relating to the size and importance of the audience reached in comparison with other communications techniques. This factor must be calculated in the same way as other projects—how much per head to influence which particular sector of the organization's identified publics. Sometimes the 'aura' or association that might be created through the publication can be an important secondary factor.

A commercial book carries the name of the organization responsible for endorsing the publishing project. It differs from other promotional literature and publications in that it usually carries a cover price and is distributed through bookshops, newsagents, educational or other publishing outlets. Most endorsed publications are produced by specialist divisions of commercial book publishers. These publications can vary from popular best sellers (in Britain the *Guinness Book of Records*, *Wisden's Cricket*, are good examples) to the esoteric and specialized reference work whose sales may only be counted in hundreds (Blue Circle's publication, *Designing in Concrete*, is a good illustration of this type).

A separate category is the information booklet produced directly by the sponsor. For example, British business researchers, Dun & Bradstreet Ltd, was one of the first financial institutions to prepare and issue a booklet on the pitfalls of managing a small business and how to avoid them. This was created as part of a promotional campaign. It generated considerable goodwill and attracted attention to the business information services that Dun & Bradstreet offers. This initiative has been successfully emulated and developed by, for example, many banks.

Many public utilities and information bureaux sponsored by generic industry bodies also produce information booklets which may carry a cover price. A sponsored book, however, normally carries the name of the commercial publisher and is distributed through normal book outlets.

The revenue from few sponsored books covers the total cost to the sponsor. Some sponsored titles in popular consumer areas are financed on the basis that a royalty to the sponsor is paid by the publisher. Therefore, sales above a certain minimum number actually create a direct return. More usually, the sponsor funds the up-front costs in return for an agreed quantity at no cost or a discounted price. Few organizations are likely to find a new market sector that can be tapped to create a run-away best seller. Therefore, most sponsored publications are likely to need some degree of subsidy. The book must justify its cover price in terms of value to the reader and generate some sales or it will not be highly regarded. An overpriced or unsuccessful book will not reflect well on the sponsoring organization.

In evaluating a joint-venture publication exercise, it is essential to agree the right subject. Some companies simply wish to lend their name to a publishing venture which might not otherwise have been financed. Their prime objective is to create publicity and awareness—the *Dunlop Book of Facts*, might be an example.

The majority of sponsored books cover areas where there is a close association with the interests of the sponsor. The Co-op retail organization sponsored a series of low-cost household guide paperbacks which were just right for their market. At the other end of the scale, champagne makers, Veuve du Vernay, produced an entertainment book which was intentionally very glossy and expensive. Sponsored publications are usually written by independent specialists—such as the *Philips Guide to the Electronic Office*. Sometimes they can be written by a staff man working on the book as a special promotional project.

The calculation of the cost of sponsorship of a book is dependent on a number of factors—these include the quantities the company might need for promotional use, the potential commercial book sales, the length of life of the publication and whether the sponsor wants to see a financial return. When planning the promotional campaign, sponsored publications should certainly be evaluated. They are most effective where the aim is to reach an identified market and present the organization's credibility in a permanent and impressive way.

As with all areas of communications, the professional public relations adviser needs to be able to identify when and how to use print as the most cost-effective technique. Despite the development of alternative communications techniques, the clarity, integrity, permanence and 'transferability' of print make it an essential element in most campaigns.

PLANNING FOR PUBLICATIONS

Their role in the programme

1. As always, have we agreed on the audiences, the messages, the communications objectives, the existing and optimum public attitudes?
2. Where will publications play a role in the broader communications programme?
3. Can we identify which type of printed item will be best to reach each audience group?
4. How will our direct and controlled communications through company-produced print be related to indirect communications through, for example, the grapevine, conferences or the media?
5. Can specific communications objectives be drafted that will help plan each proposed item of print?

Promotional brochures

6. Who is responsible for preparing literature to support the sale of products, promotion of services, maintenance and after-sales services of the organization?
7. Have we prepared a complete list of all such print requirements covering, for example, everything from the prestige range brochure, through individual sales leaflets to in-pack instructions and parts lists?
8. Has this been checked with all relevant executives including marketing, sales, advertising, service, distribution, maintenance, stores, consumer advisers and so on?
9. Can this literature be prepared to a coordinated brief relating to style, use of colour, logo, sizes, aura, messages, cross-references and so on?
10. Does this indicate ways to get the maximum from the budget, for example, printing some items together or using some artwork more than once?

House journals, internal

11. Have we identified the audiences with whom we wish to communicate through the medium of a house journal?

12. Do we have a clear idea of their backgrounds, social positions, attitudes, languages, religions, nationalities, loyalties and other relevant factors?
13. Will this help us decide whether it is practical to produce one broad-appeal publication: such a publication but with local or special interest inserts, or a series of separate publications perhaps in regional, national or subject-matter editions?
14. If we take each sector in turn, can we identify communications needs to help guide us in drafting the editorial policy, for example, more product information, explanation about policies, discussion of issues?
15. Can we also establish attitudes towards the organization to help us agree on content and style, for example, are our readers indifferent, enthusiastic or potentially hostile?
16. Have we all the information possible about other sources of news that will be affecting the opinions and attitudes of our readers?
17. Can we now draft an editorial policy covering such areas as:

    (a) editor's responsibilities,
    (b) sources of material,
    (c) any copy approval procedures,
    (d) access to management information,
    (e) coverage of contentious issues,
    (f) the available editorial resource,
    (g) copy style and editorial stance,
    (h) any feedback provision, such as letters, fax, telephone hotline or contributed articles?

18. Have we a clear indication of the frequency of publication and the space that will be necessary to cover the areas agreed?
19. What is the balance between news, feature copy and picture elements in this proposed publication?
20. Do these factors help us decide which print format might be most suitable:

    (a) newspaper: punchy, news orientated, urgent, topical, suitable for big print runs,
    (b) magazine: feature orientated, more in-depth reading, possibly more suitable for colour and low frequency,
    (c) bulletins: fast, low-cost, very topical, direct style but limited editorial authority?

21. Will the organization need more than one type of publication, for example, a newspaper for production staff, a magazine for international agents and bulletins for the salesforce?
22. Do we need to recruit a professional editor to handle such publications?
23. Can we draft and agree with personnel and relevant divisional heads the specification of this position?

24. Will the editor report to the line manager of the division requiring the publication or report within the public relations function to the chief executive?
25. Have we agreed procedures for monitoring the communications effectiveness to assess performance and any necessary budget adjustments?

External journals

26. Can we control the issuing of any internal publications to external audiences ensuring the relevance of the editorial content and style?
27. Have we defined the attitudes that exist among the actual/potential readers of our external publications?
28. Do these factors indicate the need for a separate external publication and possible style, frequency and format?
29. Can we run through the steps already discussed to evaluate the policy, the necessary resource and the coordination of the publication with other of our house journals?
30. Does our editorial policy ensure that this publication will have editorial authority and that it will project our organization in a way consistent with corporate objectives?
31. How will the editor exercise his editorial judgment over the suitability of material, particularly when this may be proposed by more senior managers?
32. Have we considered a cover price to establish the value of the publication and help recover some of the production costs?
33. How will we distribute the external publication to primary audiences (say customers or shareholders) and secondary audiences (say MPs, MEPs or suppliers)?
34. Are we planning to use outside, by-lined contributors?
35. Can we achieve any media interest in the publication and its contents, for example, by issuing advance copies or selected articles to key editors?

Special reports

36. What audiences are we trying to reach, to develop what attitudes through the presentation of what information?
37. Have we agreed on the frequency, quality and content of these publications and the impression of the organization we wish to create?
38. For our annual report have we established the necessary coordination between the chief executive, the financial director, the public relations adviser, external financial professionals and the printer?
39. Can we benefit from the investment in the annual report by extending

the distribution of this important overview of the organization to other influential audiences?

40. Can we ensure that there is a consistency in style, presentation and messages between the annual financial report, the corporate brochure and other special reports, for example, by producing these through the editor's or public relations adviser's department?

Sponsored books

41. Do we plan to produce our endorsed title ourselves or through the sponsored books division of a commercial publisher?
42. Have we (or our proposed publisher) researched the market for such a publication and evaluated potential interest?
43. Who will be controlling this project and deciding the editorial policy, content and style?
44. Will the author/editor be a member of the organization, on the staff of the publisher, or a commissioned professional?
45. Has the budget been calculated, including the up-front costs and the potential for recovering costs from sales or royalties?
46. What cover price will be set to position the book in the market and what discounted price will apply to copies supplied for our promotional activity?
47. Will such a publication be cost-effective in promoting the organization and/or its products and services?
48. Are we creating a new publishing venture or lending our name to an existing publication?
49. Can we estimate the life of this publication and the possibility of needing updated editions?
50. How will our publication be distributed and can the publisher estimate the number of outlets and volume of sales?
51. What promotional support will the publisher put behind the title and how will this be coordinated with our public relations efforts?
52. Is the publication suitable as a trade giveaway or prize or to be featured in proposed advertising?
53. Can we merchandise this project by sending complimentary copies to shareholders, industry bodies and opinion leaders?
54. Is the publication date firm so that it can be included in the promotional calendar and coordinated with supporting and other promotional activities?
55. What procedures have we established to measure the effectiveness of the publication in its contribution to corporate communications objectives?

Other print

56. When planning broad communications programmes are we properly evaluating the contribution of other company-produced print items?

57. Do we differentiate between advertising material and print which is produced to achieve a public relations aim, such as creating community goodwill or educating the market?
58. Are we clear which department is responsible for producing which types of print and which budget is involved?
59. In our programme have we considered such print items as:

calendars and diaries	stickers and badges
posters and wallcharts	induction notes
educational leaflets	company history
trade term glossaries	reprinted articles?

60. Have we established the necessary coordination system to ensure all items support communications objectives and their cost-effectiveness can be assessed?

TWENTY-THREE

SPONSORSHIP

PUBLICITY IS ONLY ONE BENEFIT FROM SPONSORSHIP

Publicity is only one criterion when assessing the potential value of sponsorship. There are many different types of sponsorship and, at the planning stage, it is helpful to appreciate the basic differences. Perhaps the most frequent reasons why organizations undertake sponsorship are publicity, entertainment opportunities and favourable associations. Some sponsors want only one of these, some want them all, others a combination of these elements.

Each factor can be evaluated separately. Publicity (in terms of name or brand exposure) can be measured in the same way as other media. Entertainment costs and opportunities can be calculated. Even the favourable aura or association that reflects on the sponsor with some activities can be evaluated fairly accurately. The potential sponsor needs to be disciplined in deciding objectives and preparing sponsorship requirements before becoming enthused by one of the hundreds of opportunities that always exist. One reason why so many commercial sponsorships operating at present in the UK (and in many other countries) are *not* effective is that the discussion has focused too early on the activity; consequently, the excitement created has tended to cloud the original objectives.

Organizations must keep clearly in mind exactly what they are trying to achieve. In Britain, Gillette pioneered some areas of sports sponsorship for publicity reasons and achieved outstanding success, for example, supporting 'knock-out' cricket. Later, the company amended its methods of projecting its involvement when it discovered that a proportion of the audience it was trying to reach did not automatically associate these sponsored events with

....the potential sponsor needs to be disciplined in deciding objectives

the products—some even thought that Gillette was the name of a long-forgotten cricketer! Several national companies have also become concerned about the increase in the real cost of running certain national sponsored events, mainly designed for trade entertainment—particularly as a proportion of the trade buyers being entertained were existing customers who already had established relations with the company.

Consideration needs to be given to whether the organization's identity is to be strongly established with an event—some of the best opportunities require a commitment over several years. Taking over the sponsorship of an event that is already closely associated with another commercial name can create significant initial problems. Additional promotional efforts may be needed to establish the new sponsor's name. Because of the limited opportunity to create new events, most sponsors add their names to an existing activity. (The British Dunlop Masters golf tournament may have been an excellent promotional activity but it involved the sponsors in all the logistics of organization and this was one of the major reasons the company withdrew.)

Taking an existing event provides a ready-made promotional opportunity with the minimum of organizational demands. It has the disadvantage that it becomes more difficult to associate your name with an event that previously might have carried somebody else's name. However, where an existing sponsor has not renewed an option such sponsorships can be picked up at modest cost. For example, the prestigious Burghley Horse Trials, which achieve considerable national publicity and provide good entertainment opportunities, became available one year due to the withdrawal of Land Rover through the economic pressures at that time on sponsors.

CONSIDER NEW OPPORTUNITIES

The public relations adviser should consider activities never sponsored before. There can be opportunities for the sponsor to create something completely new. For example, in the UK this was achieved with Embassy in such areas as snooker and darts, or with Just Juice and basketball. Shell created a whole new area of public interest in Britain when they established the challenge for the vehicle that could achieve the maximum mileage from a gallon of petrol. Groups of schoolboys, engineers, enthusiasts, technical colleges and others took up the challenge and the event achieved national media coverage. (One year alone, the record was raised from 2000 to 2700 miles from a single gallon!) Scottish Amicable stepped in to support the low-profile but well-established British baseball league with excellent results for the sponsor.

Opportunities are not restricted to major commercial companies. For example, the professional body, the British Association of Industrial Editors created the 'Communicator of the Year' awards. This was successfully established, despite the fact that other organizations might have been as well placed to initiate such an idea. The presentations achieve national coverage and provide the association with a unique opportunity to entertain opinion leaders.

In the US, Denny Griswold, through her publication the PR Newsletter, has established a series of awards for public relations professionals that have become highlights of the public relations calendar. The International Association of Business Communicators has its prestigious Gold Quill awards for organizational communications. In the UK, Ilford runs the prestige 'Industrial Photographer of the Year' awards scheme. The Chartered Institute of Marketing has its annual marketing awards, the Institute of Public Relations its Swords of Excellence, the PRSA has its Silver Anvil.

SOLUS VERSUS COOPERATIVE BENEFITS

A particularly successful event was sponsored by the Plain English Campaign and the National Consumer Council. They held an annual award for the most outstanding examples of gobbledegook. Winners have included government departments, a bus company and an electrical manufacturer: for their efforts they received a suitable trophy—a golden bull statuette. At the same time the panel of judges made awards to the producers of good documents. Journalists delighted in publishing the results, particularly when they were unexpected: one year the best documents were produced by two insurance companies, a local authority, and a government department!

Another important sponsorship consideration is whether the organization wishes to have the sole benefits (and costs) of the sponsorship. For example, Pasta Foods created significant benefits from a subsidiary sponsorship of the London Marathon. Their participation provided opportunities to put over the fact that pasta is a high energy food. In addition, the eve-of-marathon pasta banquet created unique media opportunities for the company. This was all achieved without the need or cost of solus sponsorship. In contrast, some of the sub-sponsors of such events as the Bob Hope Golf Classic in England, which ultimately folded, had to watch carefully to ensure that their identity did not get lost in the overall media noise.

If publicity is the objective, the public relations adviser needs to be certain that the media coverage will reach those audiences that are relevant. For example, it is arguable that an up-market sport like show-jumping may not be of as much interest to potential customers of double glazing as soccer might. How close is the profile of the followers of the activity to the profile of the target market? More golf events are organized because it happens to be the chairman's favourite sport than because this is an appropriate vehicle for the sponsor.

The relative importance of the publicity and entertainment opportunities need to be balanced. Some activities—power boat racing, for example— provide good publicity but limited entertainment opportunities. Golf can provide both.

For some sponsors, the entertainment opportunities are the most important. Music and the performing arts can be particularly effective in entertainment terms. The sponsorship of classical concerts by TI was recognized as being good for community relations and employee goodwill but was primarily designed for the trade hospitality opportunities. BMW supported classical concerts in stately homes to provide dealers with customer entertainment opportunities. Rhone-Poulenc supported classical orchestra concerts to create attractive customer evenings.

When can the venue be decided by the sponsor? Some sponsorships are national events and their location is part of their appeal—Henley, the

Windsor Horse Show and many of the horse racing classics are good examples. Compare the benefits of a single national event with a series of regional activities. The BMW concerts took place in stately homes around Britain, every one an attractive place to host an evening. The UK Speedway Championships are fought at stadia located in major cities across the UK. A series of cycle events sponsored by Kellogg took place in a number of British city centres. The Milk Race cleverly combines a national event with major regional participation: it creates both publicity and entertainment opportunities for the Milk Marketing Board—as well as directly associating their product with a clean, energetic and stimulating sport. Part of the prime sponsors costs are recouped by offering subsidiary sponsorship of the route stages.

THE IMPORTANCE OF THE LOCATION OF EVENTS

Some events are committed to a fixed time and place, such as Wimbledon or Royal Ascot and the football Cup Final. Sports such as ice hockey, speedway, motor racing and horse racing have to take place at specially built facilities. However, there can be far more flexibility with golf and tennis. Sponsors of some tennis tournaments have a large degree of control over where the finals take place—and these may not even be at an accepted tennis venue and could be at such places as a conference centre or the National Exhibition Centre. Similarly, Kellogg had a degree of choice over the city centres where they wanted to run their cycle races.

Swan Vestas, the world's number one match brand, sponsored an outstandingly successful angling competition. This associated neatly with the open air identity of the product. Because angling takes place on rivers throughout the UK, this provided excellent regional public relations opportunities.

Similarly, the sponsor had an influence in the choice of location for the concerts organized for the Royal Philharmonic tour. These still had to take place in cities that had a large theatre or concert hall, though chamber music, small orchestra tours and art exhibitions can be effective in a wider range of venues.

There may be other factors that reduce the sponsor's control. The participation of key personalities or the need to fit the event on an international calendar can create limitations—for example, with show-jumping, golf and tennis. This may not be a restriction with events organized mainly for entertainment, such as private golf days, squash, darts, snooker and many of the sports training clinics.

Sports opportunities have tended to be dominant in sponsorship partly because of their broad audience appeal and partly because of the more commercial nature of the organizers of most of these activities. But there can be substantial opportunities in the visual and performing arts.

RELATE THE ACTIVITY TO THE MARKET

The sponsoring body should identify the activity closest to the likely interests of the audience that the public relations manager wishes to influence—this might identify whether it should be painting, sculpture, opera, ballet, drama, mime, jazz or classical music. Some activities can provide publicity and entertainment, as well as reflecting well on the organization. Some sponsorships need to be national in impact; others are more relevant to the development of the organization into the area of community relations: some may be both.

There may be even more scope for imaginative sponsorship in the educational sector. Well devised schemes can create good media interest and project the company well—though with very limited entertainment opportunities. Sponsorship is possible through the organization providing educational grants, study courses, travel awards, the provision of educational facilities, the funding of professorships, research and many others. Educational sponsorship is possible at sixth form, graduate, postgraduate, adult education and professional development levels. In the UK, computer manufacturers have sponsored training schemes for business students, food manufacturers have supported dietary research projects.

Philips Business Systems identified the benefits of an educational activity directly related to their business development. This was combined with valuable publicity opportunities when they helped the Industrial Society put together a series of seminars on coping with the electronic office of the future. Acorn Computers sponsored a series of round-Britain scientific lectures in cooperation with the Operation Raleigh organization.

Some companies have achieved substantial benefits from supporting activities in the area of human endeavour, such as exploration, record attempts, challenges and adventure—the Transglobe expedition, supported by Bowring, is an example. The *Daily Mail* sponsored the trans-Atlantic race. The Milk Marketing Board aided the world altitude record attempt for hot-air balloons. World record attempts in every area are substantially supported by sponsoring organizations.

The sponsorship activity need not have a direct connection but it should project the company in an appropriate light. Some notable potential football sponsors withdrew from the sport because of the declining standards, both on and off the pitch. One famous UK consumer manufacturer declined to put its brands behind snooker and darts events—despite the excellent TV publicity opportunities. The company was concerned about associations with activities so closely related to smoking and drinking.

While media exposure through, for example, television can be measured, these figures need to be treated with caution. There are rules on the use of brand names in sponsored activities featured on British television. The exposure of the name does not always relate to the audience perception.

Some logos are seen only as patterns and are not registered as brand names. In some sports the activity is so intense that little attention is paid outside the centre of action—such as in soccer or motor racing. Others are more leisurely and brand names do register—with snooker, darts or indoor showjumping.

BE CRITICAL IN COST-EFFECTIVENESS EVALUATIONS

The most critical question to ask relevant to sponsorship is the cost-effectiveness of the activity. The total real cost must include both direct and indirect costs. As a broad guide, a publicity-sponsorship usually incurs £1 of exploitation costs for every £1 of direct sponsorship. It might also require a further £1 in management time. Therefore a payment of £100 000 to secure sponsorship could eventually cost the organization closer to £300 000. From this sum, it is possible to calculate the cost per thousand of reaching the direct audience (those who attend the event) and the indirect audience (those who might be exposed through media coverage). Sometimes, if the event is of a prestigious or innovative type, a factor can be allowed for the favourable aura created.

The calculation is simpler with an entertainment opportunity. The cost can be divided by the number of guests who will attend and an assessment made on whether this is cost-effective. The direct costs of entertaining a guest in a private marquee at Wimbledon may seem very reasonable at, say, £200 per head; however, it is possible to incur over £1000 per head in indirect costs. Some private boxes at first division football grounds cost ten times the rate for the equivalent number of individual seats.

There can be no set answer to the question of what is a good sponsorship. Public relations advisers to potential sponsors should establish the relative importance of entertainment, publicity, goodwill and favourable associations. The financial calculations should be related to the usual basic factors—who are we trying to reach, what attitudes are we trying to shape, which messages do we wish to communicate and how will we monitor our effectiveness?

If the activity is carefully selected and controlled, it can be a most powerful technique. If not, it is a waste of money and a diversion of scarce management resources from more important communications areas.

SELECTING A SPONSORSHIP

1. Before we consider any particular sponsorships, have we reminded ourselves of whom we are trying to reach, our objectives, messages, existing attitudes and so on?

2. Are we clear that potential sponsorships must be evaluated on performance criteria and not enthusiasm, excitement or pressure from the chief executive?
3. Can we clearly establish the target audience for which we might be considering sponsorship as a method of communication?
4. Are we looking for publicity, prestige, entertainment opportunities or some combination of these?
5. Should we consider separate sponsorship activities for different audiences with different objectives?
6. Can we compare any nominated sponsorship event with alternative techniques, in relation to their ability to meet defined objectives?
7. Do we wish our organization's name to become closely associated with a particular event?
8. If so, do we wish to make a commitment for a number of years ahead?
9. Would we consider the opportunity of attaching our name to an event that has had a previous sponsor?
10. If so, should we check with the organizers and the previous sponsor why they are withdrawing?
11. Would we prefer to add our name to a new event or one that has never been previously sponsored?
12. If so, how can we check on such factors as potential audience, exposure, public and media interest and so on?
13. Do we wish to become involved in the logistics of organizing an activity?
14. If so, can we calculate the additional costs and demands on executive time that this will involve?
15. If not, can we evaluate the professional efficiency with which the event is likely to be organized, for example, on the track record of the organizers in other areas?
16. Do we want an event that has some relevance to our areas of activity, for example, directly, such as running and a health food maker, or indirectly, such as ice-skating and a freezer manufacturer?
17. Alternatively, do we want an acceptable association such as the healthy aspects of outdoor sports, the youth element of soccer, the up-market appeal of yachting, the intelligence of chess and so on?
18. Alternatively (or perhaps additionally) are we looking just for maximum exposure of our name to our target audience?
19. If the publicity aspect is likely to be the main benefit, can we quantify the audience exposed to our name, its breakdown in age, socioeconomic categories, geographical location and so on?
20. Can we separate the direct exposure of those who attend, those who will see posters and publicity and those exposed via media coverage?
21. If media coverage is a factor in our cost-justification, what guarantees do the organizers offer?

22. Is it possible to check their track record in previous years, look at the actual media coverage, and obtain the views of media representatives?
23. Is any part of the sponsorship cost related to promised or implied media coverage?
24. Has such coverage been confirmed, such as live TV coverage or is it subject to negotiation?
25. Are there restrictions on the use of our name likely to be imposed by media covering the event?
26. Does the agreement clearly specify that our name will be used in the title of the event and always used whenever the event is mentioned, for example, the ABC Grand National?
27. In what other ways will our name be used in activity relating to the event, for example, on posters, stadia boards, tickets, programmes and so on?
28. Is ours a solus sponsorship or are other organizations likely to be involved?
29. If so, are we prime sponsor and do we have the right of approval over subsidiary sponsors and their proposed activities?
30. What permanent record will the organizers give us of the event and the benefits to us of our sponsorship?
31. Can we ask them to give us an assessment after the event of the effectiveness and ways it might be improved in successive years?
32. Should we make the achievement of some agreed performance criteria a condition that will affect the continuation of the sponsorship in successive years?
33. Will our initiative be helping establish an event that will later have a real commercial value and where we need to ensure we have first option on future sponsorship?
34. If entertainment is important to us, what special facilities will we have as sponsors, such as:

royal patronage	guest souvenirs
VIP receptions	executive transport
special guest facilities	meeting the celebrities
reserved parking	presentation of prizes
starting the event	video or film record?

35. What flexibility might there be over the choice of venue to suit, for example, our organization's location?
36. Are we planning for one major event or a series, such as regional stages, preliminary rounds or home and away events?
37. How might the proposed dates relate to our promotional calendar and is there any flexibility on these timings?
38. Have we evaluated the opportunities for promoting this participation through our other communications channels, such as the house journal, advertising, and so on?

39. Can we calculate the total cost for the package including the sponsorship cost, executive time, exploitation costs and relate these to the original objectives?
40. Before next year's euphoria takes over, can we schedule a postmortem after the event to evaluate its cost-effectiveness, the extent to which it met the objectives and how we might develop the activity in successive years?

SPECIAL EVENTS

CREATE EVENTS THAT GENERATE ATTENTION

With imagination, the public relations professional can create his own public relations opportunities through the development of special events, including openings, celebrations, anniversaries, seminars and competitions. The London Marathon was mainly created through the enthusiasm of Chris Brasher and a handful of people who wanted a fun, popular sporting event: sponsorship was added later as a method of making it all happen. In contrast, the Milk Race was created specifically to meet the objectives of the organizers, the Milk Marketing Board.

A good public relations programme has room for dozens of small ideas, as well as the occasional big one. Are there natural activities within the company's year that could become special events? As an illustration, the introduction of a new product is an opportunity for a launch. But, if the public relations adviser is in at an early stage of the planning, new products create far more opportunities to get key audiences involved. Let us look at an example based on an actual recent case-history. A manufacturer produces, say, electric kettles. Research has identified that these are viewed by the buying public as dull products. The replacement market is very modest and not growing.

This would seem to be a marketing opportunity to create a more exciting model with some performance benefits. It might even have an element of 'fashion' in its design and pick up sales through making other models look dated. As the existing product sales are important, it might be proposed to introduce this alongside the current models—rather than as a replacement for any established model.

The public relations manager should be involved in all of these discussions to make a contribution relating to market awareness and potential attitudes. He would also help in the shaping of the original research. Public relations also needs to be considered in the development of the brief for the new product.

The obvious support activity might be say, a press launch, for the new product; some incentive scheme for the sales team; a sales conference launch; perhaps some trade public relations activity to back-up the trade press advertising; a sales promotional scheme, and so on.

So far, so good ... but very routine. An imaginative public relations practitioner would use the introduction of the new product to improve communications with many audiences directly, as well as through media relations. It is helpful if such planning can run parallel to the product development—which is one reason why the public relations specialist needs to be involved early. By the time the product is ready for introduction, the manager responsible for public relations will have developed a plan not only to introduce a new product, but for the company to reinforce its reputation across a broad spectrum of influential publics.

USE EVENTS TO REACH BROADER AUDIENCES

One simple event like this can produce a dozen opportunities. For example, suppliers could be invited to a special presentation of the product, including a factory tour and lunch with the production director. A factory open day might be held to coincide with the introduction of the new product. Employees might be given the opportunity of inviting their wives, husbands and families to a gala-day, complete with marquee, brass bands, entertainers, sky-divers and a whole programme of family fun.

The launch of the product might be timed so that it comes just a month before the agm. This meeting would give an opportunity for a display of the company's newest product to shareholders—perhaps showing the stages in its development and design, prototypes and test models, as well as the complete press, radio and television launch coverage. Special gold presentation versions of the model might be given to long service employees, selected pensioners, shareholders, major customers or wholesalers.

Regional introductions in all the major cities might be organized for retailers. These presentations would give an opportunity for retailing personnel to meet senior company management and be treated as VIPs. Wholesalers could be invited to participate in a trade competition which included, say, prizes of holidays to faraway places. This might be tied in to a series of individual presentations to main wholesalers and their staffs.

A simple product introduction has become the foundation for a broad range of communications activities involving many audiences on whose goodwill the organization depends. Vent-Axia of England created news interest in their ventilation fans by arranging a ceremony where the director presented the first ever model to the Science Museum. The Fisher Body Division of General Motors took their anniversary and organized celebrations that involved all 65 000 employees at 27 plants, plus retired personnel, families, trade partners, media and opinion leaders.

WHEN TO INVOLVE ROYAL PARTICIPATION

In the UK, some activities planned by the public relations specialist will be of such national importance that they may be suitable for consideration as a royal event. In the UK, members of the royal family are involved in all aspects of the life of the nation; this means that under the right circumstances they participate in public events that are organized by businesses, charities and social groups. (However, no members of the royal family will lend their name or endorsement to a commercial activity except under the strictly controlled conditions that apply to a Royal Warrant: this is granted to companies who provide products or services over a period of years to a member of the royal family and to the satisfaction of the royal household.)

Members of the royal family open new factories or inaugurate major public works or social projects such as dams, airports, public amenities and so on. The public relations adviser needs to have a clear idea of the type of event where the attendance of a member of the royal family may be possible. There is a simple procedure for making application to Buckingham Palace. The press secretary at Buckingham Palace will give advice relating to inviting members of the royal family to attend events.

The diaries are planned well in advance and therefore early requests are essential. It is also helpful to know the expected movements of members of the royal family: a particular regional or overseas visit might provide opportunities to include the event that the public relations adviser has in mind. A great degree of flexibility over dates is necessary to give the best possible chance for the activity to be fitted in to busy royal diaries.

Although the public relations adviser may be responsible for the planning of the event, the formal invitation must go from the head of the organization, addressed to the appropriate private secretary. (A helpful guidance paper on the running of such an event is published by the PRCA.)

CONSIDER THE USE OF CELEBRITIES

Sometimes the use of a public figure such as a showbusiness, sporting or political personality can lift an activity. Look at the event from the point of view of those you are trying to influence. Does it have a natural news value?

Is there a personality within the company who would act as a focal point? Will the story get media coverage in its own right?

Personalities can add new impact to some events. For example, launching a new microcomputer may be of sufficient interest to gain coverage in the electronic, office and business publications. If it is coming from an interesting new company or an established giant this may add news interest. However, 'yet another microcomputer' may have very limited news value.

Suppose that one extra feature of the microcomputer is that it can talk back. It does not use synthesized voice: the owner can record his own vocabulary which the machine uses when replying. In this case, the addition of a personality to the launch might begin to create news interest for radio, television and national press. The product demonstration could be given a new dimension. A relevant personality might be a famous stage star or Hollywood actor with a very distinctive voice. Alternatively, it could be the cabinet minister reponsible for this sector of business. In either case, the computer that talks like Robert Redford or Margaret Thatcher has to have some news appeal!

Let us consider another illustration. The opening of a new laboratory may be undertaken by your director of research or managing director. This may be fine if the aim is just to create a warm glow among those immediately involved. Unless your executive is able to make some major announcement, it is unlikely to raise much of a ripple beyond the immediate local scene. Is this a case for using a personality?

USE LATERAL THINKING TO IDENTIFY 'NEWSY' PERSONALITIES

This leads on to the second point to consider. By what criteria do you select your personality? Remember the 'who, what and why' rules. Look at your audience, their ages and interests. Review the messages about your organization you are trying to project. Then pick somebody who reflects this aura and will appeal to your identified audience. If they are young junior managers in the motor industry, for example, then will they relate to an ex-racing driver from a decade ago? Would he project your organization as you would wish it to be seen? If he is a legendary figure that they will never have the opportunity of meeting, perhaps. If he is living in the past then he will not be right. A specialist academic dealing in industrial psychology may be very exciting to one group and tedious to another. A support player in a TV soap opera may be magical to some and unknown to others.

An easy way of judging whether you have selected the right personality or not is to imagine the conversation that will take place when your guests get back home. Will they talk excitedly about the person they met that day? Will they respect your company for this opportunity?

If the laboratory we considered earlier represents a major investment in a serious sector of research, then a stand-up comic may not be appropriate. In contrast, imagine that the laboratory is looking into the process of ageing. The head of research has published a paper which suggests that, among other factors, laughter is a way of keeping this process at bay. Under these circumstances, a stand-up comic may be appropriate—perhaps as a double act with the more serious head of research!

THINK ABOUT COST EFFECTIVENESS

The value of the personality to the event should not be judged by the cost to obtain his services. (Indeed, many public figures will only participate if they can support the activity and usually require no fee other than the direct expenses of travel.) If a fee is appropriate, this is usually reasonably negotiable. Sometimes, an expensive personality will be available more modestly if some effort is put in to minimizing the inconvenience. If the helicopter or limousine actually picks him up at home a more modest fee may be acceptable than if he is expected to make his own travel arrangements.

The cost can be more modest if the event fits in with an existing schedule: flexibility on dates can improve the chances of getting your personality and saving cost. Of course, if you make extraordinary efforts you have the additional expense involved. But, of equal importance, you are more likely to see your celebrity on the day. The more meticulous your arrangements, the more likely that the personality will take it seriously. Assess any fee in terms of the value to your organization, the pictures, the excitement, the publicity and so on, that will be created at your event.

The skill is in identifying the right celebrity. The world's largest manufacturer of harmonicas, Hohner, helped create an event that attracted press, radio and television coverage. Their public relations consultancy had been looking for personalities to stimulate public interest in harmonicas. The public relations director on the account spotted a brief mention in a report that the then eldest congressman, 81-year-old Claude Pepper, played one for relaxation.

Congressman Pepper was delighted to be enrolled as an honorary life member of the Society for the Preservation and Advancement of the Harmonica. As well as creating excellent pictures, Mr Pepper played his presentation harmonica for radio and TV newsmen at a ceremony organized in Washington. The appeal of this event demonstrated the skill in identifying the right public figure happy to support the campaign objectives.

Do not be tempted to graft a famous face onto your activity just because it is famous. The personality must have relevance. As we have discussed, the personality does not have to be in showbusiness—or even famous. The public relations adviser might give consideration to the director of the professional body most closely associated with the research involved; or a well-known popular scientist; or a broadcaster on science matters; or an author on such subjects. If it has consumer implications, then the director of a trade or consumer association might be suitable.

Do not always go for the obvious. Try a little lateral thinking. Your personality might be a machine—a robot, for example—or an animal. GEC once used the parrot which held the world talking record to launch a new communication system. Air Products used a troop of penguins for a new refrigeration process. One chemical manufacturer invited the distinguished vice-chancellor of a famous university to open a new laboratory.

Do be sure that the personality does not overpower the situation. Even if you succeeded in persuading the well-known Hollywood star to open your laboratory, it is possible that the news stories would be all about his latest romance. They may not even mention the laboratory.

Make sure the event, the speeches, the involvement of the personality are all closely related and integrated. Make sure that the best picture opportunities only happen at the opening ceremony. Do not allow your personality to get involved in interviews that are unrelated to the activity you are organizing. Bring your personality in to your event and then get them away—and, apart from the event, keep them away from the media. Get the maximum value from your investment in the personality. One leading British industrial company sponsored a charity golf day and the four famous show business stars invited planned to play golf in a foursome. It took some firm but diplomatic persuasion by the public relations consultant to break them up to play separately with the business guests.

It can create a lot of impact to create an unusual arrival for your personality—hire a stage coach, bring them in on the back of a tandem, an open-top Bugatti or the traditional chauffeur-driven Rolls-Royce—make it a vintage model, if appropriate. Boulton & Paul brought sports personality Dickie Davies in to open a new joinery centre in a scarlet helicopter: those attending were not aware that the helicopter had picked him up only a quarter of a mile away!

Make sure your personalities are fully briefed on what they are expected to do, the timing and any special arrangements that need to be made beforehand. Do they need to wear something appropriate? Will they be making a speech? Who is writing this? Do they need to bring anything special? Are they to make a presentation? Will they be cutting a tape? Who will be looking after them? When will they be paid and how?

Make sure you get good photographic coverage. You can produce pictures that will have many uses—framed copies for the boardroom or reception of the company; copies for all the personalities involved; a picture story for the trade press; a photospread for the company newspaper; a mailshot to customers who were unable to attend.

A well chosen personality, well-briefed at a well-organized event, can make your organization the talking point of the industry. At the same time, considerable goodwill can be created among those guests invited to attend to meet your celebrity. And good follow-up using the pictures of the event can make those who did not attend wish they had!

THE IMPACT OF SPONSORED SEMINARS

A separate area of special events run by a sponsoring organization is the private conference or seminar. These can be a powerful medium for influencing a direct audience. There will be many areas where the experience and knowledge of the organization would be of interest to some of the publics.

The running of a seminar or conference enables the organization to inform and educate these key groups. At the same time, if effectively run, it can generate valuable goodwill. There are few more effective communications techniques because of the immediate and positive opportunities for feedback. Indeed, the reactions of delegates will provide helpful information relating to attitudes, awareness and knowledge of the organization's activities.

A company-sponsored seminar, conference, open-day or special event can provide excellent opportunities to create goodwill among selected audiences. The Institute of Public Relations publishes a helpful checklist on organizing events. If properly run, the special event can position the organization as the pacemaker in its field, a respected authority in its industry and the team as one with flair and imagination ... not bad for a public relations effort!

USING EVENTS IN THE PROGRAMME

1. Have we got agreed communications objectives before we start looking at special events?
2. Can we look at the calendar of activity and identify those occasions where we need to create a special event to generate interest and/or news?
3. Should we organize a brainstorming session with colleagues from marketing, sales, personnel and other relevant departments to develop ideas for such events?
4. How can these ideas be developed so that they are relevant to the broadest audiences possible, for example, the new product presentation to customers, shareholders and factory neighbours?
5. When, during the campaign, might it be helpful to use a personality?
6. Could a personality be involved with a whole series of related activities,

rather than just one event, for example, the star of the TV commercial meeting the trade, touring the factory and so on?

7. Is the event of such significance that we might wish to consider inviting a member of the royal family?

8. Alternatively, would we wish to approach a leading public or political figure and would this be acceptable to our identified key audiences?

9. What association do we wish to project between our special guest and our organization or products and are these valuable and relevant?

10. Might our 'celebrity' be a piece of machinery or an animal, for example, a computer, a satellite link, King Kong or Lassie?

11. How will we project this involvement to the broader audience beyond those VIPs invited for the day, through media relations, the house journal, a special film and so on?

12. Can we extend the use of the celebrity to other promotional activities, for example, he opens the store, has lunch with the staff, presents the sports cup, hands our charity cheque to the local children's hospital and so on?

13. Have we organized every detail of the event and prepared an agreed programme?

14. Is each activity costed and the total agreed as the budget for the event?

15. Has a proper briefing session been arranged with our celebrities so they know exactly the role they have to play in the detailed programme for the day?

16. Have the local or trade media been advised of the programme and given opportunities they may require for special pictures and/or interviews?

17. Have we agreed the nominated executive to be responsible for the complete master plan including:

    (a) catering and hospitality,
    (b) site facilities,
    (c) briefing and run-through,
    (d) budget and assessment?

18. When planning a special event have we looked through earlier checklists (particularly media conferences) and the guidelines in this events chapter to ensure we cover all arrangements, particularly those relating to:

    (a) timing and venue,
    (b) theme and printing,
    (c) invitations,
    (d) publicity and photography,
    (e) presentations and papers?

19. Can we ensure that an assistant is also nominated to record those areas that might be improved if the event is repeated?

20. Have we established how we will monitor success in meeting the

objectives relating to the event and how this might affect decisions and budgets relating to successive years?

Event planning

Efficient organization is essential in planning any major public relations event. There are a number of basic factors the public relations adviser must cover.

Date and time Check with the calendar that there is no obvious clash of dates. Talk to the news agencies, trade associations and other sources to ensure that you are not in conflict with other events. Keep an option on a number of dates to ensure VIP attendance. Decide on start and finish times.

Critical path Prepare an overall masterplan. This must allow sufficient time for the planning of all activity. Develop a critical path plan. This will identify decision dates for all key elements to ensure they are ready on the day.

Theme Identify any theme and brief the designers who will be interpreting this theme in displays, print and exhibitions. Select relevant speakers, celebrities or special guests.

Invitations Put together an invitation list. Include the direct audience (the shareholders, the customers, wholesalers or whoever) as well as other guests (such as the local media, VIPs, opinion leaders in the community and so on).

Venue Book the venue and all the necessary hotel arrangements, lunches, overnight accommodation and so on. Confirm these arrangements before the critical path is agreed.

Media relations Prepare and issue the press invitations with outline details of the event. Ring round as a follow-up to the invitations. Check who would be likely to attend. Make the arrangements for the press, presspacks, news stories, special travel, telephone, press office, background material, photography.

Print Produce a list of necessary printed items. Prepare the brief. Appoint the printer and/or designer. Obtain quotes and detailed production schedules for each item.

Displays Plan the necessary display, conference set or exhibition material. Appoint the designer and contractor. Brief them, including coordination with print and theme elements. Obtain quotes.

Presentations Agree speakers and prepare a brief for each. Put together the programme. Check the physical resources including the public address system and closed circuit TV, audio-visual aids, recording facilities, names for platforms and so on. Arrange rehearsals.

Papers Ensure all speakers prepare written presentations. Obtain approvals from any external speakers to use their material in public relations activity. Prepare copies as required.

Hospitality Confirm who will greet your guests, will look after them over lunch. Check any special VIPs who require attention. Confirm arrangements for the visitors' books, presentations to senior guests, bouquets and gifts.

Facility inspections Check on the guides, their briefing, the tour itineraries, labelling and identifying of machinery, noise levels, safety, security aspects, lapel badges, rehearsals, timing and so on.

Staff briefing Talk to all support staff and contractors. Brief them on the theme, style, policy and objectives. Ensure they know how to cope with contingencies. Stress the importance of attention to detail.

Consistency Make sure that everything is related to the theme, including the colours, selection of the flowers, displays, presentation sets. Check that the staff are wearing the right badges and overalls, there is special clothing and headgear for visitors, the vehicles, badges, signs, visitors' flags, banners are prepared.

Travel Confirm all arrangements covering cars, coaches, aircraft, special trains and so on. Make sure guests have location maps, and there is suitable signage, parking facilities, the police are advised. Provide any necessary back-up transport.

Catering Check your list of guests and make sure the appropriate arrangements have been made for lunch, breakfast, coffee, tea, dinner, special service, place layouts, menus, master of ceremonies, music, toilet and cloakroom facilities.

Information Prepare any material for other media such as advertisements, posters, exhibits, product displays, visual aids. Brief local bodies that may be involved or affected, such as the chamber of commerce, city council, trade associations etc.

Photography Select and brief the photographers. Cover pictures on the day, special requirements for the slide presentation, press pictures of the event, shots for the record album, the framed memento for the boardroom. Allow for any recce, special processing facilities, lenses and lighting required.

Overseas requirements Arrange interpreters, translation, presspacks in alternative languages, captions and displays. Confirm arrival times and dates and plan for delays/cancellations. Check that no material is unintelligible or offensive to foreign nationals. Advise caterers of any special requirements.

Memento Organize the memento of the occasion for guests. This may be a gift, a signed book, bound copy of the papers presented, photographs, or as appropriate.

Run-through Check the final plan looking for timing and budget anomalies. Organize any progress planning meetings. Confirm individual staff responsibilities. Relate the final plan to the objectives and correct any discrepancies.

Contingency Plan for wet weather arrangements covering umbrellas, duckboards, awnings and weather insurance. If the transport could be affected, organize a contingency programme. For example, if the VIP party is travelling by air, allow for alternative train transport and a delayed start.

Budget Prepare final costings on all agreed activity. Compare this with the original budget allowances. If there are any budget anomalies, advise management. Cut back activity or amend budget if necessary.

Follow-up Issue appropriate material to those unable to attend. Check any further requirements of the media. Obtain cuttings and broadcast transcripts. Issue thanks and appreciations. Check bills against quotes.

Assessment Have a briefing session immediately after the event. Analyse the successes and failures. Prepare a report on these so that the next event can benefit from this experience.

TWENTY-FIVE
EXHIBITIONS AND PRESENTATIONS

WHICH CATEGORY?

Exhibitions fall broadly into three categories: they are either a solus display by one organization; a cooperative presentation arranged between a number of organizations or by a trade association; and, most commonly, a commercially-organized event where many exhibitors buy space to reach a ready-made audience.

The solus display The company which made *only* electric kettles might find it difficult to attract an audience to a product exhibition. In comparison, a company that is distributing a wide range of products or services can often justify its own exhibition. For example, many electrical wholesalers, appliance manufacturers and business systems suppliers organize major displays of their own products. They treat these exactly as if they were participating in a commercial exhibition venture; this means they have to consider carefully the audience, the location, the professional level of display, transport, catering, accommodation and other facilities essential for public comfort and convenience. Such displays may well be of a touring type, visiting regional centres.

The cooperative event There can be advantages in a group of manufacturers or suppliers, welfare bodies or charities pooling their resources. This will enable the basic set-up and organization costs to be spread. The participants will also be able to create more interest and attract a broader audience.

Some trade and professional bodies are now extending their annual conferences by organizing exhibitions which run at the same time.

The commercial exhibition By far the most common option is the commercial exhibition venture. The decision to participate in such exhibitions needs to be very carefully considered. The only acceptable reason for participating in an event is the commercial benefit it will produce. The exhibition 'habit' is not enough to justify this participation. Nor is the blackmail threat of 'you can't afford *not* to participate' ... unless it can be firmly established that this would be to the commercial disadvantage of the organization.

A commercial exhibition is probably far closer to a public relations exercise than it is to an advertising or sales promotional activity. It really *is* presenting the face of the organization to important publics.

Decision factors How do you decide whether an exhibition is a possible solution to your communications and/or marketing objectives? The two key factors are audience and cost—and the first of these is the problem.

The calculation is simpler with the solus (one company) or cooperative event. In most cases, the audience will be known because it is invited. Is it worth the expenditure to reach these people?

The calculation is more difficult with the commercial exhibition. Let us assume that this is an exhibition in which your organization has never participated. You are considering this for the first time: remember the principles of who, what and why?

Check the aims and objectives, as identified by the organizers. Compare their outline of the audience with the profile of your potential customers. Talk to other, previous participants to see whether the quality of the audience delivered actually matched the promise. Discuss with relevant trade media their own views.

The audience delivered Make a calculation of the total real audience that you think you are likely to reach by participating. Be ruthlessly realistic. If you are to take a corner booth in an exhibition dominated by the giants of your industry, it is not realistic to expect that the half million visitors boasted about in the promotional literature are going to tramp across your few square feet of coconut matting. You may be lucky to *see* five per cent of that audience and only one per cent might become involved with your display.

Even if you are convinced that there is a valuable audience, you still need to make another calculation. How much of this audience would you be reaching through your other promotional work? For example, does your company work in a specialized trade where your sales representatives are regularly meeting the same people who will be attending the exhibition? Or is the audience being attracted to the exhibition a completely new sector of your market?

It is important for the executive responsible for advising on the exhibition to attempt to make a calculation of the value of the audience. Try to make a realistic estimate of the numbers of visitors to your exhibition and their level of importance, in terms of business. Let us look at a sample calculation. The main figures you need are the anticipated total audience, the number and stand size of other exhibitors and the real cost of your company's participation.

If it is a new exhibition, you will have to rely on information given by the organizer. These will be predictions, so treat them with caution. If necessary, reduce the audience figure by a factor to allow for the organizer's optimism. If it is an existing exhibition, check previous attendance figures. Assess attitudes to this exhibition. Make an adjustment (up or down) for any factors that might influence the total anticipated audience—an economic decline in your sector, for example, or the improved publicity budget allocated by the organizers.

You will now have a figure for likely total attendance. For convenience, let us assume that this is one million people. Discuss with other previous exhibitors, the organizers, your own sales personnel and relevant editors on the make-up of this total audience. Make an estimate of the proportion that you could reasonably describe as true prospects.

Let us asume this is 50 per cent. Your real total audience is now 500 000. Try to determine how many discussions on average each visitor might have with exhibitors: discount passing traffic as this is of no measurable value to you. Suppose, as might be reasonable, each visitor on average has a discussion on stand with ten exhibitors. This means that there will be a total of five million stand discussions from which you want your commercial share. From the organizers' floor plan you will be able to obtain details of the total number of exhibitors. Say this is 1000. Then, all things being equal, each stand would expect to enjoy 5000 (calculated, 5 million ÷ 1000) stand discussions.

However, all things are not equal. The big names might reasonably be expected to attract the largest proportion of real customers—possibly on the basis of 20 per cent of the exhibitors attracting 80 per cent of the business. But let us be more precise than the 80/20 rule. One approximate indication of the importance of each exhibitor will be their stand size. Say your stand is one-tenth the size of the big industry names. If the industry leaders were to get 80 per cent of the business discussions, the small exhibitors would share the balance of the 20 per cent of stand discussions.

Therefore, only 20 per cent of the total of the stand discussions is available to you. This is 20 per cent × 5 million, which equals 1 million. These discussions have to be shared among the 80 per cent of smaller exhibitors like yourself and these total 800. This will give you a maximum potential of 1250 business discussions on your stand.

A more accurate estimation can be made if you can obtain actual figures. Find the total exhibition floor space being sold. For a show of the type we are using as an example, 25 000 square metres might be reasonable. Divide this into the total stand discussions figure, calculated above, which was five million. This will give 200 (calculated, 5 million ÷ 25 000) stand discussions per square metre. If your stand is, say, 10 square metres your real total potential is 2000 stand discussions.

Now, discuss the appeal of your display with your marketing colleagues. Estimate a factor to represent this appeal: you may feel you can target for 150 per cent of this potential or 50 per cent. But be realistic: it is difficult to undertake an activity that will lift your figures above 100 per cent of the potential. For simplicity, let us assume you agree to target conservatively for 50 per cent. This will give you 1000 business discussions on your stand. This is what you are paying for—*not* the one million visitors in the organizers' publicity.

Compare this audience with the total real cost of participation. This will be the direct costs, transport, advertising, mailing, hotel, travel and other expenses, plus the costs of all executive time in planning, organizing, staffing and follow-up and an allowance for lost business through, for example, taking the sales team off the road. (Staff costs are vital: at exhibitions, why do so many companies think their personnel come free?)

If participation in real terms will cost the organization £20 000, then each stand business discussion will cost £20. How does this compare with other face-to-face sales opportunities for your organization?

Of course, this is a calculation to try to anticipate the real commercial benefit of participating. There are many other factors such as publicity awareness, favourable aura, salesforce motivation and so on. Here are some aims for a manufacturer at an appropriate exhibition. In an actual case, these aims should be quantified and expressed as objectives, as outlined earlier:

1. To improve awareness of the company.
2. To attract potential customers.
3. To reinforce relationships with existing customers.
4. To identify new potential sales outlets.
5. To introduce new products or services to existing customers.
6. To strengthen relations with trade associations and industry leaders.
7. To position the company in terms of price and competition.
8. To evaluate market attitudes towards the company.
9. To demonstrate practical support for distributors.
10. To create sales leads and enquiries.

Such objectives need to be defined before the practical aspects of participation are undertaken. The commercial viability of the exhibition will be influenced by such factors as stand costs. It is recommended that initial calculations are carried out using an estimate of possible costs: then when the potential viability has been established, actual design work can begin and quotations can be obtained. The reason for this approach is that the best display in the world is only as good as the quality of the audience who will see it.

Exhibition sales training Members of the exhibition team need to understand the rather special techniques that apply to handling enquiries on the stand. A commercial organization may have a sales training manager to handle this area, but it is useful for the public relations adviser who may have exhibition responsibilities to understand some of the principles.

For simplicity, let us consider an exhibitor with products to sell—though the same principles apply to a charity appeal or environmental lobby stand. Even trained personnel used to creating opportunities find it difficult to develop effective stand discussions. Under no circumstances confront a visitor by saying: 'Can I help you?'

This has to be one occasion when a closed question should never be used. Open questions that show interest and stimulate a response will enable the executive to develop the conversation.

For example, ask ... 'How do you feel about the new colours we have introduced on these models for this year?' ... 'Are you more interested in our domestic or industrial range?' ... 'Could you give me your opinion on our new flavour range we are testing here?'

At this early stage do not risk a question that might be answered with a negative, for example ... 'Do you like our new colour range?' ... 'Would you try our new flavours?'

Equally, wait before asking questions which might appear too direct ... 'Are you in the wholesale or retail trade?' ... 'Are you planning to buy at this exhibition?'

If the public relations adviser is in doubt about instructing stand personnel, he or she should consider appointing a specialist training organization to run an exhibition familiarization course. This can be invaluable, even if the team have participated in a number of exhibitions in the past. Also there are a number of training films available which can be helpful including, in the UK, 'How not to exhibit Yourself' from Video Arts.

MONITORING VISITORS

Review the procedures for staff to monitor visitors to the stand, to provide a valuable list of potential interest. Exhibition follow-up activity will be directed towards these people. Certainly, they should go on to the organization's prospect mailing list. From this information, it will be possible for the public relations adviser or exhibition executive to analyse the effectiveness of this participation.

Each member of the stand staff must complete a record form for each visitor. Then the cost of achieving each stand discussion can be calculated; remember, this was the original justification for participation. Check how the reality measures up to the prediction. This helps identify any error in the calculations so that they can be corrected for future estimates.

At some time after the exhibition—say, six months—check which of these prospects has been converted into actual business. How much of this might have arisen from other activities? The cost of obtaining this business can be worked out.

As well as the quantitative assessment of performance, the exhibition executive needs to make some qualitative appraisal of the value of participation. This might cover checking on media interest, attention and measuring the actual coverage; checking the most effective stand in terms of public appeal, press interest and so on; trying to assess the publicity value of participation or awareness of your stand among exhibition visitors; evaluating your staffing levels to cope with visitors; identifying peak times and best days for visitors to enable you to adjust the staff roster; interviewing stand personnel to record their observations.

The final assessment must be to relate the outcome to the identified objectives. How close did the exhibition perform to the figures that justified participation? Anything above will be a bonus. Say 10 per cent or 15 per cent below target level might indicate that participation could be worthwhile but better efforts are required. Anything below this would suggest there might be better ways to achieve these objectives.

Therefore, if you are in, give it the maximum: if not, get out and put your efforts somewhere more worth while.

Exhibitions and related presentations can be a central element in a broad public relations campaign, but they must be evaluated on their merit. The cost/audience factors should be calculated and compared with the alternative techniques for reaching the target publics.

PLANNING FOR EXHIBITIONS

1. Have we identified why we wish to consider an exhibition or a presentation and the audience we are trying to influence?
2. Are we considering:

   (a) our own display or series of displays,
   (b) a touring exhibition on train or special vehicle,
   (c) participation in a scheduled commercial exhibition?

3. If our event, can we calculate the total cost in terms of outgoings for venues, travel, hospitality and the executive time involved?
4. Has the organization got the staff to handle the logistics?

5. Are we clear what audience we will be reaching and that this will be a new audience not already familiar with our case?
6. If we are considering the touring exhibition, will we be the only exhibitor carrying the total cost?
7. Or will we be sharing costs and audiences with other participants?
8. Are they complementary or competitive to our interests?
9. If we are evaluating the commercial exhibition, will this bring us to the attention of a valuable new sector of the audience that matters?
10. In all cases, have we carried out the cost-efficiency calculations to enable us to compare events and decide which is most appropriate?
11. How are we proposing to staff this exhibition or presentation?
12. Have we nominated an exhibition manager to be responsible for the stand, the staff roster and on-stand behaviour?
13. What special training or briefing do we need to provide for our exhibition staff?
14. Are we planning to undertake any attitude research or competitive evaluation during this participation?
15. Have we produced and agreed the timetable relating to the build up to the exhibition, the event and the follow-up?
16. Have we agreed the publicity efforts needed to inform the primary audiences of our plans—customers, wholesalers, retailers?
17. Are all our trading partners, suppliers, agents, distributors, aware of the exhibition and their role in the activity?
18. Can this participation be used to improve relations with secondary audiences by, for example, inviting selected employees representatives, civic leaders, MPs, MEPs, union negotiators and so on?
19. Will we be checking on competitor activity and using the event to gain intelligence about, for example, their marketing or product development plans?
20. As always, by what criteria will we be measuring the effectiveness?

Exhibition effectiveness Two publications from the Incorporated Society of British Advertisers provide some useful guidance on evaluating the effectiveness of a participation in an exhibition and these are *Guide for Exhibitors* and *Value Analysis in Advertising: Measure of the Effectiveness of Exhibitions and Trade Receptions*.

There are a number of key stages that the executive responsible for the exhibition will need to consider:

1. An outline budget allocation needs to be drafted.
2. The coordinator of the project has to be appointed.
3. A decision has to be made on the location within the exhibition and stand size.

4. The exhibition manager responsible for liaison and control of staff must be nominated.
5. All other departments need advising of their own responsibilities, which might include production of models, special painting of prototypes, personnel requirements and so on.
6. The brief for the stand contractor and designer must be drafted and agreed.
7. Contractors must be invited to tender.
8. A schedule must be drafted to cover all necessary print, photography and illustrations of the displays on the stand.
9. The manpower requirements need to be evaluated covering participation in the exhibition, including a duty roster, accommodation, transport and so on.
10. Briefing sessions should be run by the coordinator for the stand manager and all staff, including a run-through of the check list and duty roster, the preparation of guidance notes on dealing with enquiries, logging visitors, enquiry forms and so on.
11. The exhibition catalogue copy and/or advertising must be prepared.
12. The advance news story and press liaison arrangements should be agreed, including invitations to stands and/or press receptions at the exhibition.
13. All material should be delivered to the contractor as scheduled, including company items such as models, products and so on.
14. The arrangements must be confirmed for the special receptions for staff, key customers, press and so on.
15. Final briefing for stand staff should be scheduled to cover rehearsals, discussion on awkward questions and difficult customers, confirming the details of the roster, reminding colleagues of the objectives and ending with a motivational appeal.
16. Agree all procedures for follow-up after the exhibition.

TWENTY-SIX

ADVERTISING

USING ADVERTISING AS A PUBLIC RELATIONS TECHNIQUE

It has been argued—not just by public relations people—that advertising is a part of public relations. Certainly, advertising can be one of the most powerful methods of influencing the attitudes of audiences of importance to the organization.

Both public relations and advertising should be working to a consistent communications policy. As advertising requires special skills and frequently requires major budgets, this activity is undertaken by specialized agencies who resist inroads into their responsibilities. The public relations adviser may have the confidence of the chairman of his organization, but may still operate with a modest budget and limited resources: to undertake the broad public relations responsibility, the public relations adviser will have to have influence over advertising policy.

Of course, even under such circumstances, it will still be essential for the advertising to be carried out by professionals with independence and strong views on their craft. The public relations executive will differentiate between the monitoring responsibility and the implementation of the advertising.

Should the advertising become a direct responsibility for the public relations specialist he will need to enlist professional assistance. This can be through the appointment of an advertising manager or the selection of an appropriate advertising agency. This is increasingly the position among charities, trade associations and non-profit bodies where all communications are conducted through the public relations channel.

With commercial organizations, much of the advertising effort will be directed towards sales support. Consequently, it is natural that it should be monitored and controlled directly by the marketing personnel. In these cases, it is the public relations adviser's responsibility to ensure the advertising is consistent with the agreed corporate communications policy.

Separate to promotional advertising, there are some sectors where the most effective means of communicating with company audiences may be through the medium of advertising. These corporate advertising efforts are frequently planned to help an organization become better known and regarded. In such cases, advertising can present messages quickly and powerfully.

Care needs to be taken in the messages projected. BP ran a £20 million campaign to demonstrate its commitment to environmental issues—one damaging by-product was a series of news articles which attempted to prove the company had a less than satisfactory record in this area.

Such corporate campaigns are never cheap. Deciding what to say and where takes the time of top advertising professionals. By their very nature, such advertisements need to be high profile and appear in expensive surroundings, such as large spaces in prestigious publications or pricey slots on national television. Results are difficult to measure without costly research and are unlikely to generate tangible results such as sales. When money is tight the corporate campaign is the first to go.

There are other problems. Standing up and being counted can be risky, like standing up and being shot at. Communication is only working if it invites feedback. To quote a few recent examples, if you decide to call yourself 'the listening bank' then the first time a customer has a complaint the event can become bad news. One student was threatened with the police over her overdraft and the bank manager involved found himself in the national news! When Avis state 'we try harder' then they need to prove it with every contact with their customers. If Japan Airlines say 'To be prepared is everything', then they had better be prepared next time something unexpected occurs. If Toshiba forget to enclose an instruction leaflet, do you care if they're 'in touch with tomorrow'? When ICI were 'The Pathfinders', salesmen late for an appointment were met with comments like 'What was the matter—couldn't find the path?'

Making such statements firmly positions the organization but carries clear dangers. The only wise course before embarking on such corporate campaigns is to be sure that they are the correct method to achieve the objectives. The promises must be real and checked out thoroughly; in the UK, we still smile at British Rail 'getting there' or the ludicrously glitzy television 'wonderful world' of Woolworths.

Above all, such campaigns must spring out of the corporate communications strategy and reflect the corporate personality. In other words, they should only be initiated by the corporate communications adviser and working 'on strategy', not 'on whim'.

COORDINATE ALL THE ELEMENTS

All facets of the promotional activity need to be integrated. For example, a company which is closely involved with the public sector may be using a public affairs campaign to develop relations with senior government officials and ministers; a public advertising approach could be used to reinforce this. Through the pages of selected national newspapers, a specific message can be orientated towards senior civil servants, local government officers, cabinet ministers, MPs and MEPs.

Corporate advertising can also be an effective way of strengthening relations with suppliers, attracting potential recruits, reinforcing relations with distributors, confidence-building among such publics as shareholders, trading partners, customers and employees.

An outline brief for a corporate campaign for, say, an electrical motor manufacturer, might include the following broad aims:

1. To inform graduates and experienced industry managers of the career potential within the company.
2. To develop awareness of the company throughout the distribution network.
3. To remind senior politicians of the contribution of the company to the national economy.
4. To educate relevant government departments on the importance of the product sector.
5. To project to opinion leaders, pressure groups and local communities, the social responsibility of the organization.

The advertising agency will discuss with the company's communications manager those areas where direct advertising could contribute to the broader communications effort. Their observations will include an assessment of the viability of such a strategy using advertising, the cost-effectiveness of alternative tactics and the potential media. From such discussions, the agency will be able to prepare realistic advertising objectives and recommendations on how they might be achieved.

Corporate advertising is frequently strategic but it can be used tactically; a company which is under attack from a consumer group or fighting a takeover bid can very rapidly put over its case through the advertising columns of the national press.

It must be remembered, such advertisements are not only read by the direct audiences concerned but they are also read by other media personnel: a powerful advertisement can help create a wider debate of the subject and put over a stronger news angle. Potentially, this advertising effort can strengthen the public relations activity being undertaken through media relations channels. (See Chapter 12 on financial relations, covering the reservations on this technique.)

There are many areas where advertising and public relations can work most effectively together to form a perfect marketing mix. In such cases, the advertising may be deployed as a medium of communications to meet public relations objectives. Sometimes public relations will be deployed to support advertising. Whichever way, each craft is stronger when operating with the other to coordinated objectives.

USING ADVERTISING AS A PUBLIC RELATIONS MEDIUM

1. Have we decided, as a policy, that all advertising will be the responsibility of the public relations function?
2. Or are we only considering that part of the advertising effort that is aimed at meeting public relations objectives?
3. If the former, what are the lines of responsibility between the public relations adviser, the advertising manager, the agency, and those departments for whom the advertising is undertaken, notably sales, marketing and personnel?
4. Has the public relations adviser adequate staff and expertise to handle this responsibility?
5. If the latter, do we appreciate the circumstances that may require advertising to achieve public relations objectives, for example, when complete control is required by the organization over the media, the timing and the message?
6. If we are using such corporate advertising to handle an emergency situation, is it consistent with how we have projected the organization to date?
7. Could we develop alternative communications in future to reduce the need for contingency corporate advertising?
8. In other words, are we concentrating adequate resources on a continuous basis towards developing goodwill and favourable attitudes among corporate audiences?
9. Do we require a different advertising agency to handle the corporate activity with the public relations adviser or do we use the same one that handles sales and marketing support?
10. How will this advertising budget be agreed and controlled?
11. Who will be approving the creative copy platform, media selection, the schedule?
12. Is some direct response element to be built in, for example, requests for the annual report or special booklet, an invitation to ring an information number, and so on?
13. As a separate issue to corporate advertising, has the advertising agency received a copy of the corporate communications objectives so that all product advertising is projecting messages that are consistent with these aims?

14. What arrangements have been made for the heads of public relations and advertising to coordinate the timing of their activities?
15. What method will be used to evaluate the effectiveness of the corporate advertising in changing attitudes among the identified audiences?

TWENTY-SEVEN
AUDIO-VISUAL

In broad terms, audio-visual aids can be described as those items which rely on sound and pictures to assist speakers. (They usually work together, though not always: during a London communications workshop, a radio producer included a quadraphonic demonstration through multiple speakers located around the room. Using sounds only, he presented a clear and moving story without words.)

Similarly, it is possible to produce an audio-visual aid that is visual only. (Perhaps the early silent films fitted into this category!) This visual-only technique has been updated by the production of silent films and tape/slide presentations without sound commentaries. Usually, these use only pictures to convey the information: the sound track has no commentary but just adds atmosphere. Perhaps the most famous example is the Pirelli promotional film, *The Tortoise and the Hare*. This used music and effects but no dialogue. It achieved the distinction of television and cinema showing on its entertainment value alone. A film sponsored by Norwich Union looked at the life of Norwich and used no commentary or voice-over, just sounds of the city at work and play.

The use of audio-visual techniques in public relations programmes can be divided into two broad categories—first, support for a live speaker and, second, the presentation of a complete message in a self-contained format.

A research project undertaken by a manufacturer of projection equipment showed that, after three days, 15 per cent of the message might be remembered, on average, when presented in an oral form; 40 per cent might be remembered when presented in a written form and 75 per cent when the message used both sound and vision together. There is still a lot of research to be undertaken in this area but common observation will show that a message reinforced visually will have more memorability.

Flip chart Perhaps the simplest visual aid in general use is the flip chart. These are large pads of plain paper usually mounted on an easel or frame. To a large extent these have replaced the old blackboard—though not the whiteboard, which can be drawn on with coloured ink—or the electronic whiteboard, from which hard copies can be printed at the touch of a button.

With a flip chart, the presenter can build up a picture or can use prepared sheets to illustrate the points as the case is developed. Cues can be written lightly in pencil, say, in the top corner of each sheet. Therefore, the speaker can work without obvious notes.

However, if the speaker is proposing to use sheets which have been prepared in advance, there is little value in the use of the flip chart. The case can be better presented on boards which will have more impact and a longer life.

Equally important, with flip charts some speakers cannot resist illustrating every minor point or writing down occasional words: this becomes irritating to the audience. Any audio-visual should *add* an extra dimension to what is being presented and not simply repeat it. Used properly, a flip chart can involve the audience; they are able to see the picture taking place in front of them. They will be able to feel the spontaneity of the presenter; he can maintain eye contact with the audience but, as with all techniques, it needs skill and practice.

Slides Transparency slides are more expensive than the use of boards or a flip chart. They can have impact, particularly, where the speaker is presenting photographic material. The most common format is 35mm, usually in a projector with a slide or carousel-type magazine. Always use glass and not card-mounted slides as the latter bend, can absorb damp and the focus shifts as they warm up in the projector.

Again, some basic rules apply. Do not simply use the words that the speaker is going to say. Summarize the points into short sentences with active verbs. Modern electronic desk-top publishing systems have dramatically brought down the cost of high-quality, presentable slides. Never drop below this standard, for it will not be acceptable to the audience. Make sure the slides are clearly, cleanly and professionally produced.

Today, most projectors have magazines so that the slides can be arranged in advance. Remember when you want the information on the screen: you may need blanks in the magazine when the speaker is talking without requiring illustration. Include the blanks where necessary and run through the slides. Make sure your speaker knows how to cue and use his slides. It is wisest to use only horizontal or vertical slides (for *all* speakers at a session) so that the screen can be set up to accommodate the *whole* image.

Overhead projectors These were originally designed to help in lecturing and are most versatile. They use transparent sheets and can reproduce photography or graphics in colour or black and white. Pre-prepared transparencies can be combined with those that are written as the speaker progresses—using spirit pens.

Simple slides can be prepared through photocopiers on to transparent sheets. A small audience in a lecture may forgive the speaker's scrawny handwriting as he illustrates points: they will not forgive such standards in pre-prepared transparencies. These must be up to professional standards. Again, new desk-top publishing systems can help produce attractive, economic overhead transparencies.

Epidiascope This machine projects an image onto a screen but has the ability to show a three-dimensional or opaque object and does not require the light to be shone *through*—in other words, it will show the pages of a book, artwork, small objects and so on. This hardware is very expensive and rather rare. However, it is invaluable for such uses as technical lectures where actual items, samples or small products need to be shown to a large audience.

Of course, all the items described above are really visual aids without any audio element (other than the speaker!). It is useful to look at the audio-visual techniques which are commonly available:

Tape/slide These are generally based upon 35mm or 6 × 6cm slides in magazines and use a pre-recorded soundtrack on tape. The tape contains pulses which provide the signals to the projector to move on to the next slide.

The simplest format will use one slide projector. Slightly more versatile is the twin slide projector: this allows dissolve between slides, avoiding a blank screen. The hardware is bulky, fairly costly and requires some modest operator training.

Major tape/slide presentations using three, or even 300, projectors are quite possible: these are usually controlled by a computer programme and are only suitable for major productions in fixed locations. Invariably, they require a big budget and a commercial production house.

Cine film Film is both high in sound and picture quality and still has some advantages over video. It is available in a number of formats, the most common being 35mm, 16mm and 8mm. The public relations adviser would almost certainly need to bring in a professional production house.

Film still has the advantage that all projectors for each film format are compatible and universally available. Film can be shown in any country in the world; it can even be shown on projectors with their own independent power source.

Many commercially-made training and sales films exist. Alternatively, film can be used as a means of communicating specific messages to specific audiences. While the initial cost of cine can be high, the advantage of film is that it can have a long life and can be most impressive. Language sound-tracks allow film to be used in overseas markets. The production of a foreign language commentary or commentary updates are relatively inexpensive. Lip-sync (where the actors are filmed speaking) is more expensive than a separate soundtrack.

Filmstrip Tape and slide presentations can also be put onto filmstrip format. The continuous closed-loop format is practical at exhibitions where a slide programme can be left running continuously. These systems require the minimum of attention.

Cine film can also be prepared into a closed-loop cassette for showing on portable equipment (such as Fairchild or Technicolor).

Radio Private radio is mainly used for limited, person-to-person contact such as with citizens band or radio telephones. However, larger organizations (in the UK, United Biscuits and many hospitals), have developed private radio stations as part of their overall communications activities. These do not broadcast but are relayed over private lines, in some cases to more than one location. While they are primarily for entertainment, they can have a news function and some limited information feedback.

Tape Of course, sound can be used alone but is rarely a technique to support or replace a speaker—though some dramatic personal presentations have been produced where the live speaker has been backed by a track, usually in stereo, of appropriate sound effects and music. This requires a very professional speaker.

A more frequent use of tape, which does not strictly fit into this audio-visual section, is where an audio magazine is produced, usually on cassette.

Private television Closed circuit television (CCTV) systems have no broadcast element but can be used to show pictures remote from the viewer. For example, the opening of a new plant, the launching of a ship, the commissioning of a piece of equipment—all can be covered by video cameras with the pictures seen live in, say, a VIP reception area. Pictures can be transmitted by direct cable connection, hired public telephone lines, local electronic-news-gathering systems (ENG as used by broadcasting television stations) or by satellite.

CCTV is often used in conjunction with video recording so that the pictures can be edited or used at a later date. This is particularly relevant to training, for example.

Video presentations Video offers sound, colour, movement—in much the same way as film. Production tends to be less expensive as the equipment is simpler to use and does not require such large crews. But video still does not yet match the highest qualities of film. Again, it is essential to use professional production houses.

There is increasing standardization in video. Prepared programmes can be recorded onto cartridge tape of suitable format and used in colour video players. The video disc is having some impact in the educational and industrial markets, because of quality and ease of distribution.

Every member of today's audience is trained to expect the highest standards. They all watch the best video production possible on their television screens every night. Poor direction, poor scripting, poor lighting or other potential faults will detract from the power of the message.

Technique selection

Start by identifying the audience to whom you are trying to talk. What are you trying to achieve? Make a list of the resources and requirements. Will you have speakers to present the case or has the presentation to be self-contained? How professional or experienced will they be? Is there existing video material or film footage? Are there many locations where presentations need to be made? Have you historical and archive material? Does the case to be explained require sound and colour? Is movement essential? Would animation be of help? Where will your audience see this presentation? How large will these audiences be? Would sophisticated hardware be available? Does the presentation need to be in different languages? Are there personalities that need to be featured in it? How many copies will be required of the presentation? To what length might it need to run? Will it require updating? Over what period of time will it be used? What sort of feedback do we require? How long have we got for production?

Such questions will identify which of the audio-visual techniques will be best—and the likely budget that you may need to allocate. The following notes make some suggestions on which techniques might be most suitable for different presentation opportunities:

Flip Chart Suitable for personal talk to a small group of managers by a competent speaker. Also for lecturers, discussion meetings—particularly where more than one member of the group may be putting material together. Normal room lighting is possible, therefore effective where visual audience contact is necessary.

Overhead projector Best when speakers need to use slides on which information is written. When using pre-prepared slides, suited to a larger audience, particularly where pictures need to be projected under daylight conditions. An example might be a seminar for 40 or 50 people using a mixture of handwritten slides, photographic material, charts and graphs.

Slides, single magazine or carousel, self-operated Ideal for a lecture situation but where a larger number of colour photographs need to be used. An example might be an illustrated lecture by the export director on an overseas visit; an examination of the use of corporate identity around the company; a study of housing round the world, using slides taken from stock and library material. Virtually no training needed, though subdued light is necessary.

Slides, tape-driven using dissolve Excellent for a prepared presentation to an audience of 20 upwards, particularly where it will be repeated. Advantageous where a professional voice-over is necessary. Invaluable where a 'theatrical-type' atmosphere is helpful. Needs subdued lighting. Cannot be set up quickly and has limited transport capability. Brilliant picture quality is possible and easy to update. Needs some small degree of training. Equipment can be hired. Major programmes may require a production house.

Film strip Average quality pictures can be used with or without pre-prepared voice-over and therefore suitable for desk-top presentation to small groups. Cheap to reproduce copies, so suitable for use by salesforce or international representatives. Also ideal for exhibition use where a series of slides are to be shown continually. Virtually no skill required. Appropriate hardware essential.

Radio Useful medium where entertainment is required, such as in production units. Can use tapes or staff personnel. Hardware very expensive and operation costs high. Consider the alternative of piping in a commercial radio line—for example, the local radio station—with an additional facility to insert company news items, live or on tape.

CCTV Suitable for the remote opening of facilities, relaying ceremonial occasions or demonstrations which can be projected to a larger sized audience. Also, suitable for training, projection of speakers to overflow audiences or big-screen projected pictures of speakers. Needs expensive hardware and skilled operators—though both can be hired.

Film Quality pictures possible, though needs substantial budget. Use of movement invaluable in some situations. Copies easily and cheaply reproduced. As the sound track is separate, can be produced in language versions. Not easy to edit or update and therefore more suitable where a longer life can be anticipated. Good film is very impressive. Uses might include the introduction of a new building product which has to be explained to groups of architects, suveyors, local authorities and builders. Or, the background to a successful conservation project presented as a human-interest story to diverse audiences. Hardware and skilled personnel essential but complete production can be quoted and bought from a production house.

Video Can be fast, can be edited and can, to some extent, be updated. Does not yet match the quality of film but can be reasonably impressive. The picture image can be projected—though this hardware is expensive. Also uses colour, sound and movement and many electronic effects are available. Video players rapidly reducing in size. Desk-top presentations practical. Some typical uses might include the presentation of a new campaign across the desk to buyers; round-up of the company's activities for showing at the agm; presentation of sales reports to the salesforce; presentation of annual results to employees ... and the recording of their comments for relaying to the directors. Hardware expensive. Equipment idiot-proof. However, professional productions do need professional crews. Packages can be bought from production houses.

The public relations adviser should become familiar with all audio-visual systems. Learn the techniques—and when to use them. If in doubt, ask for the advice of an audio-visual consultant. Use the best production house possible. Develop your skills so that your visual communications match your verbal, for that is tomorrow's way.

.... a message reinforced visually will have more memorability

Client:	*Any Charity Appeal*
Audience:	chairmen, managing directors and chief executives of large companies identified as having strong sense of social responsibility/ community commitment
Aim:	to demonstrate the benefits of supporting the national charity appeal in terms of: 1. publicity, 2. employee involvement, 3. product promotion opportunites, 4. public goodwill
Objective:	to influence a sponsor to commit £AAA to support this project
Duration:	10/12 minutes
Schedule:	research by 7 May draft script by 30 May casting by 7 June final script by 14 June location shooting by 21 June studio shooting by 27 June music, sound, dubbing and editing by 14 July delivery to client by 21 July private preview 24 July public presentation 25 July
Outline:	a weekend at the holiday home seen through the eyes of one of the handicapped children, his first holiday ever, away from home
Message:	the concept works—and if it can achieve this success on a modest basis, £BBB could finance a national scheme
Production:	Project coordination: ABC Public Relations Director: John Smith (see attached biography) Researcher: Mary Brown Production: XYZ Video Format: recorded and edited on high band with full recognized crew (to allow possible editorial TV use). Copies to be delivered on VHS
Budget:	total cost including all research scripting, production, hire, location costs, music, fees and copies delivered not to exceed £CCC

Chart 27.1 With a major video or film production, it is helpful to gather all the key elements together onto one briefing sheet. This can be circulated to all executives involved and ensures maximum understanding and minimum problems that might affect the production schedule. This briefing sheet, based on an actual production, is for a charity feature on video to raise a substantial fund to finance a new appeal.

USING AUDIO-VISUALS

1. What is the audience for this presentation in background, age, social position and so on?
2. Are the aids we are proposing appropriate for the size of audience and room?
3. Will the speaker be operating all aids or will there be a separate technician or operator available?
4. Is it possible to get into the room earlier to set up all necessary equipment, test, focus and adjust volumes?
5. Have we allowed time for a rehearsal to check the operation of the equipment, aids and timing?
6. Can the level of room lighting be controlled and who will do this?
7. Have we considered the main options relating to choice of audio-visual aids including:

flip chart or cards	tape/slide programme
whiteboard/feltboard	filmstrip
overhead projector	film or video
slide projector	cctv?

8. Have we suitable internal resources or external suppliers to ensure we can produce the most appropriate and cost-effective support for our speakers?
9. Have we checked the speaker training notes, at the end of Chapter 30 on speakers' panels?
10. Are we using aids to support a speaker or are we putting the emphasis on a presentation introduced by the speaker?
11. If the former, can we check that the audio-visual assistance does not dominate the presentation?
12. If the latter, can we ensure that the presenter knows how to introduce the tape/slide or film, handle questions and still establish his personality?
13. Have we run through the overall presentation to ensure that it is at the right depth and sets the right tone for the audience?
14. Is our speaker properly trained and equipped with all the facts, company policy and authority to deal with all issues that may be raised at the discussion stage?
15. Have we checked the training notes on presentation skills in the radio and television section?
16. Can we arrange for someone to assess the presentation, to give a view on its effectiveness and methods of improvement for the future?

TWENTY-EIGHT

RESEARCH

CAMPAIGNS START WITH RESEARCH

Public relations is dependent on an input of information—or perhaps, more accurately, intelligence (assimilated and interpreted information). The ideal campaign is based on facts not assumptions. It is impossible to change attitudes effectively unless the public relations specialist has identified what attitudes already exist. In discussions with managers of the organization it is not always easy to obtain a full and honest picture. In some cases, personnel may not wish to reveal problems that might reflect on their professionalism. More often, they might not be aware of important facts.

However, unless the public relations adviser insists upon having the correct information, he will not be able to develop the recommendations that will be necessary to improve the situation. In Britain, it has been estimated that over 90 per cent of *The Times* top 1000 companies (presumably those who know what they are doing) regularly use research to find out more about subjects about which (it might be supposed) they already know enough.

Experienced managers know the dangers of basing decisions upon personal observation. We all know that we tend to see what we want to see, hear what we want to hear. It is almost a truism, as an illustration, that every company thinks it is better known, better understood, better supported than it actually is.

To quote an actual case, a large British industrial company introduced a new corporate identity. This was adopted on all stationery, every factory, every vehicle and every uniform. After a period of time, much to the consternation of the management, a survey showed that some 50 per cent of *current* customers of the company did not recognize the new identity. It realistically puts public perceptions into perspective: if your existing customers do not know who you are, what chance do you stand with your prospects?

INFORMAL RESEARCH CAN BE INVALUABLE

Normally, there is considerable information which can be gathered by the public relations team through informal research. Talking to people can be invaluable. If you are supposed to be improving employee relations, talk to employees. Get round and about and be seen. Create opportunities for people to expand on their ideas and views with you. Be available by attending the company club, going to the annual conference, sitting in on sales meetings, attending the sports day, and so on.

Consider putting together a committee to represent the various operating sectors. Structure an agenda to talk through the areas where you would like views. Leave plenty of opportunity for colleagues to raise their own areas. Convene the panel on a regular basis so that it performs a continuous monitoring operation. After a period of time, each member of this discussion group will be carrying out their own discussions within the company. You will be getting representative views from a far wider spread than could ever be achieved by yourself.

Organizations have available a large number of sources of invaluable information about the attitudes of important publics; many of these are never tapped. These are the professional advisers and trading partners who observe reactions to the organization. Confidential discussions with such specialists as banks, accountants, solicitors, union leaders, the advertising agency, suppliers, professional bodies, financial analysts, trade editors, stockbrokers, careers officers, even government officials and civil servants—all can put a fresh perspective on many aspects of the organization's operations. Get a view of how competitors and other peer organizations are performing in comparison with your organization. (The positioning of your company in this group can be a measure of the effectiveness of the public relations work: this can be checked as the campaign develops.)

The objective of this research will be to establish the gap between how the organization is seen and how it would like to be seen—the public relations credibility. Get members of your team to develop this habit of asking and listening. Carefully read reports, literature and brochures. Check on complaints and talk to personnel about the reasons people give for leaving the company. Collate all such information into an informal report.

DESK RESEARCH IS THE STARTING POINT

In every sector of human activity there is a wealth of published material. This can include textbooks, publications, government statistics, journals, existing reports and so on. Many organizations maintain an information library while public or trade association libraries can be an invaluable additional source of information. Basic statistical information is available from dozens of public, industry and professional sources.

For example, in the UK, it is possible through the public library, to check on the directors of companies, the acreage of grain growing in each county, the number of radios per household, how much per head is spent on packaging, the average number of TV hours watched by women over 55...

Build up reference files on information you are likely to need. Train your staff in desk research. Where necessary, use professionals but ask them to work in your own offices so that members of your team can develop an appreciation of the techniques involved in gathering desk research. Build up your own library of statistical industry information, company data, trends and product information, available for media and company use.

FORMAL RESEARCH

Broadly, research breaks down into those areas which just give guidance and those which are statistically valid. The guidance information should not be used to make substantial decisions.

One widely-used research method is the in-depth interview. This can give helpful guidance on awareness, perception and attitudes. Discussion groups extend this idea by giving a selected group the opportunity to explore an area under guidance from the research leader. Though they may not be representative, discussion groups can give useful indications where more substantial research might be undertaken. They can also help the researchers in drafting questionnaires to be used in any proposed subsequent survey.

Statistically-valid research results are obtained when the size of the sample and the method of sampling give a response that is to within an acceptable level of accuracy of the predictable response from the whole audience. This requires the sample to be selected to represent the larger universe being investigated—in terms of age, occupation, income or other relevant factors. The public relations adviser is recommended to turn to a professional market research organization to assist in these areas. Even in modest surveys, the professional can often produce the results at no more cost than the public relations department. In some cases, the professional can draft the questionnaire, advising on the method of sampling and analyse the results.

One consultancy was asked to evaluate the audience for a group planning to tender for a radio station franchise. The budget would not allow the statistically-valid research that was necessary. However, the budget would allow the hiring of a professional to put together the questionnaire, to plan the research and to supervise the work of a team of university graduates recruited to undertake the interviewing. However, amateur interviewers must be used with caution and only under strict supervision.

Limited surveys

The type of survey that might be undertaken by the public relations department would be one where there was a defined and limited audience. This might include investigations into employee attitudes towards working conditions, benefits and so on.

Let us look at another example. A well-known group of garages in southern England held the franchise for a major manufacturer but offered servicing facilities and used car sales for any make of vehicle. A simple analysis of sales figures showed that servicing and used car sales for other makes were very low. There were some simple questions that arose. Was the strength of the car franchise being projected so well that it implied the company was not interested in other makes? Was there public feeling that if the garages could service one particular make they might not have the experience to tackle others?

The company asked their public relations advisers to investigate these areas. They organized a modest survey to evaluate these potential problems. They decided to check attitudes among known existing customers themselves but to use a professional research company to evaluate potential attitudes among the motoring public at large.

The questionnaire to customers was structured on a simple tick-box basis. It required no more than a minute or two to complete. Five hundred customers were mailed and a response of just less than 30 per cent was achieved.

This tended to confirm some of the points already identified. The answers also raised one or two fresh points, including concern about the quality of the company facilities being reflected in the high servicing prices charged. On the basis of this preliminary assessment, the professional market research company was briefed to investigate broader public attitudes. The final results of the professional survey demonstrated that there was concern among many motorists over the technical competence of the garage to service other makes; also, there was very limited awareness of their interest in servicing these.

Consequently, a public relations programme was structured which included regular mailings to customers, a shift in the emphasis in the advertising to include other makes, open days, showroom displays and special offers on services on other makes. The result over a 12-month period was that the total service business for other makes rose from less than 10 per cent to 22 per cent. In value, turnover for servicing non-franchise cars doubled during the same period.

Drafting the questionnaire

It is possible to bias the response strongly in the direction you wish by the shaping of the questions. Emotive, or biased questions or those which only allow a limited number of answers can produce a substantial shift in the response. It is possible to structure a postal questionnaire so that you only get a response from those who will support the case you may be trying to improve; this may be interesting but it is not real research.

As an illustration, the motor group mentioned earlier used only closed questions in their preliminary study. An open question would be 'What factors are important to you when choosing a garage to service your car?' A closed question would limit the answers, for example, by asking 'Rate these factors in order of importance to you in choosing a garage to service your car...'. They *could* have included a question that might have produced more flattering results. 'Do you feel it wiser to go to a well-known company with full facilities and staff to service your car or to smaller, one-man operations that may not have the resource or capabilities?'

Given just the choice of ticking a box which says agree or disagree, more people are likely to agree. The response could be biased the opposite way if the question had been put 'Would you prefer to have your car serviced at a small, caring garage with low overheads rather than one of the big, impersonal chains?'

The point for the public relations adviser to remember when approving the questionnaire is that any bias must be avoided. Do not use open questions for substantial surveys that require statistical analysis but give tick box alternatives. Consider the use of semantic differential; here respondents are given the opportunity to answer a question by indicating their strength of feeling, 'The service staff of ABC Motors are helpful.' The answer to this question would be a series of boxes to tick which would cover ... agree completely ... agree slightly ... uncertain ... disagree slightly ... disagree completely...

Similarly, another area for potential confusion is to ask how often people undertake an activity or purchase a product. Reject vague wording like 'regularly'. To one person regularly might be once a month, while to another it might be once a day. Where your survey is evaluating prices, make sure you give a range and ask people to be specific. 'For the product described, I would be prepared to pay £1, £2, £3, £4, £5.'

The research specialist should only ask for information that can be known by respondents. For example, in one mushroom survey undertaken by a national research body, housewives could recall with accuracy how much they had paid for the product. However, the quantities that they claimed to have bought were widely different from the known quantities sold. This was later discovered to be because mushrooms had previously been sold generally in 4oz quantities. Housewives had been less accurate in observing when they bought 8oz or 6oz packs.

Be suspicious of any questions which ask people to explain their motives. Many may not know their motivations and all will be tempted to rationalize.

PUBLICITY USE OF RESEARCH

Often, the public relations adviser may not be running the organization's research but should be given the opportunity to have an input. Add in questions which will produce information that will have some public relations value. For example, a survey to establish consumer attitudes to a new brand of a processed food was undertaken some six months after it had been introduced. The public relations specialist included a question which asked respondents to rate the value of foods of this type, in comparison with values prevailing some years before. Over 85 per cent felt that value had improved. Although of limited marketing value, this fact provided a news angle for the consultancy in drafting a story.

In such cases, when the results of surveys are issued, it is essential that the public relations executive does include full details of the source of the information. In the UK, it is the recommendation of the Market Research Society that selective extracts from research should not be used unless the whole information is published or available.

Any study being undertaken for marketing and other commercial purposes should be considered for its public relations value *before* being planned. However, many organizations wishing to focus attention onto their business sector will commission surveys *solely* for the potential news value of the findings; indeed, there can be few areas of human activity where well-prepared information is not of interest to people working in or concerned with that sector.

Such surveys can often attract wide media coverage and, in the UK alone, commercial organizations have researched the amounts given to children in pocket money, who performs which domestic chores in the family, attitudes towards status symbols, views of other European nationals, favourite foods in different regions and many others.

It is often possible to develop surveys that produce both important commercial information *and* have useable news value.

'IMAGE' AND RESEARCH

Though image is an uncomfortable word for most practitioners—with its suggestions of the structured aura—it is widely used and understood. But, as David Bernstein has sensibly observed, 'A company cannot "create" an image. Only a public can create an image, in that it selects those thoughts and impressions on which any image is based.'

Possibly the most important principle in effectively projecting the corporate personality is to identify and understand the opinions and views of the key audiences. Research is a sound way to evaluate these perceptions. The right programme to build the reputation (or image, as many would have it) can only be planned on the basis of a proper knowledge of how the organization is seen. Bob Worcester asserts that research is good for corporate communications and that corporate communications is good for research. All the evidence is that the importance of corporate reputation is growing ... and will continue to grow. MORI asked directors of Britain's top 500 companies (largely chairmen and chief executives) about the importance of corporate image to them. A resounding 75% said that it would increase over the years, while *just one* expected it to decrease. This trend was confirmed by a survey among senior corporate communications directors, conducted by HR&H Consensus on behalf of McAvoy Wreford Bayley. Some 70% reported significant increases in corporate communications budgets.

Are they right to attach such importance to the corporate reputation? Worcester confirms that other research evidence suggests that they are. Consumers for instance, are not as enthusiastic for new products as some advertisers would have us believe. Rather, they are conservative and much influenced by reputation. Almost seven out of ten adults in the UK believe that 'a company with a good reputation would not sell poor products'.

APPRAISING PUBLIC RELATIONS INVESTMENTS

Research can be used to test the effectiveness of public relations campaigns, just as it can any other promotional investment. As an illustration, Mars, the snack manufacturer, sponsored the London Marathon for some years as part of its broader communications efforts. Recall levels for Mars sponsorship grew dramatically over the three years. By the end of the period, over half the public could spontaneously name Mars as sponsor of the event, rising to three-quarters after prompting with a short-list of company names. Those aware of the Mars sponsorship were also significantly more favourable to the company, suggesting the activity had created both measurable awareness and an improvement in attitudes towards the organization.

Though this is an example relating to a major investment, the same principles can be applied to such activities as shareholder relations, good neighbour projects and even modest trade support campaigns.

When considering research on attitudes towards the organization, the public relations adviser should evaluate the effectiveness of the public relations communications in shaping attitudes. Such research will help develop the programme as well as providing a benchmark against which to measure progress. Over the coming years, we will see more serious attention paid to research. Public relations programmes that are research-based are demonstrably more effective—and while the research may involve some cost, through focusing the public relations efforts, it can improve cost effectiveness.

USING RESEARCH

1. Have we discussed with all managers their perception of the attitudes that exist towards the organization?
2. Can we balance this with any existing research relating to attitudes?
3. Is there research we have commissioned relating to other activities of the organization that might have implications in our communications area?
4. Should we discuss our research requirements with a consultant or professional research organization?
5. Have we undertaken any formal research that might give us the attitudes of important audiences?
6. For example, do we have a procedure for monitoring views and opinions of our employees?
7. Could we form a panel to review internal opinion on key company issues?
8. Have we talked to external bodies (such as our trading partners and agencies) regarding market and other attitudes towards our organization?
9. Do we have a procedure for regularly undertaking desk research for published information which might provide useful guidance?
10. Are we aware of the main sources of existing information including:

publishing houses	research institutes
records offices	educational bodies
government departments	professional societies
public libraries	trade unions
chambers of commerce	national statistics
trade associations	and others?

11. Should we appoint a research manager or research assistants to work with existing communications staff?
12. Should we retain an external research body on a regular basis?

13. Have we established an information library and the relevant reference files?
14. Do we undertake formal research when planning policy in new areas where attitudes will be of importance?
15. Do we understand when surveys for either guidance or statistically valid research are most appropriate?
16. Can we undertake our own preliminary investigations before commissioning full-scale research?
17. Would in-depth interviews or discussion groups be relevant at this stage to help plan the major investigations?
18. Can we obtain professional advice on the best stages to progress in the development of a short-term and long-term research programme?
19. Can we incorporate questions in scheduled research which will help create news material for use in our communications programme?
20. Should we establish a separate communications research budget, objectives and assessment procedures or combine this within other organizational research activity?

TWENTY-NINE

PROFESSIONAL AND TRADE GROUPS

Every organization employs executives who have ambitions to succeed within their own professional sectors—as well as in the broader framework of the company for which they work. Take advantage of this potential energy available from personnel on the payroll; the public relations executive needs to evaluate the possibility of key executives developing activities which will help in community and corporate relations.

All organizations should give serious thought to encouraging their employees to take an active part in relevant trade and professional bodies. Participation in such groups improves the effectiveness of the executive, broadens his experience—and can often provide opportunities for the company to project itself to important opinion leaders.

Selected executives can be encouraged to present papers to meetings of their groups or branches, to present speeches at annual conferences, to invite groups of their professional colleagues to inspect their own company at work and so on.

Company resources The organization can offer resources to these groups, including facilities for meetings, catering, secretarial and administrative support. Every presentation has a publicity value and usually this can be used to create a good local news story. Sometimes it might be suitable for a technical or trade journal. This produces a return for the effort the company is investing; the employee also sees that his company is supporting his professional development.

The organization needs to have a policy on these areas. This should be agreed with the personnel department. Managers might be allowed to charge their subscriptions to the organizations if they take an active part—for example, by sitting on a committee or acting as an officer for the local branch. The company might also make a contribution towards local travel, entertainment and other direct costs.

The company should also detail resources that it might make available. A method that the executive should follow to obtain company resources needs to be agreed. Again, the personnel director and the public relations director may decide this between them.

As an illustration, the company could make one evening a month available for professional groups to inspect facilities. This might be followed by an informal buffet supper in the staff dining room. In one month the organization might be presenting the marketing story to the Chartered Institute of Marketing, the following month, the personnel story to the Institute of Personnel Management and so on.

Standard presentation If the company is going to undertake these activities the public relations advisers should produce a standard presentation on the company. This might be on tape/slide or video. It should be in a format that can be shown to a general audience, perhaps 'topped and tailed' by the appropriate executive.

This might be supported with a brief package for company executives serving as officers on approved bodies, covering notes on the company; information sources; a standard check list; details of catering arrangements and other facilities; media relations sources and how to involve these; draft standard letters to be sent out confirming arrangements, inviting speakers, notifying the press, and so on. Produce for executives a standard advisory form to be completed when requesting facilities. Copies of this would be sent to members of the company who will be involved in organizing back-up public relations, security, production visits, personnel, catering services and so on.

Two case histories One small professional consulting firm undertook a limited programme of talks to professional groups. At the end of the first year, they found that the 12 partners had given between them 22 presentations to civic and opinion leaders in their community. This averaged out at less than one presentation every six months for each of them. But, together, they had succeeded in directly reaching and impressing some 1500 senior opinion leaders who would have been very difficult to reach by any other method.

A city in East Anglia once ran a campaign to inform the professional groups about a major new housing development. On advice from their consultancy, they chose the technique of individual presentations by a team of eight managers in the development department. The executives used a professionally prepared tape/slide presentation. For this they were professionally trained in presentation techniques. In the year they gave in excess of 80 presentations to an estimated total audience of 5000 community leaders, all members of relevant professional bodies. Attitudes were favourably improved and the initial investment was recovered many times over.

The public relations adviser is wise to remember that one of the most powerful resources available can be the members of the team within the organization. Check these notes alongside 'speakers panels' as these two techniques can often be run together.

INVOLVING VOCATIONAL GROUPS

1. Are there audiences relevant to our communications objectives that we could reach through their professional affiliations?
2. Can we list the professional or trade bodies where the opinion leaders within these audiences might be in membership?
3. Do we have executives in *our* organization who are in membership of any of these bodies?
4. Are we prepared to encourage them to take an active part and support such participation?
5. Could we, for example:

   (a) pay subscriptions and associated costs,
   (b) offer meeting rooms or secretarial facilities,
   (c) provide a venue for the annual general meeting,
   (d) suggest speakers, papers or facility visits,
   (e) invite their students to a factory reception,
   (f) donate a trophy or annual prize?

6. Should we consider organizing a programme for visitors to inspect our facilities, which could be adapted according to the trade or professional body concerned?
7. Could we arrange for such items as:

   (a) a printed tour leaflet or handbook,
   (b) a trained guide (perhaps a pensioner),
   (c) notices at key parts of the plant,
   (d) transport facilities,
   (e) a visitors' reception area,
   (f) appropriate catering or hospitality,
   (g) a memento, such as a company history?

8. Have we discussed these areas with all relevant departments, particularly personnel, production and security?
9. Is it possible to set a maximum budget on the cost of this activity, including the management time to be deployed?

10. Have we investigated methods to control demands on our resources, for example, a diary for visits limited to each Friday afternoon or one day per month?

11. Does the regularity of this activity and the potential goodwill that can be created suggest that a standard presentation on the organization might be helpful, for example, a film, a video or tape/slide?

12. Can we introduce a standard application form and checklist when an executive wishes to take advantage of these facilities, to ensure that this is approved and all departments involved in arrangements are properly informed?

13. Will there be opportunities to create media coverage locally and in the respective trade or professional journals?

14. In which case, do we need to budget for photography for these stories to record the visits allowing for prints for the press and our own visitors' gallery?

15. Can we establish a procedure for making a record of all such visits (including a visitors' book), media coverage, letters and so on, so that at the end of each year we assess the effectiveness of this effort?

THIRTY

SPEAKERS' PANELS

USING COMPANY PERSONNEL AS PROs FOR THE ORGANIZATION

.... one of the most powerful communications
techniques is face-to-face presentations

One of the most powerful communications techniques is face-to-face presentations. In Chapter 29 on professional groups, we looked at how members of an organization could be motivated to develop their own involvement with professional and trade bodies. This concept can be taken one stage further by the development of a speakers' panel. The idea is that the organization forms a small team of senior managers who will be encouraged to present its view to audiences of importance to the organization.

The creation of a speakers' panel involves several factors; the organization has to find the right people to represent it; they need to be briefed and encouraged; they will need some degree of training: the organization will have to identify opportunities while establishing a procedure for declining some invitations; finally a system has to be established to follow-up these opportunities and get the maximum return for the company.

Selecting the speakers The public relations adviser can follow certain guidelines in selecting the right people to represent the organization. A check back at the corporate public relations objectives will clearly show those audiences that are of importance. This will give some indication of the type of background that the ideal speakers will have.

These are likely to be a number of specialists required to talk to a range of different groups. This is a strong advantage. For a start, it means that a range of perspectives can be put on the company's operations. It also means that there is less individual load on any particular person.

It is not necessary to go for the most senior man—unless he is the best qualified. However, it can be helpful to talk confidentially to the personnel director for a second perspective on the candidates you may be identifying.

Check each nomination against the agreed criteria. The following are suggestions: has he a strong commitment to the company; is he likely to be employed in the same area for a reasonable length of time; does he have the enthusiasm; has he the right personality; is he articulate: has he home/family commitments that would prevent an occasional evening presentation; would he get the support of his departmental head in this work?

When you have identified the most likely candidate from each of the areas, make a confidential approach. Be specific about the amount of commitment that you will expect from them. Identify the backing that each candidate will get. With your more junior colleagues, outline the contribution this will make to their career development.

But be very factual. It is not an easy job: it demands dedication. The rewards for the individual are substantial in terms of improved confidence, greater experience of public speaking, a better profile in the business community and enhanced promotional opportunities.

Support for the panel Having identified the candidates, the next stage is to give them a detailed briefing on their responsibilities. It is best if this is a written document. It should cover the training, the follow-up and support that your department will be giving. At this stage, it may be advisable to mention the other members of the speakers' panel.

Some companies with training departments can undertake the training internally. If this is not possible, turn to one of the commercial management training organizations. The best training programmes will probably involve not more than half a dozen delegates.

There are gifted speakers who have the ability to capture an audience with the power of their words: few of these have acquired this ability without effort. Like many skills, it can be improved by practice, concentration, application, observation, tuition and so on.

If your speakers resist the need to develop their skills, explain the importance of this. Your panel members will have to understand the structure of an address, the use of facts, humour, how to start and how to finish. The old rules still apply—know your subject, know your audience and know yourself.

Creating opportunities The organization will create opportunities for this panel of speakers. Trade and business directories will provide a list of organizations likely to require speakers for their programme of meetings. Establish who is responsible for putting together the programme and the likelihood of their being interested in your organization.

Quite often, one phone call is enough: many of these bodies are looking for guest speakers. It may still be useful to have a simple letter put together which will outline the background on your speaker and his subject. This might include a suggestion or two of a talk that he could give.

The news angle The Institute of Personnel Management will not be interested in the development of your product—but they may be interested in how you brought together a skilled team to take an innovative idea through to market leadership. The Market Research Society might be fascinated to hear how you used sound marketing research to open up such a large potential market. The Institute of Production Engineers might prefer to hear how you have automated one of the oldest processes in engineering with a combination of Japanese and Scandinavian technology. And so it goes on . . . relate the subject to the audience needs.

Of course, your speakers themselves will identify opportunities. Every successful presentation will create invitations to others. One measure of the effectiveness of the speakers is how many invitations they receive as a follow-up.

Polite refusal While creating opportunities, it is important to have a procedure for declining politely. One of the simplest ways to do this is to ration the number of presentations in the year. In this way, rather than directly saying no, you can simply advise that your speakers are fully booked.

Alternatively, you can explain that due to pressure on the speaker's time, invitations are handled by a committee who regret they will not be able to take up this opportunity. Or members of one organization could be invited to attend a presentation which has already been arranged for another group.

Use of audio-visual Presentations can be substantially enhanced with the use of audio-visual aids. These need not be specially produced for each presentation. Nonetheless, a basic set of slides, display boards, demonstration models, flip charts and other material can be prepared and speakers trained in the use of these. A tape/slide presentation must be considered carefully; the audience want to see a speaker not just a professionally-produced show.

Meeting arrangements Be sure that the organizers are organizing properly. Ask them how they are publicizing the meeting, what invitations they have extended, how they are putting the mail-shot out, what attendance they expect on the day. Some bodies will be delighted to have a mail-shot put together for them. Your company may be able to sponsor the cost of the postage.

They may need public relations assistance in putting out an early news story and inviting the appropriate journalist to attend. They might appreciate a photograph and biographical information on your speaker for their newsletter or programme. On some occasions the subject may be of a broader interest and the invitation can be extended outside their immediate membership.

Expanding the opportunity Your company can back-up the organizers in terms of media relations, some form of handout for those who attend the meeting; this might be a short extract of the points made in the presentation. If you have a suitable product, a sample which they can take home is appreciated.

Once at a meeting organized by a professional society, the speaker from a national food company gave every member of the audience a bunch of bananas. It was much appreciated and added a lot of fun to the evening. Another speaker from a domestic appliance company presented one example which the chairman raffled among all those present. On another occasion, a year's subscription to a famous magazine was given by the publishers to the youngest student in the audience. There are many ways of creating a warm feeling towards your organization with a fresh original approach.

Finally, after the event, remember the polite thank-you letters, the news stories and pictures to be put out and the debriefing session which will ensure that lessons are learnt from the presentation.

Effectively run, speakers' panels can be an invaluable communications tool. They can be focused to generate national credibility at the highest professional levels—or directed to provide real support for community relations programmes.

OFFERING SPEAKERS

The opportunity

1. If we can examine our communications objectives and the audiences where we wish to develop favourable attitudes, can we identify those groups where we might be able to offer a trained speaker?
2. Can we list all such organizations—covering the trade and professional bodies noted earlier, but also including social, community, national and local groups?
3. Does this give some indication of the aspects of our organization that might be of most interest, for example, our consumer testing methods, our research, our industrial relations policies, our international activities?
4. Are there any existing members of our management team who are already regularly talking about the organization to external groups?
5. Can we call a meeting of divisional heads to identify other potential candidates for our speakers' panel?
6. How do they stand up against some agreed criteria, for example,

   (a) the right outgoing personality,
   (b) a commitment to the organization,
   (c) an ability to speak enthusiastically,
   (d) willingness to be trained in speaking?

7. Can we now ask respective divisional heads to approach each candidate and identify those willing and keen to assist?
8. How can we best assist these speakers to present themselves and the organization to the best of their ability:

   (a) background guidance notes,
   (b) in-house speaker training,
   (c) appropriate external courses,
   (d) proper publicity back-up,
   (e) slide or other audio-visual presentation,
   (f) assistance with organization of meetings,
   (g) suitable hand-out material,
   (h) secretarial and administrative help?

9. How will the organization create the speaking opportunities:

   (a) through trade and business directories,
   (b) news stories in appropriate trade media,
   (c) radio and television interviews with speakers,
   (d) personal letters to branch organizers?

10. Can we simplify all approaches, contacts and back-up by planning a standard procedure including, perhaps, the main letters ready-drafted on a word processor?

11. Have we agreed a system for politely refusing requests for speakers, for example, by running a diary which will control the number of occasions on which each member of the panel will speak?
12. Are we able to rotate the invitations so that the demands are evenly shared among panel members?
13. Can we provide each speaker with appropriate audio-visual support and thorough training on how to use these items?
14. Have we agreed the methods to keep a note of each presentation, which speaker, the audio-visual and hand-outs used, the actual attendance, any publicity or follow-up?
15. From this information can we make an evaluation of the effectiveness of these presentations related to our original objectives, particularly how we might amend and develop the programme for successive years?

Speakers' notes

There are many excellent books on presentation, but a few simple guidelines on speaking may be helpful.

Advance information

1. What is the make-up and size of the audience?
2. What is their background knowledge?
3. Can I assess their likely attitude to me?
4. How long will my talk be?
5. Do we have questions at the end?
6. Is there a chairman to handle these?
7. Am I meant to be informative or entertaining?
8. Who will be introducing me and how?
9. Should I be using any visual aids?
10. Will the media be at the meeting?
11. What is the meeting room like?
12. Will I need a microphone and what type?
13. Am I talking from a table, a lectern or platform?
14. Will I be talking before or after eating or drinking?
15. Are there other speakers before or after me?
16. How has my talk been advised to the audience?

Preparation

1. Why am I giving this talk to these people?
2. What do I want to achieve when I have finished?
3. How will I collect ideas and facts on this subject?

4. Can I use index cards to marshall the information?
5. Are there additional research or information sources?
6. How can I relate my subject to my audience?
7. Should I be using jokes or anecdotes?
8. How much can my listeners absorb?
9. Should I speak from headline cue cards?
10. Is it necessary to read or memorize this speech?
11. How can I stimulate interest right from the start?
12. Do I expect audience reaction to the presentation?
13. Will I be able to adjust the talk as I progress?
14. Have I run through and rehearsed my talk?
15. Can I shorten any long sentences to help presentation?
16. Am I using positive statements, active verbs?
17. Can I privately tape my talk to analyse later?
18. What should I be wearing for this occasion?

Presentation Have I reminded myself of these key points?

1. Stand up straight but comfortably.
2. Look at the audience as often as is reasonable.
3. But look at people in different parts of the room.
4. Avoid excessive gestures.
5. Keep my voice bright and clear.
6. React naturally to anything unexpected.
7. Have a joke or anecdote for an emergency.
8. Keep the language relevant to my audience.
9. Do not use jargon or 'in' expressions.
10. Vary my pitch but keep my pace steady.
11. Pause after each important point.
12. Practise to drop any 'ums' or 'ahs'.
13. Smile as often as is relevant.
14. Talk across the top of the microphone.
15. Watch the audience to gauge reactions.
16. Have a strong point or story on which to close.
17. Know when to close questions.

THIRTY-ONE

ISSUES PLANNING

UNDERSTAND ISSUES AND CRISES

Even within the smoothest running organization there will be crises for the public relations specialist to handle which have been created by circumstances 'beyond management's control'. Some of these problems may arise from matters that will be of general public concern. In such cases, there is usually little doubt about what has actually happened. For example, a road tanker laden with chemicals has crashed and a motorist has been killed. Sad to say, this accident may not be of great news interest outside company circles, or the area where it happened and among friends and relatives of the unfortunate people involved.

What might make the incident of broader public concern would be the facts behind the news. Who owned the tanker? There might be greater news interest if it were an organization with a questionable environmental record. What product was it carrying, how well was the vehicle maintained, what is the safety record of the operators? Any good reporter would want to ask those questions and any good company would be sure that they had the answers. The pressures on the public relations system can be immense. It is the responsibility of the executive concerned to ensure that there is a well-organized and clearly-understood communications procedure that will swing into action immediately the incident occurs.

What might happen if your chairman were killed in a road accident? Suppose raiders held a director hostage; a fringe group set fire to a plant; an international executive were to be arrested on an export mission; a trade union leader singled out your organization for criticism in a major public television debate; animal activists put poison in one of your food products;

an employee sabotaged a critical production process; chemicals from your plant escape into the atmosphere or into a local river. Could your public relations system cope?

Mishandling emergencies can be very expensive and ruinous to reputations. The Exxon Valdez disaster in Alaska cost that company billions in clean-up and reparation activities—though its reputation suffered even more through criticism of its operations procedures that allowed the tragedy to happen and its slowness to respond. One measure of public condemnation of the company was that an estimated 39 000 Exxon customers destroyed their credit cards after the incident.

Mishaps can have other serious consequences. In the US, for example, companies are regularly taken to court for negligence. This is happening increasingly across Europe and other markets. Personal liability can also be involved; officials and directors of the parent company of Townsend Thorensen faced legal actions in the UK following the sinking of their cross channel ferry and the tragic loss of life.

THE ISSUES AUDIT

Management should be responsible, sensitive and enlightened enough to realize that no company or organization—least of all a multinational with status and recognized achievements—can operate in today's climate without the highest standard of public responsibility and accountability. Public acceptance of the operations and managements' attitudes will significantly affect that company's commercial performance. These perceptions will be shaped by how a company behaves in the public eye—and, in particular, how it is seen to react to a crisis which may affect employees or the public safety ... or which might have an impact on health or the environment. Today's organizations are publicly accountable in a way that they have never been before.

Appraise all eventualities that could affect operations

The imperative for each organization is therefore to assess and analyse all issues and crises likely (or even unlikely) to be experienced and to formulate plans to deal with them positively. While these will not necessarily guarantee commercial success, there can be no doubt that, without such policies, long term success will be jeopardised. An efficient communications programme is an essential element of this response.

It might be helpful to look at a few of the terms used in this important area. A *crisis* (something which used to be called a contingency!) might be an immediate incident such as fire, explosion or spillage, where speed, efficiency and reassurance are crucial. An *issue* is a longer term consideration—for example, an eventuality which is likely to affect the operations of a company and the way it does business. Many issues can create opportunities and not just problems, for an issue may be positive, negative or neutral. As an illustration, a positive issue might be a new market opportunity or the growth of a market sector; a negative one, say, rising public resistance to a product or an industry; a neutral one could be proposed changes in legislation on packaging.

Over recent years, however, these concerns have come to a head on one broad-ranging topic: the environment and safety. The necessity for responsible and rapid crisis communications management has been given an added importance and urgency by public concern over 'green' issues. These concerns are central to the business economy and their significance continues to increase.

Every company and organization has a role to play and is expected to be both ethical and responsible. The development of public understanding, the power of the media and the influence of public opinion have shown that *the public can change policy*. Such issues are of international importance and companies cannot perform to different standards in different communities unless they are prepared to risk public criticism. As an illustration, for how long will third world governments tolerate the sale of medical, chemical and construction industry products (such as, at the time of writing, asbestos sheet) long since banned in the industrialized sectors of our world? How will manufacturers defend lower safety standards for their products or in their factories in different markets when these dual-standards are exposed to a concerned public? Will world opinion allow pollution from some countries to unbalance our world ecology, simply because their economies are not so developed?

High profile industries need effective support

While these observations are applicable to all companies, it is probably true that pharmaceutical, energy, mining, transport, chemical and other sensitive sectors have found themselves in an increasingly exposed position. The chemical industry, for example, bore the brunt of environmental criticism for many years, some ill-founded, but some justified. Sections of the green lobby even question its very existence. It is not sufficient for the chemical industry's professional bodies—such as the UK's Chemical Industries Association—to answer on behalf of its members. Companies are themselves expected by the public to make their own stands. Too frequently in the past, industry statements have been seen by the public and other opinion formers as abdications of responsibility by the individual companies.

It is the job of the public relations adviser to help his organization behave ethically and to communicate effectively. In monitoring public concerns, he will have a clear view of what is acceptable and what is not; he must present this perspective to his management colleagues so they can make the necessary business decisions. He must be involved in such discussions, particularly where there is a difference of opinion or where changes to meet public concern are uneconomic or likely to take some time. If he is to explain properly his company's position to the public and to the media, he must not only know the background but must be able to defend the decisions—because he was a central member of the management team evaluating the options. The public relations professional will find it difficult to support his colleagues if he is fundamentally out of step with their views; and, if neither side can reach an acceptable compromise, then it might be time for him to move on to a position where he can give 100 per cent support to his management.

Plan the internal, external and issues programmes together

Sometimes the research to identify the issues, clarify the organization's stance and prepare the necessary policies can be run alongside other communications work—not just for economic or practical reasons, but to ensure that issues-management is integrated into management thinking at all levels and is not just a bolt-on extra.

The public relations professional will have set up continuous media and public relations programmes to convey agreed messages, aimed at local business leaders, opinion forming groups, the press and site neighbours. As outlined in the community relations section, such a programme will include a series of planned activities aimed at encouraging a balanced and positive attitude. The organization must be seen to be involved with and committed to the community, as well as being an important and responsible employer. Very often, the communications audit to look at internal and external channels of communication and their effectiveness, can be run in parallel with an issues audit. Attitudes held within the company will need to be assessed to evaluate the employees' needs. The attitudes reflected will then influence the scope and scale of the internal activity that is undertaken; such interviews can also be used as the opportunity to identify many of the issues likely to affect the organization and appraise its readiness to cope with these.

Identify issues before planning crisis management

Public concern over site incidents (and off-site problems) highlight the importance of establishing a planned, tested and comprehensive crisis communications infrastructure as a priority for almost every organization. Obviously safety, welfare and emergency notification issues relating to potential crises should be standard in any organization involved in manufacturing or using potentially dangerous materials or processes. However, without a matching communications procedure, any organization can be highly exposed and vulnerable.

Such a crisis communications programme must be implemented in a rigorous and sustained fashion to ensure maximum effectiveness; it is also essential that it is fully supported from the top.

Use a questionnaire to guide interviews

Preliminary research can be carried out among managers and members of the organization's team through the use of a simple questionnaire; it is not normally necessary for this questionnaire to be completed with full written answers to every question. It should be intended to provoke thought and discussion. Respondents should feel free to write notes, answers and/or comments, as they consider appropriate. The public relations manager can then use this document as a basis for further discussions, with the results of the interviews compiled into an overview report.

The type of question to be posed might be:

1. Very briefly, what does your department do and what process/procedures are involved?
2. Is there a readily accessible database covering all the health and environmental hazards/implications/potential side effects of all your products, chemicals etc? If so, what form is it in and where is it kept?
3. What are the crises that could happen involving those processes that would either trigger the company's emergency procedure and/or be likely to result in adverse outside publicity? ... such as explosion, fire, spillage, theft, vandalism, sabotage, pollution, or employee/visitor accident etc.
4. ... and so on.

The questionnaire needs to be constructed to cover the circumstances of the organization, but all would probably need to cover such areas as emergency procedures, legal restraints or requirements, relations with neighbours and other key audiences, agreed communications procedures and the competitive position.

Ensure the plan includes specific action points

When the surveys are completed, the recommendations are likely to include practical recommendations on the action to be taken, covering:

1. Teams trained to respond in an emergency
2. Contingency programme covering logistics/communication skills necessary to deal with problems

3. Public relations plans to deal with range of crises, minimising impact, tailormade to the company's needs
4. Crisis team's work and home telephone numbers in a printed format
5. Insurance/legal/personnel advisers' involvement
6. Areas in which competitors may exploit situation identified
7. Media information as precise as possible and regularly updated
8. Pre-prepared standby statements and analysis of these might affect company reputation
9. Possible media reaction to every contingency situation
10. Policy on official/public relations/record photography
11. Procedures manuals/stickers/posters available at appropriate places on all sites
12. Procedures to monitor and record situation to assess efficiency and ways of improving it in future
    ... and others as appropriate in each case.

Test procedures with an emergency drill

As part of setting up an effective crisis communications programme, an emergency drill or exercise should be considered. This would be run 'for real' with an explosion or other crisis situation reported with simulated damage and fake casualties. The police and emergency services need to be contacted and involved in the exercise, which would test all aspects of the emergency procedures from security to first aid, including dealing with media and external enquiries.

The public relations team might consider acting as journalists from local and national media, both on the telephone and on site. This will test the procedures and way in which the emergency is handled. It would also be their job to prepare a full debriefing report on the crisis procedure, how effectively the situation was handled, lessons to be learned and changes to be made to future procedures.

Check the public relations resources needed

The public relations adviser should identify which colleagues might form a contingency team. Certainly the public relations adviser should head this team and take personal responsibility for all media activities. He will need the back-up of staff to gather the information and draft statements. In turn, they will need secretarial back-up to type and telephone news stories, handle telex, photocopying and so on.

Direct access to security personnel may be necessary to control entry to sensitive areas, direct the traffic, organize parking and provide facilities for camera crews and so on. An official photographer is absolutely essential.

This material may not just be required for news use but for a full record of the handling of the incident.

MEDIA LIAISON

Management needs to appreciate the responsibility the public relations adviser must have if he is to cope on-site with any emergency situation. Decisions have to be taken quickly, often on the spot. With electronic news gathering (ENG), material for television can now be on the screens almost as quickly as with radio. The organized public relations adviser needs to have an instant media procedure to cover collecting information, providing a spokesman and being ready and available to make comments.

The public relations adviser might need to provide television reporters with visual material. If for safety or security reasons the camera crew cannot get to where they would like to see what is happening, the public relations adviser may produce charts or graphics. It is not a good idea to use this as a technique for keeping them at bay, for they will simply hire a plane or helicopter to get the shots that you are trying to prevent. (See Chapter 20 on radio and television.)

SUPPORT RESOURCES

There will be some physical resources that you will need to call on at short notice. The public relations adviser must be completely in control and ensure that there is no restriction on his ability to handle the situation. Facilities that might be required would include:

1. Support staff, information gatherers, secretaries, messengers.
2. Typewriting, telex and telephone lines.
3. Media briefing rooms which will need to be in a secure area. For a major event this might require catering, toilet and telephone facilities.
4. A communications centre where all information will come in to one point and from where all news material will be issued.
5. Above all, cooperation from colleagues. This can only be ensured by arranging it in advance.

In any organization, there will be areas where management decisions can create situations that will result in controversy and, potentially, adverse news. The effective public relations practitioner will be advising management on the public relations implications of any policy at decision-making time. Much of this advice can be very unpopular.

Who wants to hear the public relations manager questioning the advisability of deceptive packaging, economies in staff welfare, blind eyes turned to contraventions in safety regulations, the introduction of an extra noisy late night shift, the odd few barrels of gunk down the drains, the undisclosed golden handshake to the retiring director, the dubious deal with the African dictator—or the cracked cups in the canteen?

A recent analysis among large organizations of the problems which created public relations difficulties identified the most common. These were safety situations, welfare conditions, industrial relations, consumer affairs, unfavourable financial results, sensitive overseas markets, redundancies, foreign investments in unpopular areas, product durability, neighbourhood relations and, of course, environmental disturbance. Significantly very few were 'beyond management control'.

Nonetheless, a coordinated plan is necessary to cover all such areas and the others identified by management colleagues. The final plan should cover both the direct and indirect audiences. The aim of this is to prevent the creation of an information vacuum with an important audience. Speculation or unauthorized information can often be more damaging than the actual facts. For example, it may be preferable for the shareholders to be advised that technical production problems will cause temporary closure of a line ... rather than for them to speculate on the prospects of the whole manufacturing process being shut down. Employees may need advising of the dozen redundancies rather than gossiping about hundreds.

The central factor is for the organization to be in control of information, wherever this is possible. Reactions to published bad news or speculation can never be as effective as taking the initiative in communications.

The personnel department must establish methods for advising all staff of their responsibilities both in coping with potential problems before they arise and actual emergencies—including alerting management and setting in motion the agreed communications systems. This will involve a procedure for advising members of the public relations team; they will need to offer advice as well as handling any media requirements.

Part of this communications system will include instructions for all plant locations on action to be taken in an emergency, including how to advise the public relations personnel. These notices may be in the form of site stickers, posters, or procedures manuals: they must include telephone numbers where a responsible member of the public relations team can be reached, 24 hours a day, 365 days a year.

The effective introduction of an issues analysis policy and the resulting crisis procedures is one of the most important responsibilities facing the public relations practitioner. It will be a challenge to his skill and persuasive abilities; it may not be popular. But it will be the biggest service he can offer his organization.

Any Company Ltd
Address. Telephone

Site location address
Telephone

EMERGENCY ALERT PROCEDURE

In the event of an emergency, it is the responsibility of all employees to advise the senior manager on site.

If that is *you*, put in operation the following procedure:

1. Take the immediate steps necessary, as covered in your training, to:
   (a) protect the life, safety and welfare of any endangered colleagues
   (b) protect company property and interests

2. Either yourself or (if occupied by the consequences of the emergency) a responsible colleague must telephone:
   (a) during working hours:
       (names and telephone numbers)
   (b) outside normal working hours
       (names and telephone numbers)

These personnel are trained to advise you on how to cope with any eventuality. They are available 24 hours a day, 365 days a year; but as these are their home numbers, and one or more may be away, keep calling until you get a response.

Remember
(a) Do not wait until you have all the information relating to the incident
(b) If possible call from a company telephone on company premises where you can be reached later
(c) Do not talk to any journalists or personnel outside the company, other than any emergency services in attendance, until you have the necessary instructions.

Chart 31.1 An emergency procedures card or small notice should be given to every employee and posted on every company notice board at every location. It will not be needed until the emergency arises and that will not be the time to go hunting through files. This is a suggested layout.

PLANNING FOR ISSUES AND CRISES

1. Have we a clear view of the issues that are likely to affect the organization over, say, the next three years?
2. Can we check management's views on these, develop a stance and get this agreed?
3. What prepared statements do we need to cover the organization's attitudes to these possibilities?
4. Should we consider a full-scale issues audit of all operations on all sites?
5. Could this be run in parallel with communications or green audits?
6. Through the interviews, as part of the audit, can we agree all emergency situations that could cause a crisis in company operations?
7. What is likely to be the reaction of each of our key audiences should the organization experience an emergency situation?
8. In other words, can we crosscheck between audiences to ensure we consider all communications needs, for example: a takeover bid will not just affect shareholders, but employees, neighbours, and suppliers; a plant accident not only employees, but customers and trade associations?
9. What emergency situations might the organization experience?
10. What systems exist at present to handle such emergencies?
11. Are these coordinated and do they cover the media and communications aspects?
12. Has a divisional head the authority to inform audiences outside his divisional responsibilities; for example, with a production mishap, who advises the customers?
13. Can a central communications plan be agreed to coordinate all information channels within the organization and with external audiences?
14. Has the public relations adviser a clear central role in handling such communications?
15. At what stage and how is he alerted to a problem?
16. Does the system allow for personal absences due to holidays or illnesses, in other words, will it alert responsible management and public relations personnel 24 hours a day, 365 days a year?
17. Is the importance of the media and communications aspects appreciated by personnel at operating level, for example, drivers or operators?
18. Have they clear instructions on what they should do in an emergency situation?
19. Do we have agreed procedures for handling information and dealing with media enquiries?
20. Who is authorized to act as an organization spokesman?
21. Have we given the coordinating executive the authority (written if necessary) to deploy whatever resources are required to handle the media and communications related to the incident?

22. Do all members of management appreciate the importance of the organization handling the media calmly, efficiently and positively, during and after a crisis?

23. Would an analysis of potential problem areas indicate where we might be investing in improving attitudes to ensure goodwill would carry us through a problem, for example, a more positive projection of our environmental, safety and employment policies?

24. Do we have an adequate budget available to handle the communications aspects of any emergency situation?

25. Have we procedures to monitor and record the handling of any contingency so we can assess the efficiency of this operation and ways it could be improved for the future?

FIVE

Figure 32.1 Media campaigns can be reinforced by direct presentations to key audiences where the effectiveness of the communication of a message can be directly measured. Key business presentations to over 2 000 people in one venue can be organized in many major cities. Picture courtesy of Haymarket Publishing.

THIRTY-TWO
MEASURING RESULTS

METHODS OF APPRAISAL

The value of public relations will only be appreciated by management when specific performance objectives are set and the action undertaken can be demonstrated to have achieved measurable results.

There are many factors relating to the public relations performance where measurement can be made before and after the campaign to quantify the results. These measures can also indicate the cost-effectiveness of the activity undertaken.

Some of the more frequent measures include:

Budget The completion of activity within the agreed budget and timescale

Awareness An increase in the knowledge of the organization among the defined audience

Attitude A shift in opinion or attitude towards the organization

Media The level and tone of news coverage during the period under review

Position The placing of the organization in the market among competitors

Response The number of enquiries and/or leads generated by the campaign

Share price The value that the investor puts upon the company

Sales Any change in sales volumes or prices that can be related to public relations alone

Advertising agencies and many other professional advisers are expected to quantify the effectiveness of their work. This must also become the norm within public relations. Some consultancies are using sophisticated methods to calculate the audience exposed to favourable messages ('opportunities to see' as our advertising colleagues would describe this).

Both public relations directors and consultancies are increasingly using formal attitude research for pre- and post-campaign measurement. As chairman of *Countrywide*, Peter Hehir, said, 'Public relations professionals who complain about the low status accorded them but don't try to give their proposals a scientific platform, continue to bite the hand that starves them.' The position identified by research will only be part of the appraisal. Any change in awareness, or shift in opinion, needs to be related to the resources deployed to achieve it ... to appraise its effectiveness and, indeed, its cost-effectiveness.

Although a quantified measure must always be best, almost any measure is better than none.

INFORMAL REVIEWS OF COST-EFFECTIVENESS

Broadly, such practical assessments will fall into the subjective or objective categories. Certainly if the goals for the public relations performance were originally set only as aims, then there is not much point in taking the assessment beyond the subjective stage. Though, even this can be valuable.

One well-established subjective measure is to hold a performance review towards the end of a programme of activity and before the detailed planning of the next stage. This needs to involve all the people who contributed to the original discussions and helped in preparing the aims—this might include personnel, production, marketing and international directors. Each representative invited to attend this meeting should be given ample advance warning and asked to obtain some assessment in the change of attitude in any sectors for which they are responsible.

The meeting will then look at each of the aims originally defined and will discuss whether there is any evidence to support any improvement related to the targets. As an example, the marketing director might have prepared for the meeting by talking to distributors and asking them for views of the company's approach to the market. He will find it is better not to ask directly about, say, news coverage, but rather about the influence that the coverage might have had on the targeted audience. An increase in coverage would not necessarily be recognized by the trade as better media relations.

The marketing director should select a representative range of distributors with whom to discuss this change in awareness. He might cover, for example, larger and smaller wholesalers—northern and southern—or some appropriate balance.

This assessment has no real quantifiable validity. However, if the campaign has been working effectively, there should emerge clearly a consistency of view. This should be sufficient to give guidance on how to adjust the programme and perhaps, in future years, how to improve the objectives. These views might also suggest a better method of measurement, such as a more formal audit of wholesaler attitudes.

The same procedure should be adopted across all the operating divisions where public relations has a responsibility—personnel may well talk to new recruits, shop floor representatives, community leaders, and so on. Although this can never be as good as a proper objective measure, it is far better than no measure. It has been estimated that in the UK no measure of any kind is made of the effectiveness of between 60 per cent and 70 per cent of all public relations programmes. A practical first step for the public relations adviser trying to introduce discipline into activity is to start assessing subjectively and improve as the campaign develops.

One consultancy handled a modest but innovative campaign for a small packaged grocery manufacturer. The chief executive queried the effectiveness of the public relations support. At the suggestion of the consultant, he telephoned 20 retailers at random . . . and was astonished to find that all but one reported that they felt the company had become more active in the market and improved its trade support.

The impact of the public relations, therefore, was undeniable. There had been no other change in the company's approach—and there had been no new product announcements during the course of that year. As a result of this informal assessment, the public relations team were able to move the public relations activity onto a more substantial and objective basis.

CONSIDER FORMAL ATTITUDE RESEARCH

Market research specialists will confirm that monitoring the effectiveness of a public relations campaign is not as difficult as many people imagine; nor need it be an extremely expensive activity. In some cases, a sample of 100 or 200 respondents may be sufficient to get a reasonably accurate measure.

It is essential that the measure is of the public relations effectiveness and that other changes are not inadvertently monitored; for example, other influences could include an increase in the salesforce, the effectiveness of a new sales manager, the impact of an advertising campaign, the introduction of half a dozen new products and so on.

Therefore, as the original objectives will probably have been phrased in relation to some form of quantifiable awareness or attitude factor, it is this which needs to be measured. In fact, attitude surveys are probably the most valuable method of assessing the effectiveness of the campaign. On a normal annual basis, it is probably sufficient to monitor the section of the market at which the public relations is specifically aimed. However, periodically, it is valuable to look at overall public attitudes towards the organization. This is certainly useful before the start of a major campaign or, say, every five years. If it is properly constructed, the attitude survey will be of invaluable help to the public relations advisers in their planning.

Attitude research also should provide the benchmark against which future effectiveness can be measured. Therefore, it is important that it is structured to enable it to be repeated at a later stage. This will enable the results to be compared and any advance identified. It is of limited value to research attitudes among retailers, then five years later to research attitudes among wholesalers and try to draw any comparisons between them. Similarly, the same research format and, probably, research specialists should be used.

On some occasions, the research will reveal information that may affect other aspects of the company's operations that have an effect on public opinion—driver behaviour, delivery methods, complexity of paperwork, telephone attitudes, salesforce structure, corporate identity and so on. (Read also the notes on research before calling in professional advisers.)

DRAFT QUANTIFIED PROGRAMME OBJECTIVES

Some measurements of the effectiveness of the public relations programme are simple to quantify if the original objectives have been well drafted. Suppose one objective has been to improve awareness of the products at retailer level, in order to help the salesforce improve distribution; it would be possible to record the increase in the number of retail outlets where the awareness had been improved to the agreed level.

This would separate the awareness and sales objectives. In other words, sales management would be expected to take advantage of the improvement in awareness by increasing the number of stockists holding the product, say, by a comparable percentage.

Let us assume that public relations had developed product awareness among retailers from 20 per cent to 30 per cent. Then, let us suppose this additional awareness could be converted by the salesforce into actual distribution. If this potential increase in distribution were to represent sales of say, £500 000 at ex-factory prices, then we are beginning to have a figure against which to compare the effectiveness of the public relations spend.

Alternatively, we could begin to calculate how much might be expended to achieve this goal. For example, the marketing manager might feel it reasonable to expend 10 per cent of the value of the potential ex-factory sales on the promotional effort. It might be worth spending a *bigger* proportion if it is a one-off activity; for example, this might be valid if it means that once distribution has been achieved, sales will automatically follow year-on-year. If, however, the nature of the product is such that it needs *continuous* trade support, then a lower percentage might be necessary.

Consider the public relations activity undertaken to reduce staff turnover in a fast growing, high technology company. In an actual UK example, such a campaign was undertaken under a brief from the personnel director. At the end of the first complete 12 months during which this new scheme had been in operation, staff turnover had declined from 30 per cent to 18 per cent and continued down.

The direct costs that appeared to have been saved in cutting down this turnover—in terms of recruitment, training, the effect of limited performance during induction and so on—were estimated at £120 000 per annum. The total cost of the public relations campaign (not including the time of the executives, as it was run paralled with other activities) was less than £20 000. Even if the time *had* been considered, it would still have totalled less than £30 000. This investment produced a substantial saving that would be continued year-on-year.

USE THE APPRAISAL FOR FUTURE PLANNING

Whatever our limited ability to see into the future, many of us have stunning powers of seeing into the past. But hindsight can be invaluable in public relations. It can help develop alternative tactics and improve the strategy. At the end of every campaign, the analysis must identify those techniques which have worked most effectively.

Let us consider a practical example; one new public relations campaign supporting a branded packaged food included a series of presentations to housewives through tasting evenings organized across the country. These had been successful in improving awareness and directly stimulating sales. The level of sales could be positively measured in each of the towns after each of the events.

A success you might think? Not exactly, for both the public relations consultant and the client were aware that this success had taken a very substantial investment to achieve the results—and these sales improvements were only achieved in those areas where the demonstrations had taken place. As less than five per cent of the total market could be covered in any one year, it would take 20 years to cover the market. To gear up the operation would create a budget out of all proportion.

Yet, all were agreed that the technique had worked. A little bit of lateral thinking—plus a dash of hindsight—made the public relations advisers question whether it was necessary for the company to be carrying *all* of the costs and logistics of these demonstrations. An investigation showed that there were several other manufacturers undertaking similar exercises. One, in particular, was handling a product which was not only non-competitive but complementary to the client's brand. A little negotiation followed and the result was a modest financial contribution to the other company's costs, plus an unlimited supply of the product, supporting literature, recipe leaflets, and so on. The agreement covered how the product should be presented.

The end result was a far broader coverage than could possibly be undertaken by a solo effort. Awareness and sales levels were monitored and found to be comparable with earlier results. But the final costs in the second year were only 25 per cent of those in the first.

CHECK COMPETITIVE ACTIVITY

When undertaking any public relations activity, look at how other people are performing. Ensure that your press cutting service is covering competitive companies so that you can get some indication of their coverage. Try to calculate their promotional budget, find out what staff they have deployed on the activity, what the fees to their consultancy might be and so on.

Try to establish if there are any industry norms. These do not need to be solely related to your industry. It might be interesting to know how much it costs to support the sales of £10 million of sports shoes every year by comparison with the sales of £10 million of gardening tools. If there are substantial differences, why? What methods are being used by these other manufacturers? Are they better than your own?

Try talking to trade associations to see what statistics exist on promotional activities, budgets, relevant market shares and so on. If your company is number one in a market with a dominant position, should you be spending more or less pro rata to hold this situation?

Obviously, you cannot compare yourself with other people in that same market, but find a parallel market where there is also a dominant supplier. Talk to the public relations professionals involved in this area. They may be as interested in your own observations as you will be in theirs.

Whatever the results of your research and analysis, always ensure that there is a proper report prepared which is circulated to all executives who have contributed to the original planning. They will wish to know if they have spent the money effectively. They will be interested to see how well the intended results have been achieved. It can be as important if the results are *not* encouraging. The problems that will arise from pursuing the wrong course can be even worse than recognizing there is difficulty at an early stage. As with all communications, remember to ask for a response to this report.

If you have been using other colleagues to work on this subject, be certain that you have the opportunity for a full debriefing and an appraisal of their own performance related to the overall programme success. These may be members of your own team or they may be the consultancy that you are retaining. Success should be one of the factors that contributes to their motivation.

With an outside consultancy, this may form part of the renegotiation. If the consultancy has not performed to satisfactory standards, then you need to decide whether this requires a change in direction of the programme or a change of the consultancy. In either case, you will be making these decisions based on a more substantial level of information.

Success demands as much praise as failure would demand criticism. Where the public relations work of colleagues is successful, recognize it. Praise can be the most motivating aspect of work. It does not cost a lot, but it pays dividends. The public relations adviser will gain far more satisfaction from performing to objectives. The value of his contribution to the development of the organization can only be assessed if it is measured. Good public relations demands effective measurement.

MEASURING RESULTS

1. Are our original objectives written in such a way that they indicate the factors we can measure to evaluate our public relations performance?
2. Have we checked back through Chapter 28 on research to remind ourselves of some other methods of measuring results?
3. Do our objectives relate to factors that can be achieved through public relations (awareness, for example) rather than those that require sales, marketing, advertising or other input (sales levels, for example)?
4. Have we a programme or performance reviews where, at the end of each campaign, divisional heads discuss the effectiveness of the public relations in supporting their operation?
5. Do they monitor attitudes among representatives of their key audiences?
6. Where we cannot yet obtain a substantial objective measure, can we consider subjective indications, for example, reactions of wholesalers or feedback from the salesforce?
7. Remembering that public relations is the organizational discipline responsible for the management of attitudes, have we considered how an attitude survey might help us plan and develop the campaign?
8. Could we look at professional market research assistance in writing objectives and measuring public relations performance related to these?
9. Can we allocate a realistic budget to this measurement and could it be effectively combined with a measure of other influences, such as advertising?
10. Should we look at benchmark studies to see how we are progressing?

11. Can questions relating to public relations effectiveness be incorporated into other studies and surveys, for example, a personnel study into graduate attitudes?
12. Is it possible to relate any improvements to the financial benefit achieved so that the cost-efficiency of the public relations can be calculated?
13. Are we comparing our communications performance with our competitors or other leaders in similar fields where there might be some established criteria or industry norms?
14. Are we assessing how efficiently we are deploying the resources of the public relations department, for example, in use of executive time?
15. Could we rewrite next year's communications to include a measurable factor relating to:

shareprice	enquiries for literature
awareness	sales leads
staff turnover	job applications
media coverage	or others?

16. Should we form an assessment committee to represent all operating areas to give us a broader perspective on communications effectiveness?
17. Have we a procedure to relate the performance of public relations in the annual assessments of the relevant staff?
18. Could this be extended to the annual review of consultancy performance?
19. Have we asked the staff/consultancy to prepare a report of the utilization of the budget which we can circulate to senior management colleagues?
20. Can we check on performance in relation to the original objectives so that for successive years, objectives, budgets and performance criteria can be adjusted?

THIRTY-THREE
SUMMARY

No organization can succeed unless it can create understanding and support. This goodwill must be developed among those people who help maintain its existence—the employees, volunteer helpers, shareholders and those external audiences to whom it is providing products, services or the satisfaction on which its ultimate success depends.

In the structure and running of every successful organization there are four major elements—ideas, people, money and support. And of these, support is the most important. Support can be created, whereas ideas are constantly recycled; sadly people come and go; money can be obtained, at a price, anytime. But it is because support is fundamental to success that public relations is fundamental to the successful running of any organization.

The management of the company is not making a choice whether to have public relations or not—there is no such choice. An organization's public relations is simply the quality of the relations between itself and the publics on whom it depends.

The organizations may be making the decision to have *professional* public relations—the planned effort to build and maintain goodwill between the organization and its publics. In other words, management has to decide whether its public relations should be accidental, reactive and haphazard . . . or whether it should be organized, disciplined and managed.

Individuals will strive for a lifetime to develop a reputation which will reflect well on them; they will struggle to achieve a reputation that will ensure that they are regarded with warmth by those closest to them and respected by those beyond this inner circle. The same can be true of organizations.

It makes hard-headed business sense to build a good reputation. This is a tangible asset of real value. Even more important, it is more rewarding and satisfying for us all to work for an open organization that is aspiring to ambitions that can be proudly supported by all associated with the enterprise.

.... in the democracies of the world we take communications for granted

In the democracies of the world, we take communications for granted. Public relations is part of this democracy. The right of any individual, association, company or organization to present the best case it can for itself is very important. Equally important is the ability of society to create pressure for change. Public relations has a vital role to play in both areas.

This book has attempted to look at the broad issues of public relations as they affect organizations, their structure, policies, operations and communications. The public relations person who wants to become a true professional needs to develop substantial knowledge and skill way beyond the scope of this book. However, he or she should also develop something which these pages have tried to convey about our most rewarding, stimulating and valuable craft—some passion. The responsibility is one of the most important in an organization . . . the professional management of its reputation.

Public relations is perhaps a way of life. It not only makes you feel good, by golly, it does you good, too!

READING LIST

Management

Adiar, J., *Management Decision Making*, Gower Publishing Co. Ltd., Aldershot, 1985

Buchanan. D. A. and A. Huczynski, *Organizational Behaviour: An Introductory Text*, Prentice-Hall, Hemel Hempstead, 1985

Freemantle, D., *Super Boss: The A–Z of Managing People Successfully*, Gower Publishing Co. Ltd., Aldershot, 1985

Serif, M., *How to Manage Yourself*, Frederick Fell Publishers Inc., New York, 1980

Stewart, D. M., *Handbook of Management Skills*, Gower Publishing Co. Ltd., Aldershot, 1987

Public relations

Bernstein, D., *Company Image and Reality: A Critique of Corporate Communications*, Holt, Rinehart and Winston Ltd., London, 1984

Biddlecombe. P., *Goodwill: The Wasted Asset*, The Camelot Press Ltd., Ormond Beach, Fla., 1971

Black, S., *Introduction to Public Relations*, Modino Press, London, 1989

Bland, M., *Be Your Own PR Man: A Public Relations Guide for the Small Businessman*, Kogan Page, London, 1981

Bowman and Ellis, *Manual of Public Relations*, Heinemann, London, 1977

Coulson Thomas, C., *Public Relations is Your Business*, Business Books, London, 1981

Derriman, J. and Pulay, G., *The Bridge Builders: Public Relations Today*, Associated Business Press, London, 1979

Hart, N. A., *Effective Corporate Relations: Applying Public Relations in Business and Industry*, McGraw-Hill, London, 1987

Howard, W. (ed.), *The Practice of Public Relations*, Heinemann, London, 1982
IBAC, *Inside Organizational Communications*, Longman, Harlow, 1985
Irving, R. B., *When You are the Headline: Managing a Major News Story*, Dow-Jones Irwin, Homewood, Ill., 1987
Moore, Stanley G., *Managing Corporate Relations: A Practical guide to Business Survival*, Gower Press, Aldershot, 1980
Olins, W., *The Corporate Personality: An enquiry into the Nature of Corporate Identity*, Heinemann Educational Books Ltd., Oxford, 1978
Ridgway, J., *Successful Media Relations*, Gower Publishing Co., Aldershot, 1984
Schmertz, H. and Novak, W., *Goodbye to the Low Profile*, W. H. Allen & Co. plc, London, 1986
Seitel, Fraser P., *The Practice of Public Relations*, Bell and Howell Co., 1984
Watts, R., *Public Relations for Top Management*, Croner Publications, New Malden, 1977
Winner, P., *Effective PR Management: A Guide to Corporate Survival*, Kogan Page, London, 1987

Marketing and marketing communications

Chisnall, P. M., *Marketing: A Behavioural Analysis*, McGraw-Hill, London, 1975
Davidson, H. J., *Offensive Marketing*, Penguin, London, 1975
Degen, C., *Communicators' Guide to Marketing*, Longman, Harlow, 1987
Hart, N. and Stapleton, J., *Glossary of Marketing Terms*, Heinemann, London, 1981
Hart, N., *Industrial Advertising and Publicity*, ABP, Andover, 1978
Hopkins, T., *How to Master the Art of Selling*, Grafton Books, London, 1983
Van Mesdag, M., *Think Marketing*, W. H. Allen & Co., plc, London, 1988

General

Bell, G., *The Secrets of Successful Speaking and Business Presentations*, Heinemann, London, 1987
Fisher, R., *Getting to Yes: Negotiating Agreement without Giving In*, Business Books, London, 1986
Goodworth, C. T., *Effective Speaking and Presentation for the Company Executive*, Business Books, London, 1980
Janner, G., *Janner's Complete Speechmaker*, Business Books, London, 1981
Kennedy, G., *Negotiate Anywhere! Doing Business Abroad*, Business Books, London, 1985
Ries, A. and Trout, J., *Positioning: The Battle for Your Mind*, McGraw-Hill, New York, 1980

HELPFUL ORGANIZATIONS

AA
Advertising Association
Aberford House
15 Wilton Road
London SW1V 1NJ
Tel: 071-828 2771

ABCC
Association of British Chambers of Commerce
Sovereign House
212a Shaftesbury Avenue
London WC2H 8EW
Tel: 071-240 5831

ACC
Association of County Councils
Eaton House
66a Eaton Square
London SW1W 9BH
Tel: 071-235 1200

ASA
Advertising Standards Authority
Brook House
2-16 Torrington Place
London WC1E 7HN
Tel: 071-580 5555

BAIE British Association of Industrial Editors
3 Locks Yard
High Street
Sevenoaks
Kent TN13 1LT
Tel: 0732 459331

BIM British Institute of Management
Management House
Cottingham Road
Corby
Northants NN17 1TT
Tel: 0536 204222

CAM Communications, Advertising and Marketing Education Foundation (CAM)
Aberford House
15 Wilton Road
London SW1V 8PH
Tel: 071-828 7506

CBI Confederation of British Industry
Centre Point
103 New Oxford Street
London WC1A 1DU
Tel: 071-638 8215

CIM Chartered Institute of Marketing
Moor Hall
Cookham
Maidenhead
Berks SL6 9QH
Tel: 0628 524922

CERP Confédération Européen des Relations Publiques
Rue des Petits Carmes 9
B-1000
Brussels
Belgium
Tel: 010-32 5112680

COI	Central Office of Information Hercules Road London SE1 7DU Tel: 071-928 2345
CSO	Central Statistical Office Government Offices Great George Street London SW1P 3AQ Tel: 071-270 3000
EPO	The European Parliament Office 2 Queen Anne's Gate London SW1H 9AA Tel: 071-222 0411
ICO	International Committee of Public Relations Consultants Association Willow House Willow Place London SW1P 1JH Tel: 071-233 6026
IOD	Institute of Directors 116 Pall Mall London SW1Y 5ED Tel: 071-839 1233
IOE	Institute of Export Export House 64 Clifton Street London EC2A 4HB Tel: 071-247 9812
ISB	Incorporated Society of British Advertisers 44 Hertford Street London W1Y 8AE Tel: 071-499 7502
IS	Industrial Society 48 Bryanstone Square London W1H 7LN Tel: 071-262 2401

ISP	Institute of Sales Promotion Arena House 66-68 Pentonville Road Islington N1 9HS Tel: 071-837 5340
IABC	International Association of Business Communicators One Hallidie Plaza Suite 600 San Francisco California 94102 USA Tel: 0101-415 433 3400
IPA	Institute of Practitioners in Advertising 44 Belgrave Square London SW1X 8QS Tel: 071-235 7020
IPR	Institute of Public Relations The Old Trading House 15 Northburgh Street 4th Floor London EC1 Tel: 071-253 5151
IPRA	International Public Relations Association Case Postale 126 CH-1211 Geneva 20 Switzerland Tel: 010-4122 791 0550
MS	Marketing Society Stanton House 206 Worple Road London SW20 8PN Tel: 071-879 3464
MRS	Market Research Society 175 Oxford Street London W1R 1TA Tel: 071-439 2585

NPA	Newspapers Publishers Association 34 Southwark Bridge Road London SE1 9EU Tel: 071-928 6928
NS	Newspaper Society Bloomsbury House Bloomsbury Square 74-77 Great Russell Street London WC1B 3DA Tel: 071-636 7014
PC	Press Council 1 Salisbury Square London EC4Y 8AE Tel: 071-353 1248
PPA	Periodical Publishers Association Imperial House 15-19 Kingsway London WC2B 6UN Tel: 071-379 6268
PRCA	Public Relations Consultants Association Willow House Willow Place London SW1P 1JH Tel: 071-233 6026
PRSA	Public Relations Society of America 33 Irving Place New York NY 10003 Tel: 0101-212 995 2230
SE	Stock Exchange London EC2N 1HP Tel: 071-588 2355
UKECO	The UK European Commission Office 8 Storey's Gate London SW1P 3AT Tel: 071-222 8122

INDEX

Note to readers: as the chapter headings and the checklists generally have not been noted in this index, it should be read in conjunction with the contents list at the front of the book. For example, there is a complete chapter on 'Media conferences' and a checklist, so only related references in other parts of the book are covered in this index.